DATE DUE

Bartók: Concerto for Orchestra

BARTÓK:

Concerto for Orchestra

Understanding Bartók's World

— ❧ —

Benjamin Suchoff
University of California, Los Angeles

Monuments of Western Music
George B. Stauffer, Series Editor

SCHIRMER BOOKS
An Imprint of Simon & Schuster Macmillan
NEW YORK
Prentice Hall International
LONDON   MEXICO CITY   NEW DELHI   SINGAPORE   SYDNEY   TORONTO

Schirmer Books
An Imprint of Simon & Schuster Macmillan
866 Third Avenue
New York, NY 10022

Library of Congress Catalog Card Number: 95-10440

Printed in the United States of America

Printing number
1   2   3   4   5   6   7   8   9   10

Library of Congress Cataloging-in-Publication Data

Suchoff, Benjamin

  Bartók : Concerto for orchestra : understanding Bartók's world /Benjamin Suchoff.
     p.   cm.   —(Monuments of western music)
  Includes bibliographical references (p.   ) and index.
  ISBN 0-02-872495-X (hard)
  1. Bartók, Béla, 1881-1945—Criticism and interpretation.
  2. Barók, Béla, 1881-1945. Concertos, orchestra. 3. Bartók, Béla, 1881–
  1945—Influence.   I. Title.   II. Series.
  ML410.B26S83   95-10440
  784.2'186—dc20   CIP
                                                        MN

This paper meets the requirements of ANSI/NISO Z39.48–1992 (Permanence of Paper).

For Eleanor

Contents

Part 2

CONCERTO FOR ORCHESTRA

Part 3

BARTÓK'S LEGACY

Foreword

❧

The *Monuments of Western Music* series is devoted to the examination of single works, or groups of works, that have changed the course of Western music by virtue of their greatness. Some were recognized as masterpieces immediately upon creation. Others lay in obscurity for decades, to be uncovered and revered by later generations. With the passage of time, however, all have emerged as cultural landmarks.

The *Monuments* volumes are written by specialists—historians and performers who bring to their accounts the latest discoveries of modern scholarship. The authors examine the political, economic, and cultural background of the works. They consider such matters as genesis, reception, influence, and performance practices. But most importantly, they explore the music itself and attempt to pinpoint the qualities that make it transcendent. The result is a series of comprehensive, engaging books that will be of interest to performers, students, scholars, and devotees alike.

It is especially appropriate to dedicate a *Monuments* volume to the Concerto for Orchestra by Béla Bartók, for as the twentieth century draws to a close, we can assign Bartók with greater certainty than ever to the small group of composers who decisively influenced the course of modern music. Bartók's prominent position was predicted some thirty years ago by William Austin, who in his epic survey *Music in the Twentieth Century* named Stravinsky, Schoenberg, and Bartók as the three central figures of our age. Austin credited Stravinsky with breaking the ties to nineteenth-century Romanticism through primitivist ballet suites such as the *Rite of Spring* and neoclassical works such as the Violin Concerto. Schoenberg's decisive contribution, Austin said, was the formulation of the twelve-tone system, which provided contemporaries with a viable alternative to traditional, tonal-based composition. And Bartók's great accomplishment, Austin pointed out, was the creation of a new international musical language, one representing an appealing synthesis of East European folksong and West European art music. Certainly no work can better illustrate the brilliant success of Bartók's achievement than the Concerto for Orchestra.

Bartók's early training at the Budapest Academy of Music pointed toward a traditional career as a piano virtuoso. He studied Western harmony, counterpoint, and composition, and attracted considerable attention through performances of piano "war horses" by Beethoven, Brahms, and Liszt. Upon completing his studies, however, he embarked on an extended exploration of Hungarian, Romanian, and Slovakian folk melodies. Working at first with Zoltán Kodály, he eventually transcribed thousands of indigenous tunes, documenting musical cultures that were soon to be infiltrated by modern civilization. The use of "native" melodies in Western music was much in the air at the time, as the works of Antonín Dvořák, Percy Grainger, Charles Tomlinson Griffes, Charles Ives, and even Stravinsky attest. But it was Bartók who strove to employ local tunes not just for melodic coloration—the approach taken by most other composers—but as a source for a new musical language altogether, one whose harmonic, contrapuntal, and structural gestures grew naturally out of ethnic principles. The steady increase of interest in ethnicity during the course of the twentieth century and the resurgence of nationalism in Eastern Europe in the past ten years show that Bartók's confidence in the enduring strength of folksong was not misplaced.

The evolution and eventual triumph of Bartók's compositional style is traced in lively detail in Benjamin Suchoff's *Béla Bartók: Concerto for Orchestra*. Few are as well positioned as Suchoff to write on Bartók's life and music. For many years curator of the New York Bartók Archive, editor of the Archive Edition, and author of the popular *Guide to Bartók's Mikrokosmos*, Suchoff is generally recognized as the dean of Bartók scholars. In the present volume, he begins by painting a broad picture of Bartók's musical language, tracing the composer's classical training, his early absorption of the Hungarian musical dialect, his fusion of national styles, and finally his joining of Eastern and Western idioms. Suchoff then turns to the Concerto for Orchestra itself, devoting chapters to each of its five movements. He concludes by outlining the influence of Bartók's innovations on later composers.

The Concerto for Orchestra is arguably Bartók's greatest public work.

Certainly it is the piece in which he achieved his most comprehensive synthesis of Eastern folksong elements and Western art forms. It was written in 1943, at a time when Bartók, in the final years of his life, was aiming at a broad, international style. Composed for Serge Koussevitzky and the Boston Symphony Orchestra, the Concerto shows Bartók treating the modern orchestra like a gigantic Baroque ensemble: there are passages for highly gifted solo players, and passages for a virtuoso tutti band. With its emphasis on orchestral color, its movement through a variety of moods (in a sense not unlike the "Eroica" Symphony of Beethoven), and its joyous finale (dubbed a "multinational round dance" by one writer), the Concerto is an uplifting affirmation of the human spirit. Its amalgamation of styles makes it a work of extraordinary universality, not unlike Bach's Mass in B Minor. That the Concerto for Orchestra is now a staple of the symphonic literature is a tribute to Bartók's ability to bring modern music into the mainstream (even when that required fulfilling Koussevitzky's request for a longer, more stirring coda to the final movement).

In *Béla Bartók: Concerto for Orchestra,* Suchoff describes these and other aspects of the Concerto for Orchestra in a masterful fashion. His book deepens our appreciation of Bartók's accomplishments and enables us to see more clearly the broad dimensions of his genius.

George B. Stauffer
Series Editor

Introduction

—————————— ✀ ——————————

𝓑artók's Concerto for Orchestra (1943) embodies what one might refer to as the "total Bartók" within a context based on the composer's most classical, lucid approach to form and texture. The Concerto can serve as a musical model for identifying the numerous types of folk-music sources collected by the composer and pointing to their infusion into an entirely original contemporary musical vocabulary. It is the intention of this book, therefore, to explore the work's thematic materials and formal structures, not only to introduce the student and music lover to the intrinsic musical value of this contemporary masterpiece itself, but also to reveal its value within the broader musical world of Bartók and twentieth-century developments in general. It is toward this end that the book provides a thorough historical survey of the musical language and sources of the Concerto, a systematic analytical overview of its melodic, harmonic, rhythmic, thematic, and formal dimensions, and a discussion of the musical legacy it has left for many composers in the post–World War II era.

As an eminent music critic remarked in 1981, on the occasion of the centenary of the composer's birth, listening to Bartók's music is not "easy," for it is filled with fragmentary motifs, complicated rhythms, and, above all, the web of eastern European peasant music that underlies almost everything the man wrote. Writing about his music is equally difficult, particularly when the objective is to address a broad spectrum of readers—concertgoers, performers, students, professors, and Bartókphiles in general. Thus, the book contains anecdotal and other materials of interest to the music-loving general public, including analytical synopses of the Concerto's five movements, in the style of concert program notes, and a profusion of music examples. The main thrust, however, is a scholarly presentation, particularly accessible for any level from the undergraduate music major to the specialist in the field of Bartók research. It addresses the multiplicity of Bartók's musical interests manifest in his introspective essays and other documents on his compositions, ethnomusicological research, music theory, and related aspects of his life and works.

When in 1995 the international world of music commemorated the fiftieth anniversary of Béla Bartók's death, international symposia were organized for the presentation of scholarly studies of his compositions and folk-music works. According to so-called conventional wisdom, the half-century period marks the point in time when the greater part of the extant source materials by and about famous historical figures will have been identified, located, and made available for research purposes. In the case of Bartók, however, the marker was set many years ago, when archives were established in New York and Budapest. I have been most fortunate in having had a primary role in the construction and development of the Béla Bartók Archives for more than thirty years, as well as having had freedom of access to the holdings of the Budapest Bartók Archívum during that time, including opportunities for research of other sources at the Academy of Sciences, the Academy of Music, and other repositories of Bartók memorabilia in Hungary and other European countries. How did these truly fortuitous events come to pass? Here follows the documented narrative.

During 1953, while I was investigating bibliographic sources related to my proposed New York University dissertation on Bartók's *Mikrokosmos*, I wrote to Halsey Stevens, then professor of composition at the University of Southern California, for assistance in locating primary source materials. Stevens, whose outstanding Bartók biography appeared that year, advised me to contact Victor Bator, a Hungarian-born attorney who had been designated in Bartók's will as executor and trustee of the Bartók estate. My December 29 letter to Bator, addressed to his Manhattan office, enclosed a list of "the specific problems needed to be solved in the preparation of my dissertation." The letter continued: "Dr. Halsey Stevens has been interested in my study and has been offering valuable suggestions as to procedure. He states that his own research discloses no information, left by Bartók himself, that would be helpful in my dissertion. He suggested that you would be the only person to have the information I need, if it exists at all."

An immediate interview was granted, and on January 3, 1954, I wrote another letter that summarized the results of our discussion, among them the offer "to lend me the photostats of the *Mikrokosmos* manuscripts when they are ready. In return for this courtesy I stated that I would supply you with a list of errors, if any, between the manuscripts and the Boosey & Hawkes publication." Following the interview, Bator opened the door to a large closet, the repository for an equally large chest of metal drawers, and permitted me to open them, one after the other. I was astonished to find the drawers crammed with well-worn, overstuffed envelopes, each one marked with one or several numbers and the Hungarian title of the related manuscripts, in Bartók's holograph.

During the summer, after photographic reproductions of the *Mikrokosmos* manuscripts as well as the contents of certain other envelopes had been readied for my examination by Bator's assistants, Nike Varga and Clifford Wooldridge, my letter of August 11—the first in a substantial number of them to the trustee—reported the following:

> What I am doing now is to collect the tissue copies of the *Mikrokosmos*, the sketches and the corrected tissue copies, and assemble them, with comments disclosed by research. (I am working with the photostatic copies, of course!) The bound collection Mr. Wooldridge [the rental librarian at Boosey and Hawkes] assembled was an excellent piece of work—unfortunately it contains music that belongs to the [*Mikrokosmos*] Sketches (#59). The Sketches contain manuscripts that belong to #58 [First Piano Concerto], and so forth. Additionally, I think we have located the missing tissue copies corrected by Bartók—they must be in London if they are not in your office. (According to the letter sent by Bartók to B. & H. in London.) I listed the missing pages and gave them to Mrs. Varga to copy and mail out.
>
> I have offered to help Mrs. Varga assemble the various documents that relate to the composer. . . . I think it is a wonderful idea to collect EVERY item of information concerning Bartók. If the Estate is willing to undergo the expense, some "international" bookstore should be contacted and given the order. Magazines must be secured, or photostatic copies thereof. Universities should be contacted to determine whether theses can be copied. A method of indexing and storing materials must be devised. "Official" Bartók Estate stationary should be printed for use in the work. A new system of numbering should be made—such as Köchel did for Mozart. Publicity should be sought to promote Bartók's name, and suggested topics sent to universities having doctoral programs. . . .

And thus began my association with the Bartók estate that ultimately led to the establishment of the Béla Bartók Archives, with myself as curator and its listing in the official New York City guide of cultural institutions. Before that climactic event, however, another important occurrence literally transformed my abiding interest in musicological research to studies in Bartókian ethnomusicology. In the archives' first publication, Victor Bator's *The Béla Bartók Archives* (1963), he describes the following circumstances.

In December, 1955, the premature death of Constantin Brăiloiu brought a new task for Dr. Suchoff. I had retained Professor Brăiloiu, the great Rumanian folk-music expert, who was then living in exile in Paris, to prepare for publication Bartók's Rumanian folk-music collection. He had, by 1955, almost finished Colinde, the volume of Rumanian Christmas Songs, but because of his many other creative interests in related fields, he had done very little work on the great collection of general song materials collected by Bartók in Transylvania. Dr. Suchoff, who had helped to save from physical disintegration and deterioration Bartók's Rumanian folk-music materials deposited in the archives of the library at Columbia University, and who, in the years 1956–1958, assisted me in supporting Professor Brăiloiu in his editorial work, willingly undertook to take over and complete the exacting task of editing, prefacing and double-checking the great collection. This task involved retroactive editorial co-ordination, for unified publication, of a work which had been written by Bartók over a period of twenty years: it also involved bringing this Rumanian material into harmony with Bartók's Serbo-Croatian folk-music work, published posthumously by Columbia University Press (in which appear in many references to the Rumanian work, as well as many refinements and organizational devices which Bartok had intended to transfer to the Rumanian material).

After completing the fair copy of the five volumes of Bartók's *Rumanian Folk Music*, and my success in finding—at long last!—a publisher willing to undertake the monumental project (Martinus Nijhoff, The Hague), I concluded agreements with the Bartók estate to edit other Bartók works: compositions, essays, letters, and folk-music collections. In addition, the trustee treated me as a confidant in the various litigations that had been initiated in the late 1950s by legal authorities of the Hungarian People's Republic; it became necessary for me to serve as an expert witness in a New York surrogate's court regarding expenditures in connection with the Béla Bartók Archives in general and the *Rumanian Folk Music* publication project in particular. Although the court ruled that such expenditures were indeed justified, other aspects of the litigation continued involving the Bartók heirs—Edith (Ditta) Bartók, the widow; her stepson, Béla Bartók Jr., both Hungarian citizens; and Peter Bartók, the composer's younger son, an American citizen—and publishers and performing-rights societies in the United States, England, Austria, and Hungary as a member of the other, so-called Iron Curtain countries.

But there was another reason for the weekly conferences between Bator and myself, up to 1967. He had presciently (and unbeknownst to me) signed a document appointing me successor trustee of the Bartók estate in the event of his death. Then, in the fateful month of December, when at age seventy-six Victor Bator passed away, it became my sole responsibility as successor trustee to deal with my "inheritance": first and foremost, the conclusion of probate proceedings in connection with the Bator estate and its relation to the Bartók estate, then the overwhelming litigation, the preparation of publications, archival supervision, myriad correspondences with present and aspiring Bartók publishers and other vendors, the clamorous requests for various kinds of support from the international music community, and so on and so forth, ad infinitum.

In August 1978, long after I had placed the collected materials in a new location and renamed them the New York Bartók Archive (of the estate of Béla Bartók), I received a letter from Professor Elliott Antokoletz, University of Texas at Austin. He requested permission to study the holdings with regard to preparation of his book on Bartók's tonal language: "My analytic studies of Bartók's music would suffer to a large extent without the possibility of looking into his compositional processes through his sketches, earlier versions of certain works, and other source material, i.e., that which pertains to Bartók's ethnomusicological work." Although I had received a substantial number of somewhat similar requests by Bartók scholars, Dr. Antokoletz was the first to propose the inclusion of folk music as a source for the study of Bartók's composed works. When I realized that the limited time each of us had for his proposed visit would be inadequate for a thorough investigation of the extensive ethnomusicological sources, I offered my assistance wherever applicable. In the few weeks we were together, a friendship was established that evolved into sharing of ideas and source materials and mutual support of our individual research and publication projects. It is therewith with deep appreciation that I express my gratitude for his assistance and encouragement in the preparation of this book. Grateful acknowledgement is also made to Maribeth Anderson Payne, former editor in chief of Schirmer Books; George Stauffer, series editor of *Monuments of Western Music*; Richard Carlin, editor in chief; and Jonathan Wiener, editor, of Schirmer Books. The dedication of this volume to my wife, Eleanor, will underscore the great share she has had in helping me bring this work to fruition.

ACKNOWLEDGEMENTS

To Boosey & Hawkes Music Publishers Ltd., acknowledgement is made for music examples from the following of Béla Bartók's works: First Violin Concerto, Concerto for Orchestra, Third Piano Concerto, and Viola Concerto. Acknowledgement is made to Boosey & Hawkes Inc., New York, for music examples from the following works: Suite op. 14 for Piano, *Out of Doors*, Nine Little Piano Pieces, First Violin Sonata, Second Violin Sonata, Fourth String Quartet, Fifth String Quartet, Music for Strings, Percussion and Celesta, *Duke Bluebeard's Castle*, Dance Suite, and First Piano Concerto. To Boosey & Hawkes Music Publishers Ltd., for music examples from Britten, *A Young Person's Guide to the Orchestra* and *War Requiem*. To Boosey & Hawkes Inc., New York, for music examples from Ginastera, Sonata No. 1 for Piano.

To Universal Edition A. G., Vienna, acknowledgement is made for music examples from the following works: Suite op. 14 for Piano, *Out of Doors*, Nine Little Piano Pieces, First Violin Sonata, Second Violin Sonata, Fourth String Quartet, Fifth String Quartet, Music for String Instruments, Percussion, and Celesta, *Duke Bluebeard's Castle*, Dance Suite, and First Piano Concerto.

To Editio Musica, Budapest, acknowledgement is made for music examples from the following works: *Kossuth* symphonic poem, Sonata for Violin and Piano (1903), Piano Quintet, Rhapsody op. 1, Fourteen Bagatelles op. 6, Two Elegies op. 8b, and Two Romanian Dances op. 8a.

To Durand (Paris) S.A., acknowledgement is made for the music example from Messiaen, Preludes for Piano. To C. F. Peters Corp., New

York, for the music example from Crumb, *Makrokosmos*, vol. 1, no. 1. To B. Schott's Söhne, Mainz, for the music examples from Ligeti, *Hungarian Rock (Chaconne)*. To Chester Music Ltd. for music examples from Lutosławksi, Album for the Young, First Symphony, and Funeral Music. To CPP/Belwin, Inc., Miami, the music example from Hernandez, *El Cumbanchero*.

Part One

---❧---

BARTÓK'S MUSICAL LANGUAGE

$\mathscr{Chapter\ 1}$

CHILDHOOD AND YOUTH: 1881–1899

⚶

$\mathscr{I}$was born on March 25, 1881," Bartók wrote in his autobiography, "in a small place called Nagyszentmiklós,"[1] near the junction of present-day Hungary, Romania, and Yugoslavia. His father, also named Béla Bartók, was head of the local agricultural school. In 1880 the elder Bartók married Paula Voit (born January 16, 1857), a Hungarian girl from Pozsony (or Pressburg, now Bratislava, Slovakia) who had come to Nagyszentmiklós as a primary-school teacher. Both husband and wife were gifted musicians. He played the piano and cello, founded the Nagyszentmiklós Music League, and composed dance pieces for the league's orchestra. Paula Bartók was a fairly accomplished pianist, and gave her son his first lessons.

At the close of the nineteenth century, the town of Nagyszentmiklós consisted of about 10,000 people, for the most part Germans, Hungarians, Romanians, and Serbs. After the ill-fated Hungarian revolution of 1848, led by Louis Kossuth, against the Austrian Habsburg monarchy, government officials were dispatched to the neighborhood with instructions to institute German as the official language. Socially and intellectually, however, the influence of Hungarians like Bartók's parents was predominant, and the child was brought up with Hungarian as his mother tongue.

Although Bartók was a strong, healthy baby, he developed a chronic case of eczema that lasted five years following a smallpox vaccination at the age of three months. "The permanent itchiness, the people shocked at the

11

sight of the spots, and the many medical treatments without any result made him a reticent child," Bartók's oldest son, Béla, wrote later.[2] In a series of eleven letters to her grandson, Béla Jr., from August 14, 1921, to November 5, 1922, Paula Bartók set down an account of her son's life from infancy until his graduation, in 1903, from the Budapest Academy of Music. She recalled that his illness had no effect on his mental development:

> Once, at the age of one and a half, I played a little dance piece for him, and he listened with great attention. The next day he pointed to the piano and made a sign that I should play (he could not as yet speak). I played several dance pieces, but he only shook his little head until I played that certain piece, whereupon he gave a nod of assent, smiling happily. I put him to the test on the third day, whether or not it had been pure chance, but he behaved as before until I played the right piece.
>
> He was given a drum at the age of three, that he played with great delight. When I played the piano, he sat on a little chair, his drum on a footstool before him, and beat time precisely. When I changed from 3/4 to 4/4, he stopped beating for a moment and then went on in the right time, accompanying my playing earnestly and attentively. During special events, when Gypsies performed in our house, he listened with amazing interest. When he was four years old he played folk songs on the piano, with one finger. He learned forty songs, and when we spoke the words he immediately started to play the song.[3]

On his fifth birthday, Bartók had his first piano lesson from his mother. Two years later, his parents discovered that he had absolute pitch and could correctly recognize each tone while he was in another room.

Bartók's father died on August 4, 1888, after a protracted illness, and the little family (his sister, Elza, was born in 1885) had to vacate the school principal's residence in October and take up temporary lodging elsewhere. Mrs. Bartók returned to her former position as a primary-school teacher in Nagyszentmiklós, supplementing her income by giving private piano lessons. Her sister Irma took over the household duties.

Although Bartók excelled in his primary-school studies, Mrs. Bartók was dissatisfied with the limited educational opportunities offered in the small, provincial town. The secondary school system only offered a six-year curriculum for skilled workers that did not qualify humanities-oriented students for further study after graduation. She decided to relocate to a larger town, where her son could enroll in an eight-year gymnasium (academic high school). In 1889 the family was transferred for three years to Nagyszöllős, at the northeast tip of Hungary, which subsequently became Czechoslovak, and still later Russian, territory. The next year, when Bartók was nine, a waltz melody came to his mind in the afternoon during his mother's nap, when piano playing was forbidden. When he played it for her later that day, she realized that he had a creative talent worth nurturing, and she wrote down the composition in a six-stave manuscript book under the title Walczer Opus 1 (Example 1.1).[4]

Thereafter, Bartók composed a number of other piano pieces, including polkas, ländlers,[5] mazurkas, two sonatinas, and sections from his first programmatic work, A Duna folyása (The Course of the Danube), inspired, according to his mother, by his school history and geography lessons. His playing was heard by Christian Altdörfer (1825–1898), an organist and composer from the town of Sopron, who predicted a great future for the boy and insisted that he should be properly taught by a good master. In the autumn of 1891, therefore, Mrs. Bartók took her son to Budapest for an evaluation of his talent by Károly Aggházy (1855–1918)—a pupil of Liszt and professor of piano at the Budapest National Conservatorium—who immediately accepted Bartók as a pupil. But the mother had no means of providing for her son in Budapest or paying for his tuition. Nor did she want his general education to be neglected. On returning to Nagyszöllős, she arranged for him to go to Nagyvárad, a somewhat

Example 1.1. Bartók, Waltz for Piano, op. 1 (1890), mm. 1–16.

larger town in southeast Hungary (now Oradea, Romania), a few miles east of the present frontier. Here Bartók was able to stay with another aunt, Emma Voit, widow of his mother's elder brother.

In Nagyvárad, Bartók was registered in the Premonstratensian Grammar School, and he continued his piano studies with Ferenc Kersch (1853–1910), an organist and choirmaster of some distinction, whose chief interest was church music. Kersch's teaching was rather superficial, and he overburdened the boy with difficult pieces in an effort to mold him as a prodigy. Bartók was unable to cope with the inordinate goals that Kersch had set for him. In addition, he was on the verge of failing geography and mathematics because of favoritism toward wealthier students by his schoolteachers. When he developed eye problems in April 1892, Mrs. Bartók decided to bring him back to Nagyszöllős, and on May 1, Bartók gave his first public concert at the Royal Hungarian State National School. He played his composition, *A Duna folyása*, and it has been reported that the recital included, among other pieces, the first movement of Beethoven's Sonata op. 53 (*Waldstein*).[6] *A Duna folyása* was a remarkable achievement for a child. The time of performance is about eighteen minutes, with the 573 bars divided into three sections descriptively subtitled as follows:[7]

I (173 bars)
    1. The source of the Danube
    2. Polka: it is pleased that it is approaching Hungary
II (266 bars)
    3. Polka: still more joyful because it has reached Hungary
    4. The Danube converses with its tributaries. They answer it.
    5. Liveliest, Csárdás,[8] it reaches Budapest
    6. The Danube absorbs the Tisza
    7. It says farewell to Hungary
    8. It is at the Iron Gate. The echo of the cliffs
III (134 bars)
    9. The Danube is still sad that it has left Hungary
    10. It flows into the Black Sea

It is indeed interesting that Budapest (no. 5) is represented by the *csárdás* and the departure from Hungary (No. 9) by the *kolomyjka* rhythm schema, 2/4 ♪♪♪♪|♪♪♪♪|♪♪♪♪|♩ ♩ (Example 1.2).[9]

The young composer's debut was a rousing success. He was thought

Example 1.2. Bartók, The Course of the Danube *for Piano, op. 20 (1890–1894), nos. 5a. and 9b.*

so outstanding that the local director of education used his influence to secure the mother a year's leave to further Bartók's musical education. She made use of this opportunity to take him to Pozsony (Pressburg; now Bratislava, Slovakia), musically the foremost provincial town in Hungary, where she hoped to find a permanent post for herself. Here Bartók attended the Hungarian-language Catholic Grammar School and enjoyed the first real enrichment of his musical experience, in surroundings as congenial as they were stimulating. He was able for the first time to study piano and theory with a first-class teacher, László Erkel (1844–1896), the third son of Ferenc Erkel (1810–1893), but also "of hearing a few operas, more or less well performed, and orchestra concerts."[10] This more agreeable life was again interrupted in the autumn of 1893, when his mother's leave of absence expired and she was transferred to Beszterce (now Bistriţa, Romania), a small town at the eastern end of the country, where there was no musical life and no pianist qualified to teach him. Fortunately, even here he met Sándor Schönherr, a forester and competent amateur violinist, with whom he played duos each week, including Beethoven's *Kreutzer* Sonata and Mendelssohn's Violin Concerto, and he continued composing dance pieces for the piano.

On the other hand, Bartók's educational experiences were troublesome, not withstanding his rank as fifth out of forty-five pupils. He had to attend the "szasz" (Transylvanian Saxon) grammar school, where the instruction was exclusively in German. He was resistant and unhappy, and his resentment of the Austrian and German domination of Hungarian education and culture in later life may have begun here. Since the defeat of the revolution in 1849, Hungarian national feeling against the Austrians, who had in effect ruled Hungary for more than two hundred years, had been intensified. In 1867 the Hungarians had won a certain degree of constitutional independence and equality of rights within the Habsburg Empire, and a succession of moderate leaders, making less ambitious demands, had slowly secured considerable, further concessions. But these were regarded by the extreme nationalists as only stepping-stones to complete independence, and their impatience grew steadily. This was the political atmosphere into which Bartók was born and grew up, and from this environment, together with his early schooling, his dislike of Austrians and Germans originated.

In April 1894, Mrs. Bartók was offered a permanent appointment in Pozsony, at the practice school of the State Teacher's Training College, and her son resumed his lessons with László Erkel. Bartók commemorated his return by composing a three-movement piano sonata as the first opus in a new series of abstract compositions (Example 1.3).

Erkel was a competent if undistinguished musician, and under him Bartók made steady progress. When Erkel died in 1896, he continued his studies with another music teacher, Anton Hyrtl (1840–1914), and with János Batka (1845–1917), a librarian and writer on music. Among the

Example 1.3. Bartók, Sonata no. 1 in G Minor, op. 1 (1894).

various musical organizations was the "St. Martin Society," which organized frequent orchestral and chamber concerts, and provided the orchestra for operatic performances at the municipal theater. As a student, Bartók had cheap or free access to all of these, and also took part in some. Thus, by the time he was eighteen, he was fairly familiar with the main musical literature from Bach to Brahms, though with Wagner only as far as *Tannhäuser*. He made the acquaintance of Ernő Dohnányi (1877–1960), four years his senior, who was then a student at the Royal Academy of Music in Budapest, but whose home was in Pozsony. Dohnányi was already highly esteemed as a pianist, and had begun to make a name as a composer with his Piano Quintet in C minor, op. 1 (1895), followed a little later by his Symphony in F (1897), which won him a King's Prize. The piano quintet and the works of Brahms had a great influence on Bartók's student compositions (Example 1.4).

At this time and for several years, the emulation of Dohnányi was regarded by Bartók and those around him as the ideal at which Bartók should aim. He was spoken and thought of as a "second Dohnányi," a label that followed him even when he entered the Academy of Music at Budapest. The comparison was obvious and flattering, giving no cause for jealousy owing to the difference in their ages. "Second" meant second in time, but did not necessarily imply second in ability. Bartók in effect followed very closely in Dohnányi's footsteps when the latter went to Budapest—Bartók succeeded him in Pozsony as organist at the gymnasium chapel and as star of the school concerts. He also began to play at concerts outside the school and earn money by teaching and accompanying. His first public appearance in Pozsony was in 1896, as accompanist for a melodrama given in the municipal theater, on the occasion of the mil-

Example 1.4. Bartók, Intermezzo in C Minor, no. 1 from Three Piano Pieces, op. 21 (June–July, 1898), mm. 1–4.

lenary of Hungary's foundation. In 1897 Bartók played Liszt's *Spanish Rhapsody*, and in the following year, at a concert at the County Hall on March 15, in commemoration of the fiftieth anniversary of the 1848 revolution, he played his own transcription of three popular Hungarian folk songs.

Toward the end of the year, the question of further musical training arose. "In Pozsony, at that time [1898]," Bartók noted in his autobiography, "the Vienna Conservatorium was considered the sole bastion of serious musical education."[11] In December, therefore, he went to Vienna for an audition with Hans Schmitt (1835–1907), an outstanding piano teacher who had written hundreds of etudes and a book on the fundamentals of piano technique. Bartók was offered a scholarship, although he was not an Austrian citizen. After some consideration during the Christmas holiday and following a meeting with Dohnányi, in January he traveled to Budapest for an audition with Dohnányi's piano teacher, István Thomán (1862–1940).

> The great teacher received me with his proverbial loving interest which instantly inspires courage on the part of the beginner and gives him confidence—not only toward the teacher but also in himself. The audition was a success, the master found that I had talent, and I could return home to Pozsony with the knowledge that after I finished my last school year I would enter the Music Academy as Thomán's pupil. . . . He also recommended me to János Koessler (1853–1926) so that I could study composition, too. At that time he could not even imagine that it was going to be just "composing" that would later thrust "piano playing" into the background.
>
> I must have been a real "savage" as a pianist when I first came to Thomán. My technique was good enough, but thoroughly crude. Thomán taught me the correct position of the hands and all the different "natural" and "summarizing" movements which the newest pedagogy has since made into a truly theoretical system and which, however, Liszt had already applied instinctively and Thomán, a former pupil of Liszt, could acquire directly from his great master. Thus, the most initiated hands imparted to me the mastery of poetically coloring the piano tone.[12]

In February 1899, Bartók suddenly became ill with a lung condition. Physical activity was kept to a minimum and piano playing was strictly forbidden. With the help of daily visits by a classmate, he managed to keep up with his schoolwork and pass the final examinations in June. During the summer, his mother took him to convalesce in the Austrian subalpine climate of Eberhard, Carinthia. In September, fully restored to health, Bartók took up residence in Budapest and began his studies at the Academy of Music, with high hopes for a distinguished career as pianist and composer.

Chapter 2

SUMMARY OF HUNGARIAN MUSICAL DIALECT: 1900–1905

At the end of the seventeenth century, following the withdrawal of Turkish forces from central Hungary, Hussar officers of the Austro-Hungarian monarchy established the practice of recruiting young men by using heroic dance music performed on the bagpipe or by Gypsy bands. Designated *verbunkos* ("recruiting"), with alternating slow and fast tempos, certain rhythms are related to the Hungarian *kanásztánc* (swineherd's dance), Romanian *Ardeleana* (Transylvanian round dance), and Ruthenian *kolomyjka* (round dance). The *verbunkos*, when removed from a military setting, grew into the national Hungarian instrumental music idiom, including its transformation into the *csárdás* dance forms during the first half of the nineteenth century. The widespread public demand for *verbunkos*-styled music also led to the composition of dance suites, chamber music, and other types of serious works. But the chief propagators were city Gypsy bands, which performed their repertory "with an excess of *rubato* and ornaments."[1]

During the *verbunkos* transformation period, a folklike art song in ABA form (*Volkstümlichlied*) penetrated Hungary through the intermediation of German vernacular opera. The popularity of this new type of urban folk song led to the publication of thousands of Hungarian imitations, for the most part composed by amateur musicians of the educated Hungarian classes, which were printed with hackneyed piano accompaniments and disseminated by Gypsy bands in Austrian and Hungarian towns. These characteristic melodies, known collectively as *magyar nótak* (plural, "Hungarian tunes") and considered to be the true national folk music, were taken over in various ways by eighteenth- and nineteenth-century composers. Indeed, the Gypsy-styled *nóta* (singular) inspired Franz Liszt to create his Hungarian Rhapsodies (1839–1885) and eventually develop the unique tonal language of his masterpiece, the Piano Sonata in B Minor (1852–1853). And, in turn, it was the unique formal and tonal characteristics in these and other Liszt works that ultimately would have so profound an effect on Bartók's development.

As indicated in Chapter 1, Bartók's early musical training and knowledge were deeply rooted in eighteenth- and nineteenth-century Germanic tradition, that is, the standard repertory from Bach to Brahms. During his student years at the Budapest Academy of Music, beginning in 1899, this repertory was emphasized by his composition teacher, Hans Koessler, to the point where Bartók became discouraged with the possibilities of evolving a Hungarian style of composing. His lifelong friend, Zóltan Kódaly, recalled that

> The wave of independence following the Millenium celebrations [1896] was then reaching its climax. Public opinion demanded things Hungarian in every sphere of life: Hungarian words of command and Hungarian insignia in the army, and a Hungarian anthem instead of *Gott erhalte*. . . . Bartók, too, wanted everything to be Hungarian, from language to dress. For years he went about in Hungarian-style clothes fashionable at the time, and that was what he wore on the concert platform as well.[2]

On the other hand, Bartók's piano teacher, István Thomán emphasized the interpretation of Chopin and Liszt. Thus encouraged, Bartók in 1901 prepared Liszt's Piano Sonata and performed it at the academy concert celebrating Liszt's ninetieth birthday. The unanimous applause of the Budapest press was followed by the award of the Liszt Prize. Bartók later confessed that "I first encountered Liszt's Piano Sonata when I was a student, but at that time, although I tried, I could not like it. I felt that the first half of the exposition was cold and empty. . . ."[3] In 1902, therefore, he turned to the *nóta* as the stylistic source for expressing his intense national feelings and composed four songs on texts by Lajos Pósa, a well-known writer of popular verse. In the first song, the traditional piano accompaniment doubles the vocal part, features commonplace tonic-

subdominant-dominant harmony in the first melody section, and modu-
lates to the relative major, E♭, in the second melody section (Example
2.1).

That same year, two seemingly unrelated events provided another
route for Bartók to follow. Hungary celebrated the centennial of Lajos
(Louis) Kossuth's birth, in commemoration of his leadership during the
ill-fated Hungarian War of Independence against Austria from 1848 to
1849. And, in February, the Budapest Philharmonic presented the Hungarian premiere of Richard Strauss's symphonic poem, *Also sprach
Zarathustra* (1896). In his autobiography Bartók writes that, during the
performance,

> "I was roused as by a lightning stroke. . . . At last there was a way of com-
> posing which seems to hold the seeds of a new life. At once I threw my-
> self into the study of all of Strauss's scores and began again to write music
> myself. . . . [T]he aim was set [by a new national movement in Hungary]
> to create something specifically Hungarian."[4]

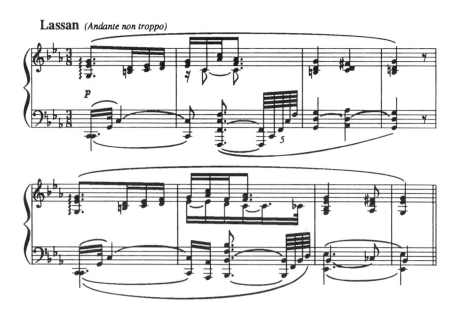

Example 2.1. Bartók, Négy dal *(Four Songs), for Voice and Piano, no. 1, mm. 1–8.*

This study introduced Bartók to the harmonic possibilities of unresolved dissonance, a contrapuntal approach to polytonal chromaticism, and the use of nondiatonic octave segments. The close of the four-part fugue exposition in the "Von der Wissenschaft" ("Of Science") section of *Zarathustra* juxtaposes the B-minor twelve-tone subject in augmented values in the bass, the G-major abbreviated reprise of the first answer in the alto, and free chromatic counterpoint in the soprano and tenor (Example 2.2).

Later, in the "Das Tanzlied" ("The Dance Song") section, the Liszt-Strauss continuum is apparent with regard to the octatonic pentachords played by the oboe. The nonfunctional chordal accompaniment in the strings, however, is Strauss's innovation (Example 2.3).

Bartók's perception of Liszt's influence on Strauss, particularly in terms of octatonicism and thematic metamorphosis, is reflected in the *Kossuth* symphonic poem, which Bartók composed in 1903. In the battle section of the work, the first two bars of the Austrian national anthem represent the motif of the Austrian army, and a fanfare motif describes the op-

Example 2.2. Strauss, Also sprach Zarathustra, *op. 30 (1896).*

("das Tanzlied")

Example 2.3. Strauss, Also sprach Zarathustra.

posing Hungarian forces. Bartók's metamorphosis of the anthem motif is the basis for a series of grotesque variations, which begin with a tritone-bounded, pentachordal segment of the C♯-octatonic scale. The Hungarian trumpet motif, in contrapuntal apposition, emphasizes the tritone, C♯–F×, which is characteristic of the C♯ Hungarian-Gypsy scale (Example 2.4).

The two motifs, seemingly discrete pitch collections, interact to form a kind of nondiatonic polymodal chromaticism, that is, the superposing of an octatonic pentachord and the nondiatonic Hungarian-Gypsy scale,

Example 2.4. (a) Gott erhalte, *mm. 1–4, and (b) Bartók,* Kossuth *symphonic poem, mm. 318–322.*

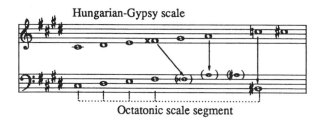

Example 2.5. Nine-tone C♯ polymode formed by juxtaposed nondiatonic pitch collections in Kossuth, *mm. 318–322.*

each with C♯ as the common fundamental tone, to form a chromatic poly-mode (Example 2.5).

The pentachord in the second bar of the anthem, whose underlying text is *Franz den Kaiser* (Example 2.4), is chromatically transformed into the octatonic configuration B♯–C♯–E–F♯–G (Example 2.6, beginning at m. 394). The juxtaposed minor seconds are a tritone apart, and they mark the first appearance of a characteristic (double-tritone) tetrachord in Bartók's musical language. This tetrachord, one of the composer's most basic symmetrical pitch constructions pervading the mature Bartók idiom, is commonly referred to as a "Z-cell."

While the variations are spun out by the tubas, the overlying orchestral

Example 2.6. Bartók, Kossuth, *mm. 393–404.*

Example 2.7. Bartók, Kossuth, *mm. 408–409.*

fabric is a remarkable approximation of Straussian contrapuntal tonality in a totally chromatic context (see Example 2.2). Then, in the next section, the octatonic "Kaiser-cell" is transformed by extension in range to whole-tone construction. The contrapuntal texture is based on inversionally related segments in the woodwinds and horns, whose axis, G♭, initiates each ascending whole-tone scale in the strings (Example 2.7).

These whole-tone passages foreshadow another characteristic configuration in Bartók's tonal language. This is manifested in the tuba and contrabass expressly as the tritone-bounded whole-tone tetrachord A♭–B♭–C–D, a fundamental symmetrical construction commonly referred to as a "Y-cell."

The work ends with a funeral march, to portray the "deepest woe and mourning" of Hungary's defeat, where the symbolic motif is a transformed theme from Liszt's Gypsy-styled Hungarian Rhapsody no. 2 (Example 2.8).

The third (last) movement of Bartók's Sonata for Violin and Piano (1903), a large rondo form that was begun during the composition of *Kossuth*, offers additional evidence of Bartók's preliminary steps toward creating a new, specifically Hungarian tonal language. Instead of Straussian polytonal chromaticism, where linear counterpoint is the vehicle for tonality in a totally chromatic context (see Example 2.2), Lisztian "multitonal chromaticism" is emulated; that is, the themes are embedded in a succession of diatonic and nondiatonic scale constructions that are based on the

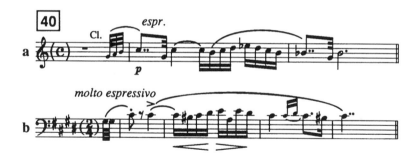

Example 2.8. (a) Kossuth, *mm. 449–451, and (b) Liszt,* Hungarian Rhapsody *no. 2 (1847), mm. 10–14.*

principal tone E or its transpositions to C, G, and B. The first theme of the movement is based on the Hungarian-Gypsy scale, E–F♯–G–A♯–B–C–D♯ (Example 2.9).

The second theme, a transformation of the first theme, has the same scale transposed to the submediant, C–D–E♭–F♯–G–A♭–B. The change in tempo replicates Gypsy style, but only with regard to alternating fast and slow rhythms. The theme and its permutations show no trace of the profuse ornaments that invariably characterize Hungarian-Gypsy performance (Example 2.10).

The third theme, which begins and ends in G major, includes varia-

Example 2.9. Bartók, Sonata for Violin and Piano *(1903), third movement, mm. 1–4.*

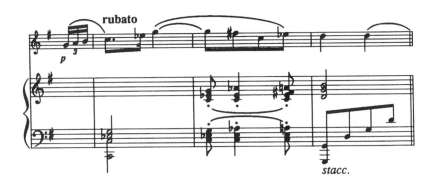

Example 2.10. Bartók, Sonata for Violin and Piano, third movement, mm. 36–39.

tions a third higher in the Hungarian-Gypsy scale (B–C♯–D–E♯–F♯–G–A♯) and the harmonic minor.[5] A transition, which includes an emphatic rendition of the tritone E–A♯, leads to the return of the first theme.

Although the fourth theme, a transformation of Theme 2, opens with the C Hungarian-Gypsy scale (also designated as Gypsy-minor scale), the tonality alternates with the so-called *kalindra* ("Phrygian") form of the Gypsy-minor scale (hereafter designated Gypsy-Phrygian scale), C–D♭–E–F–G–A♭–B (Example 2.11), and ends with a cadence in C major.[6]

Example 2.12 illustrates the first half of the retransition to the tonic key, which begins with tritone relationships of the octatonic hexachord,

Example 2.11. Bartók, Sonata for Violin and Piano, third movement, mm. 358–361.

Example 2.12. Bartók, Sonata for Violin and Piano, third movement, mm. 363–366.

B♭–C–D♭–E♭–E–F♯ (mm. 362–365). This nondiatonic pitch collection is expanded to a heptachord by the addition of A in m. 366, which results in the formation of the "tonic" octatonic tetrachord, E–A–B♭–D♯ (or the Z-cell construction referred to in Example 2.6).

Repetitions of the octatonic tetrachord (Z-cell) are followed by the entry of the violin with configurations of the whole-tone scale, B♭–C–D–E–F♯–G♯ (Example 2.13; cf. Example 2.7), which lead to the reprise of the first theme.

The last appearance of the second theme is followed by the third theme in E major. Repeated diminished-seventh chords introduce an octatonic statement of the first theme (Example 2.14).

Although the final reprise of the first theme also is in E major, the tonality is masked by motivic variations in the violin while the bass line ascent of the chordal piano accompaniment encompasses the chromatic scale. Furthermore, the coda ends with a twelve-measure section limited to

Example 2.13. Bartók, Sonata for Violin and Piano, third movement, mm. 372–374.

Example 2.14. Bartók, Sonata for Violin and Piano, third movement, mm. 530–535.

melodic and harmonic configurations of the perfect fifth, E–B, as an implicit inference of so-called neutral tonality, that is, neither major nor minor but only based on E as the principal tone of the movement.[7]

Example 2.15 is a compilation of the pitch collections, in the order of their appearance in the movement, which graphically illustrates Bartók's use of multitonality—the alternation of related diatonic and nondiatonic scales—as the means for creating a specifically Hungarian chromatic style.

When the *Kossuth* symphonic poem was premiered in January 1904, its grotesque parody of the Austrian national anthem created a sensation in Hungarian musical circles and immediately propelled Bartók into the national limelight as a composer. The Budapest music critics nevertheless complained that too much emphasis was placed on Strauss's Germanic musical language or that the composition lacked the Hungarian national melodies (i.e., *nóta*) that had inspired such great composers of the past as Schubert, Liszt, and Brahms. The next month, Bartók went to England for a performance of *Kossuth* in Manchester. This lengthy review of the concert is an interesting mixture of praise and condemnation:

> The mere fact that a young composer should attempt to follow in the footsteps of so tremendous a "Jack the Giant-killer" as Strauss would seem to betray the consciousness of great powers, and the degree of facility in handling great orchestral masses exhibited by Mr. Bartók would be remarkable in anyone, and is doubly surprising in so young an artist. His themes, too, have life in them, and in certain cases awaken a hope that in the course of time, when he shall have had enough of the Straussian chase, he may do excellent work. . . .

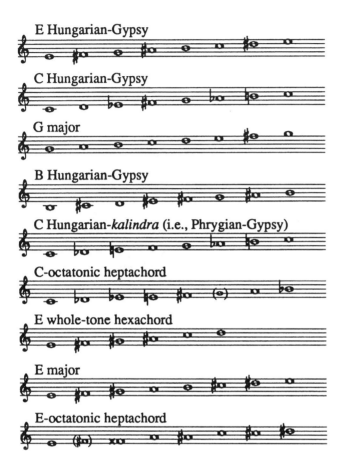

Example 2.15. Bartók, Sonata for Violin and Piano: synoptic tabulation of scalar or modal pitch collections in the third movement.

No justification of any kind can be found for such use as Mr. Bartók's of the Austrian Hymn. It cannot be pretended that the strains of that noble anthem have any fitness for musical purpose. They form a mere label, informing the listener that the reference is here to the Austrian host. Moreover, guying and degrading of the famous melody is altogether repulsive. . . . Apart from the function of the theme as a barefaced label, analogous to a piece of writing in the middle of a painted picture, "Yankee Doodle" would have served the purpose much better.[8]

In response to the suggestions of Hungarian and English critics, Bartók turned to the *magyar nóta* as a melodic source and transformed the well-known popular art song *Ég a kunyhó* ("The Hut Is Burning"), as a theme in the second movement of his next work, the Piano Quintet (1903–1904; Example 2.16).

When in the summer and fall of 1904 Bartók composed the Rhapsody op. 1, for Piano and Orchestra, a work cast in a Lisztian mold and requiring a virtuoso piano technique, he later recalled that year as the time when

> the magic of Strauss had evaporated. A really thorough study of Liszt's *oeuvre*, especially of some of his less well known works . . . revealed to me the true essence of composing. I began to understand the significance of the composer's work. For the future development of music his *oeuvre* seemed to me of far greater importance than that of Strauss or even Wagner.[9]

The rhapsody form created by Liszt, however, with its separate slow and fast movements, is transformed in Bartók's Rhapsody, op. 1, into a

Example 2.16. (a) Source melody, and (b) Bartók, Piano Quintet, second movement, mm. 479–487.

one-movement, concerto-like work with three distinct sections. The opening *Adagio molto* is somewhat similar to sonata form, with principal and secondary motifs, followed by a kind of development of the principal motif that ends with a third motif, and a reprise of the principal and secondary motifs. With only a fermata on C♯ in the piano solo as the point of demarcation, the rondo-like *Poco allegretto* begins with the third motif, which alternates with a fourth motif until the entry of the fifth motif in the full orchestra. The second section concludes with the principal and secondary motifs transformed into an *Allegro vivace*, which is followed by a *ritardando molto*. The latter tempo change leads without pause into the third section, where the *Adagio* principal motif returns briefly to close the work. Although the tonal language summarizes Hungarian musical dialect of the nineteenth century, the innovative architectonic (ABA) form of the Rhapsody heralds Bartók's turn toward Beethovenian structural principles as modified by Liszt—a stylistic synthesis that is an essential part of Bartók's later musical language.

The rhythm schema of the third motif in the *Allegretto* is a transformation of the second-theme pattern in the Vivace of Liszt's Hungarian Rhapsody no. 13. Liszt's source melody, in turn, is a Gypsy version of a widespread popular art song that was also taken over by Hungarian and Slovak peasants (Example 2.17).[10]

Example 2.17. (a) Bartók, Rhapsody op. 1, for Piano and Orchestra (b) Liszt, Hungarian Rhapsody no. 13, mm. 126–128, and (c) Bartók, The Hungarian Folk Song, *no. 73, mm. 1–3.*

The fourth motif of the *Allegretto* is a transformed (octatonic) borrowing of the first theme in the *Vivace* of Liszt's Hungarian Rhapsody no. 7 (Example 2.18).

During the summer of 1904, while Bartók was working on the Rhapsody, op. 1, he overheard a nursemaid, Lidi Dósa, singing a melody that had very unusual qualities. She was of peasant origin, born and raised in a Székely village in the southeast corner of Transylvania (now Romania).[11] He transcribed her entire song repertory, because he realized that he had discovered structural attributes radically different from those in the popular art songs that passed as Hungarian folk songs in Budapest's musical life. In the case of her song "Piros alma" ("Red Apple"), he found the use of alternating Dorian and Aeolian modes instead of the commonplace harmonic minor scale, and a truncated ABC form (2 + 2 + 3 measures) rather than the usual Hungarian-styled quaternary stanzas. And he later included her piece among the other indigenous folk melodies in his book, *The Hungarian Folk Song* (Example 2.19).

Bartók transcribed "Piros alma" for voice and piano, and sent the manuscript to the Budapest publication, *Magyar Lant* (Hungarian Lute), where it was printed in the Supplement on February 15, 1905. It is in-

Example 2.18. (a) Bartók, Rhapsody op. 1, for Piano and Orchestra, mm. 626–629, and (b) Liszt, Hungarian Rhapsody no. 7, Vivace, mm. 16–20.

Tempo Giusto

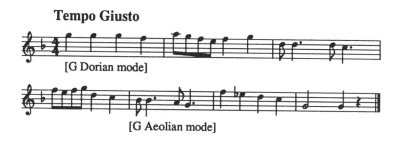

Example 2.19. Bartók, The Hungarian Folk Song, *no. 313.*

deed interesting that Bartók's transcription features the traditional *nóta*-styled accompaniment—for the most part consisting of simple major and minor chords—perhaps as a means to attract the attention of the Budapest public to its peculiar structure (Example 2.20).

Example 2.20. Bartók, Székely népdal *(Székely Folk Song), mm. 17–22.*

During August, Bartók was in Paris as a participant in the *Prix Rubinstein* competition, as pianist and composer. His failure to win a prize, particularly in composition, was a bitter experience:

> The preparation for the Rubinstein Competition gave me so frightfully much to do, and all to no purpose. There were 5 competitors for the composition prize; the works of the other 4 were below average, mine was above, hence the meticulous members of the jury, who subscribed to the principle "the golden mean," did not award the prize to anyone at all. ... [T]he worst that I expected was that someone else's work would be pronounced better than mine and the prize awarded to that person. ...
>
> ... I must say that Bach, Beethoven, Schubert and Wagner have written such quantities of distinctive and characteristic music that all the music of France, Italy and the Slavs combined, is as nothing by comparison! Even if, say, my "Funeral March" [from *Kossuth*] could hold its own in one respect or another, no nation could possibly appear in the arena with a single 4-page piece, however magnificent it might be! In short: we are still far being ready to start. Work and study, work and study, and again, work and study. Then we may be able to achieve something. For we're in a surprisingly favorable position, compared with other nations, in regard to our folk music. From what I know of the folk music of other nations, ours is vastly superior to theirs as regards force of expression and variety. If a peasant with the ability to compose tunes like one of the enclosed had but emerged from his class during childhood, he would assuredly have created some outstanding works of great value.[12]

That same month another young Hungarian composer, Zoltán Kodály, was collecting Hungarian folk songs in northern Hungary (now Slovakia). Toward the end of the year, he published thirteen of the songs, including one specimen, apparently related to a *nóta* source melody, which shows alternation of the same modes sung by Lidi Dósa in 1904 (Example 2.21; cf. Example 2.19).[13]

Struck by this similarity of modal transformation of popular art song, Bartók arranged a meeting with Kodály to discuss the significance of this type of folk song. Under Kodály's tutelage, Bartók became acquainted with the Edison gramophone—an early recording/playback device that recorded on wax cylinders—and "set out in 1905 to collect and study

Tempo giusto

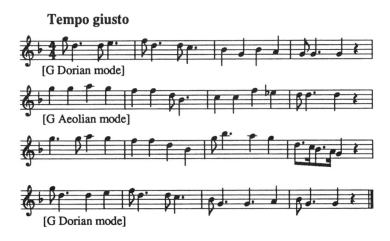

[G Dorian mode]

[G Aeolian mode]

[G Dorian mode]

Example 2.21. Kodaly, "Mátyusföldi gyűtés" (Mátyusföld Collection), melody no. 9.

Hungarian peasant music unknown till then."[14] In September 1906, during a collecting tour of northern Hungary, he recorded a quaternary Slovak folk song that he later determined was not only a variant of a Hungarian art song but also related to Lidi Dósa's truncated melody he had notated in 1904 (Example 2.22).

Bartók's analysis of the three related melodies prompted his observation that this Hungarian art song became popular among Hungarian, Slovak, and Moravian peasants to the point where it was adapted and became a peasant song. The Slovak adaptation then passed into Hungary, where it was truncated to ternary structure (Example 2.19): "This is one of the most instructive instances of changes undergone by a tune during its peregrinations."[16]

When in 1905 Bartók again took up the study of Liszt's Piano Sonata in B Minor, his previous feeling of a "cold and empty" first half of the exposition changed. As he later wrote, "The few subdued introductory bars, the main thematic group of the exposition . . . All these are among the great things in music."[17] Among Liszt's striking innovations are the contrast between the introductory Phrygian mode and the nondiatonic Gypsy-minor scale, each with G as principal tone, and the pentatonic contour of the subsidiary theme in D major (Example 2.23).

Example 2.22. (a) Hungarian popular song,[15] *and (b) melody no. 1048a from Bartók's Slovak folk-music collection.*

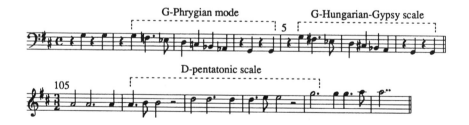

Example 2.23. Liszt, Piano Sonata in B Minor, mm. 1–7, 105–109.

The last work of this period is an orchestral composition for large orchestra, Suite no. 1, op. 3, a romantic work in five movements, whose thematic orientation more or less continues in the Lisztian *nóta* vein. The orchestration, however, is Straussian in approach: "In one long section of the Adagio there are as many as nineteen different string parts, the double-basses 'divisi a tre,' the other strings, 'a quattro.'"[18] During the next two years of "creative stagnation," Bartók applied himself exclusively to the recording, transcription, and comparative study of Hungarian and Slovak musical folklore.

Chapter 3

FUSION OF NATIONAL
MUSICAL STYLES: 1906–1925

*D*uring the spring of 1906, Zoltán Kodály proposed that he and Bartók collaborate in the collection and transcription of Hungarian peasant songs, and that they underwrite the cost of publication in a series of volumes titled *Hungarian Folk Songs for Voice and Piano Accompaniment*. Kodály would travel to northern villages (now Slovakian territory) and Bartók to Transylvania (now part of Romania) and other eastern areas. The agreed objective was to introduce the general public (that is, the educated classes) to the best examples of the indigenous rural music of Hungary, which, as described by Kodály, would be

> to a certain extent adapted to public taste by an appropriate form of musical arrangement. Folk songs should be acceptably clothed to be taken from the fields to the city. In urban costume, however, they are awkward and uncomfortable.... the accompaniment should always reflect the rural spirit of the fields and villages left behind.[1]

On June 29, Bartók set out on his first field trip to collect folk music. He recorded "Ablakomba, ablakomba" ("Through My Window") in a small town near Budapest and subsequently transcribed it for inclusion in the forthcoming first volume (Example 3.1).

Analysis of the piano accompaniment reveals Bartók's skill in adapting monophonic rural song without formulaic *magyar nóta* treatment. Instead

40

Moderato

Example 3.1. Bartók, Magyar népdalok *(Hungarian Folk Songs), no. 6.*

of the typical iv–V^7–i cadence in C-harmonic minor, the unusual VII^7–i and ii–i progressions (mm. 3–4 and 11–12, respectively) highlight the C-Aeolian folk mode, C–D–E♭–F–G–A♭–B♭.

In October, after an agreement had been concluded with the Budapest publisher, Rozsnyai Károly, to print the first volume of twenty transcriptions (nos. 1–10 by Bartók, nos. 11–20 by Kodály), Bartók extended his field trips to the Slovak language area in northern Hungary, apparently influenced by Kodály's finding of interrelations in Hungarian and Slovak folk music:

> Direct folk-contact was closest between Hungarians and Slovaks. Slovak glaziers and itinerant tinkers were always wandering about the Hungarian countryside, but it was principally as harvesters that Slovaks crowded down to the Hungarian plain. . . . Hungarian peasants would learn Slovak songs with Slovak texts, even if they did not understand a word. . . .

Example 3.2. Bartók, Slowakische Volkslieder, *vol. 1, (a) no. 11 (altered Phrygian mode) and (b) no. 31a (Lydian hexachord).*

Even greater numbers of songs were learnt by Slovak workers from Hungarians.[2]

Bartók was fascinated by the implications of his discovery that, among the Slovak folk songs collected from older performers, there was an unusual melody with chromatic alterations that transformed the Phrygian mode into a nondiatonic pitch collection, G–A♭/A♮–B♭–C–D–E–F, and another melody formed from a Lydian hexachord, G–A–B–C♯–D–E (Example 3.2).

After *Magyar népdalok* appeared in December and only a few copies were sold, both composers, furious that their costly venture to promote the dissemination of "true Hungarian folk music" was a failure, had to abandon further work on the project. The Hungarian public, customarily indifferent to "inferior"peasant music, was infatuated with *Die lustige Witwe* (The Merry Widow), the latest and most successful work by the Hungarian composer, Franz Lehár (1870–1948), which had its premiere in Vienna on December 28, 1905. Among the song hits in the operetta was the satirical *I'm Off to Chez Maxime . . . Goodbye My Fatherland* (Example 3.3).

Allegretto moderato

Da Geh'ich zu Ma - im,   da bin ich sehr in - tim,

Example 3.3. Lehár, Die lustige Witwe *(The Merry Widow), act I, no. 4, mm. 48–52.*

It is noteworthy that the most tuneful part of the melody appears as a thematic component in the first movement of Dmitri Shostakovich's Symphony no. 7 in C Major (*Leningrad*), op. 60 (1941), and in parodic treatment of the Shostakovich symphony in the third theme of the fourth movement of Bartók's Concerto for Orchestra (cf. Examples 8.5 and 8.6).

Beginning in 1907, however, a sequence of momentous events not only helped mitigate Bartók's disappointment over the failure of the collaborative effort with Kodály but had far-reaching impact on his career as pianist, composer, and ethnomusicologist. On January 18, the twenty-six-year-old "successor to Liszt" was appointed professor of piano at the Budapest Academy of Music, a position that led to his publication of many annotated editions of masterworks from the standard keyboard repertory and their subsequent performance in recitals at home and abroad.[3] Then, on May 15, the academy presented a concert by outstanding former students, including Bartók's Suite no. 1 for Large Orchestra, op. 3 (1905), and a performance by the beautiful young violin virtuoso, Stefi Geyer, with whom Bartók fell hopelessly in love. Thus, on June 28, en route to a collecting trip in Transylvania June 28, Bartók arranged a short stopover in Jásberény (a small town near Budapest), as a houseguest of the Geyer family. There he gathered a number of Hungarian folk songs and, inspired by the depth of his feelings for his talented sweetheart, decided he would compose a violin concerto for her.

The remainder of that summer, however, was devoted to the collection of hundreds of vocal and instrumental melodies in the remote Székely villages of southeastern Transylvania. He was elated to find that the Székely peasants—an enclave of Hungarian-speaking people living in a Romanian language area—had preserved ancestral Magyar folk songs hitherto thought to have been lost. The most important stylistic features of these songs are the peculiarly Hungarian pentatonic scale: a symmetrical struc-

ture, such as G–B♭–C–D–F, where the characteristic intervals are major
seconds, minor thirds, and perfect fourths; and parlando (free) rhythm.[4]
When Bartók returned to Budapest in September, he transcribed for
piano three ballad melodies that had been performed on a peasant flute,
and prepared another group of ballad transcriptions for publication in a
scholarly Hungarian journal (Example 3.4).[5]

Kodály, on the other hand, devoted the first half of the year to music
studies in Berlin and Paris, where he discovered the music of Debussy,
then virtually unknown in Hungary. He analyzed the opera *Pelléas et
Mélisande*, and following his return to Budapest to take up his new duties
as professor of theory and composition at the Academy of Music, shared
his findings with Bartók. Bartók wrote,

> In 1907, at the instigation of Kodály, I became acquainted with De-
> bussy's work, studied it thoroughly and was greatly surprised to find in
> his work "pentatonic phrases" similar in character to those contained in
> our peasant music. I was sure these could be attributed to influences of
> folk music from Eastern Europe, very likely from Russia.[6]

On November 30, Bartók returned to Jásberény for a visit with Stefi
Geyer, apparently under the impression she would accept his marriage
proposal. Bewildered at her waffling reaction—among other reasons, she
apparently had no intention of an involvement that might interfere with
her brilliant concert career—he departed the next day with the determination to quickly complete the violin concerto and present it to her as his
"declaration of love." In January he wrote that "Your *Leitmotive* buzz
around me. I spend the whole day with them, in them as in a narcotic
dream" (Example 3.5).[7]

The chromatic contour of measures 1–4, unresolved dissonance, and

Example 3.4. Uti Miska *(Miska Street),* "Székely balladak" *no.12, variant B.*

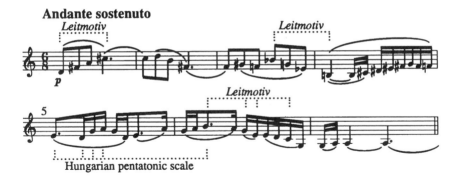

*Example 3.5. Bartók, Concerto no. 1, for Violin and Orchestra (1907–1908, op. posth.),
first movement, mm. 1–7.*

dense polyphonic texture in the fugal exposition of the first movement take
as their source of tonal inspiration the "Of Science" section in Strauss's
symphonic poem, *Also sprach Zarathustra*, (cf. Example 2.2). Where
Bartók parts company with Strauss is the unusual concatenation of the
pentatonic second half of the theme (mm. 5–7), which is based not only
on the transformation of a Székely folk-song melody collected in Transylvania the previous summer but also on the symbolism of its poetic text
(Example 3.6).[8]

Prior to Bartók's completion of the violin concerto February 5, 1908,
Stefi decided to end their relationship. Later that month, the rejected
suitor vented his anguish in the Janus-like Elegy no. 1, op. 8b, for Piano,
which for the last time looks back to the Liszt style of virtuoso piano technique—including rapid, decorative arpeggios in the left hand and alternation of flashing octaves and massive chords in both hands—and for the
first time points ahead to a new tonal language. The Elegy also reflects
Bartók's debt to Liszt as the source of thematic inspiration for programmatic purposes. Example 3.7 shows the reordered "declaration of love"
leitmotiv (the second motif in the work) preceded by a transformed borrowing of the trichord (the first motif) from Liszt's symphonic poem, *Les
Préludes*.

The programmatic content in both works, therefore, is related to
Lamartine's poem *Les Préludes* (no. 15 from *Méditations Poétiques*, 1820),

(Tempo giusto)

How I love her, love her so,_____

Why my sweet-heart is hard-heart-ed, I don't know!

Example 3.6. Ha kimëgyëk *(When I Go Out), mm. 5–8.*

which Liszt inscribed as the preface to the *Les Préludes* score. Surely the distraught Bartók found consolation in the lines that open Lamartine's poem: "What is our life but a succession of preludes to that unknown song whose first solemn note is struck by Death? Love is the magical dawn of existence, but where is the life whose first enjoyment of such ecstasy is not disrupted by some tempest?"9

Ostensibly in D minor, the tonality of the Elegy is based on what Bartók would later designate "polymodal chromaticism," that is, the juxtaposition of pentatonic, modal, and nondiatonic configurations such as octatonic and whole-tone segments, all linked to a single principal tone. In

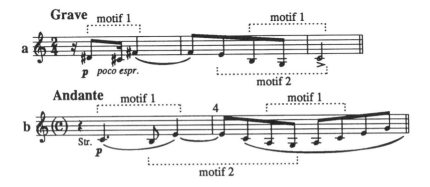

Example 3.7. (a) Bartók, Elegy no. 1, for Piano (1908), and (b) Liszt, Les Préludes *(1854).*

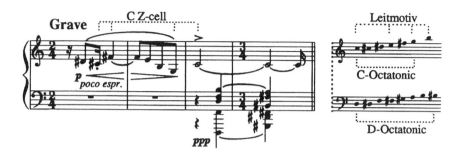

Example 3.8. Bartók, Elegy no. 1, mm. 1–4.

the first melody section (mm. 1–3) the theme has C as its end note, and the pitch collection comprises a C-octatonic hexachord, C–C♯–D♯–E–F♯–G, with B added to define the leitmotiv. Because both forms of the first motif end with the ascending interval of a perfect fourth, C♯–F♯ and G–C, respectively, the relationship of these notes as octatonic nodes, C–C♯/F♯–G, or tritone pairs, C–F♯/C♯–G, is highlighted. In either relationship, however, a C Z-cell is thus outlined, whose degrees are reordered during the work (cf. Example 3.11). The pitch collection of the chordal accompaniment is the complete D-octatonic scale, D–D♯–F–F♯–G♯–A–B–B♯. The interaction of the two octatonic collections thus yields an eleven-tone polymode with D as the principal tone (Example 3.8).

The second melody section, essentially a transposition of the first one, ends on F. Here, too, an octatonic hexachord is extended by a nonoctatonic degree, E♮, to define the transposed leitmotiv. The chordal accompaniment, however, consists of a B♭-Phrygian hexachord (Example 3.9).

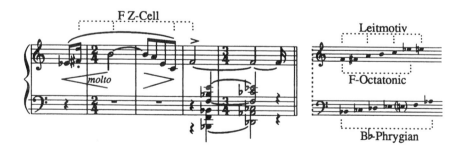

Example 3.9. Bartók, Elegy no. 1, mm. 4–8.

Example 3.10. Bartók, Elegy no. 1, mm. 19–20.

Example 3.10 illustrates the appearance of the leitmotiv, transformed into a minor configuration with a major-seventh degree. In measure 19, the juxtaposition of accompanying E-minor triads with the D♯ leitmotiv is based on discrete partitions of the E-Hungarian-Gypsy scale—a nondiatonic folk mode with two augmented seconds.

Emphatic renditions of the C Z-cell occur in measures 40–52, as explicit octatonic nodes a tritone apart, G♭–G and C–C♯, and again in the last section (mm. 85–95). These passages seem to be related to the *Kossuth* symphonic poem in terms of programmatic content, particularly in view of emphasis as well as cellular degrees (cf. Example 2.6). In *Kossuth*, Bartók represents the Austrian Army with a parody of the Austrian national anthem by transforming its diatonic "Franz den Kaiser" motive into the octatonic C Z-cell. In this way, the Hungarian composer seemingly reflects the bitter national feeling toward an unwanted Austrian king of Hungary. Thus, the Elegy may be interpreted as the emotional outburst of an unwanted suitor.

The minor sonority in the penultimate measure, D–F–A–C♯, is the transposed vertical projection of the leitmotiv broken chord, E–G–B–D♯, in measures 19–20 (cf. Example 3.10). It should be noted that C♯ resolves downward to end the work with an innovative Bartókian "consonance"—a tonic minor-seventh chord, D–F–A–C. (Example 3.11).

On March 3, Bartók purchased and subsequently annotated *Pour le Piano*, a suite of pieces (1. Prélude, 2. Sarabande, and 3. Toccata) composed by Debussy between 1896 and 1901 and considered to be his first keyboard masterpiece. He wrote,

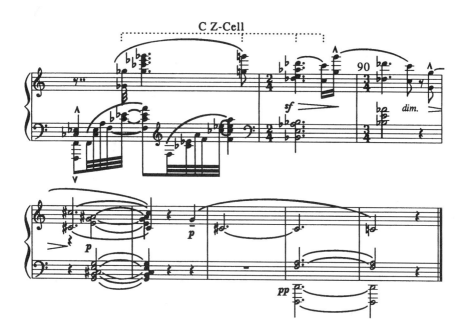

Example 3.11. Bartók, Elegy no. 1, mm. 88–95.

From the beginning of this century the young Hungarians, among whom I belonged, already oriented themselves in other domains toward the French culture. One can easily imagine the significance with which they beheld Debussy's appearance. The revelation of this art finally permitted them likewise to turn toward the French culture.[10]

The Prélude reveals Debussy's harmonic freedom, such as nonfunctional chord progressions (mm. 43–45) and unresolved dissonant intervals (mm. 91–93). The clarity of the unornamented piano writing (mm. 1–3) and the Aeolian v^7–i cadence (mm. 162–163) are other stylistic features that provided Bartók with new harmonic resources for transmuting folk music into art music (Example 3.12).

On May 1, Bartók mailed a fair copy of the violin concerto to Henri Marteau (1874–1934), an outstanding violinist who was also a composer and professor of violin at the Berlin Hochschule für Musik. Marteau returned the manuscript on May 19 with the harsh comment that "it is a composition not worth studying."[11] Meanwhile Bartók began work on Fourteen Bagatelles op. 6, for Piano, that not only "inaugurate a new style

Example 3.12. Debussy, Pour le Piano, *1. Prélude, mm. 1–3, 43–46, 91–93, 158–163.*

of piano writing," but, according to one commentator, introduce the first important evidence of his ability to transform folk elements into abstract pitch formations.[12]

In Bagatelle no. 4, Bartók applies the Debussy style of nonfunctional chord progression to harmonize a pentatonic folk song (G–Bb–C–D–F; Eb and the small-head A are passing tones), which is transposed to D as the principal tone in the transcription (Example 3.13). Because the transposed passing tones (Bb and E) are given equal weight in the accompaniment, the basic pentatonic construction is incorporated as an octave-segment of the D-Aeolian mode.

Example 3.13. (a) Bartók, The Hungarian Folk Song, *no. 7, mm. 1–4, and (b) Bartók,* Fourteen Bagatelles, *op. 6 (1908), mm. 1–4.*

The rejection of the violin concerto, following soon after the traumatic love affair, probably underlies Bartók's return to the atmosphere of Elegy no. 1 in the composition of Bagatelle no. 13. Example 3.14 shows the re-ordered, enharmonic form of the original leitmotiv, A–G♭–D–D♭ (mm. 2–3) and its transposed form, D♭–F–A♭–C. The accompaniment consists of iambic E♭- and A-minor triads, which alternate a tritone apart (mm. 23–26) and are derived from the E♭ octatonic scale, E♭–E–G♭–[G]–A–B♭–C–[D♭].

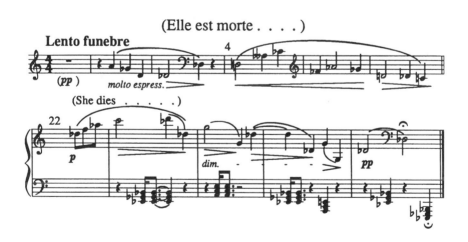

Example 3.14. Bartók, Fourteen Bagatelles, *no. 13, mm. 1–6 (L.H. not shown), 22–26.*

The unconventional structure of the piece shows a free arrangement of various sections that include octatonic and whole-tone segments.

In June, Bartók composed and signed a publication agreement for a group of pedagogical works, which he titled *Eleven Piano Recital Pieces*. The next month, however, he decided to withdraw one of them and place it as Bagatelle no. 6. Because his contract called for eleven pieces, he composed a prefixal "Dedication" as the replacement and changed the title to *Ten Easy Pieces*. The collection consists of three distinct categories: folk-music transcriptions (nos. 3, 6, 8); folk-music imitations (nos. 1, 2, 5, 10); and abstract pieces similar to Bagatelle no. 6 that are imbued with the spirit of impressionism and feature transformations of the leitmotiv ("Dedication" and nos. 4, 7, 9).

In "Dedication," a programmatic memento of Stefi Geyer, a musical dialogue takes place between the composer (whole-note configurations) and his departed beloved (melody sections). Example 3.15 shows the "declaration of love" leitmotiv, D–F♯–A–C♯ (mm. 1–4) answered by its transformed self, F♯–A♯–C♯–E (mm. 5–8). Thereafter, whole-note configurations alternate with melody sections, which incorporate octatonic and Phrygian hexachords, to produce a twelve-tone polymode with D as the principal tone. A nonfunctional dissonant progression to a whole-tone pentachord heightens the tension (mm. 41–42), but release is obtained

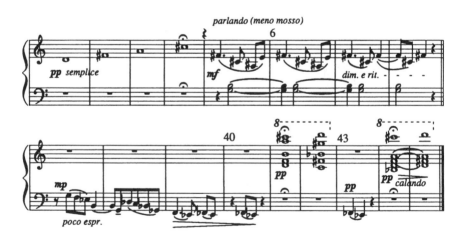

Example 3.15. Bartók, Ten Easy Pieces, "Dedication," mm. 1–8, 37–45.

when the functional leitmotiv ninth chord, B♭–D–F–A–C♯, resolves to the consonant D-major sonority—as if to signal the end of Bartók's troublesome period of mourning (mm. 44–45).

"Painful Struggle" (no. 2) represents a first effort to partition the chromatic scale into its two complementary octatonic scales and thereby create a D-Lydian/Phrygian twelve-tone polymode, D–E–F♯–G♯–A–B–C♯/D–E♭–F–G–A–B♭–C. In this remarkable piece, moreover, both octatonic partitions are further subdivided into Z-cells as the basic accompaniment (Example 3.16).

The AABA melodic construction is in the style of Slovak folk song, with emphasis on tritone intervals (mm. 3, 9, 11) and heterometric rhythm structure, as if the A sections were underlaid with eleven-syllable text lines and the B section (mm. 11–14) with a six-syllable text line (Example 3.17).

The ostinato accompaniment contains these Z-cells: D in the introduction and first melody section (mm. 1–6); F and G in the second section (mm. 7–9); G in the third section (mm. 15–18); D in the fourth section; and, in the postlude (mm. 19–21), C, E, and D (Example 3.18).

Although the first melody-section appears to be a Dorian hexachord, D–E–F–G–A–B, the F–B tritone and its accompanying Z-cell, D–E♭–G♯–A, define a D-octatonic hexachord, D–E♭–F–[]–G♯–A–B–[] (cf. Example 3.16, upper configuration). The melody section ends, however, with a pentachord of the Dorian mode. In this way, Bartók juxtaposes octatonic and modal octave segments to construct an octachordal D-Lydian/Phrygian polymode, D–E♭–F–G–A/D–E–G♯–A–B. The diverse Z-cells and, in the fourth melody section, the addition of C to form the complete Dorian mode, produce a twelve-tone polymode—the "painful struggle" whose outcome is resolved by a single principal tone, D, as the sole occupant of the last bar.

Example 3.16. Complementary octatonic partitions of the D-chromatic scale, with their component Z-cells.

Example 3.17. Bartók, Ten Easy Pieces, no. 2, first and third melody sections.

During the first week in October, Bartók visited a scenic area in the Turda region of central Transylvania, including a day "making merry" at the fairgrounds in the village of Torockó (now Rimetea, Romania). There he met some Romanian peasant girls from nearby Podeni, who agreed to sing for him while he notated their songs.[13] He was astonished to hear such structural peculiarities as narrow range, three-section melodies in the Phrygian mode, emphatic rendition of pentatonic scale degrees, heterometric parlando rhythm, and refrain lines with unintelligible text syllables. And he was especially struck by the young age of his informants: their songs reflected the preservation of a centuries-old repertory and performance style that Bartók had previously encountered only among old women in Hungarian and Slovak rural areas. He decided to add Romanian musical folklore to his growing collection of Hungarian and Slovak materials—a momentous determination that not only had primary impact on the development of his innovative musical language but eventually changed his ethnological emphasis from haphazard collecting to scientific

Example 3.18. Z-cell ostinato components in Ten Easy Pieces, no. 2.

investigation and brought him international recognition as an outstanding scholar in the field of comparative musicology.

DISCOVERY OF THE ROMANIAN FOLKLORIC MOTHER LODE

Bartók's odyssey to collect folk music in Romanian villages began July 17, 1909, in the Bihor region of central Transylvania, near the border of Hungary proper. In a two-week period, he recorded 320 vocal and instrumental melodies, among them "the most exotic melodies I have ever heard [whose peculiar melismata are] veritable coloratura arias."[14] He was "elated by the opportunity to come in contact with pure, uncontaminated material" performed by peasants in isolated areas where there were few schools, a scarcity of transportation, and rare contact with "modern urban culture."

> For miles on end, in these parts, there are entire villages with illiterate inhabitants, communities which are not linked by any railways or roads; here, most of the time the people can provide for their own daily wants, never leaving their native habitats except for such unavoidable travel as arise from service in the army or an occasional appearance in court. When one comes into such a region, one has the feeling of a return to the Middle Ages.[15]

Example 3.19 illustrates four melodies from the folk songs collected in July, which Bartók published in his first study on Romanian folk music.[16]

The melodies, sung by different performers, have parlando rhythm and narrow range as common characteristics. No. 3, sung by two girls (ages sixteen and seventeen), is a binary Christmas carol in the Phrygian mode. The tonality therefore suggests that the melody may have originated as a winter-solstice song, possibly pagan. No. 26, sung by a young man, is a pentatonic three-section melody, isometric (eight-syllable text lines) and isorhythmic (eighth-note values) throughout. These structural characteristics are typical of the ancient Hungarian folk songs Bartók recorded two years earlier, in the remote Székely villages of Transylvania. No. 144, sung by some girls, is an isometric quaternary with heterorhythmic text lines, in

Example 3.19. Bartók, Chansons populaires roumaines du départment Bihar (Hongrie), *Bucharest, 1913, nos. 3, 26, 144, and 199.*[16]

the Lydian mode. Note the emphatic rendition of the tritone (B–F) in measures 4 and 8, which is also characteristic of many Slovak folk songs.

The most interesting melody is no. 199, also sung as a duet by the performers of no. 3. This type of three-section, heterometric mourning song is usually sung by a mother at the grave of a married daughter or on the anniversary of the daughter's death. It is particularly noteworthy that the pitch collection, including the grace note in the fourth bar, is a heptachord of the G·octatonic scale, G–A♭–B♭–C♭–D♭–E♭♭–F♭. While it is sheer coincidence that octatonic segments occur in Romanian folk music as well as in abstract art music,[17] Bartók's earlier use of them in the accompaniment of folk-styled works (i.e., Example 3.18) was indeed prescient. After his return to Budapest in September, he composed the first of his Two Romanian Dances op. 8a, for Piano, inspired by a unique type of instrumental dance melodies he had also collected in July and secure in the knowledge that octatonic configurations were authentic means for accompanying monophonic folk tunes (Example 3.20).

Example 3.20. (a) Bartók, Chansons populaires . . . , *No. 362, mm. 18–23, and (b) Bartók, Two Romanian Dances Op. 8a, No. 1, m. 3.*

The Romanian melody, a *joc* (dance) performed on a *Drâmbă* (jew's-harp), is made up of twin-bar motifs, such as the rhythm schema, 2/4 ♫♫♫|♫ ♫♫ |, shown in Example 3.20. Bartók collected many such pieces of indeterminate structure, which have one or more motifs that are irregularly repeated throughout the piece and without any plan or coordination.[18]

Bartók's composition, although based on original thematic material and structured in rondo form, uses the rhythm schema in Example 3.20 and others borrowed from similar Romanian dance pieces. In measure 3, beat 4, the motif and its ostinato accompaniment form a Z-cell, C–D♭–F♯–G, which serves as an octatonic tonal center for confirming C as the principal tone of the work. The individual staves, however, show emphatic rendition of specific modal degrees: a tetrachord, G–F–E♭–D♭, from the C-Phrygian mode in the upper staff; and a tetrachord, B–C–F♯–G, from the Lydian mode in the lower staff. When the accented F♯ is added to the motif, the tetrachords interact to form the C Z-cell. In this ingenious manner, Bartók creates a new tonal language by linking modal and octatonic tetrachords to form a Lydian/Phrygian polymode based on a single principal tone.

Romanian peasant music also includes melodies that have a tetrachord with a single augmented second (Example 3.21). Peasant performers, however, whether Romanian or (less frequently) Hungarian, do not play

Example 3.21. Bartók, Chansons populaires roumaines . . . , *no. 65, mm. 1–12, and no. 189, mm. 1.10.*

or sing melodies whose scales contain two augmented seconds, such as those featured by urban Gypsy musicians.[19]

The tonality of no. 65, a heterometric three-section melody based on G as the end (principal) note, is particularly interesting. The first melody section (mm. 1–4) is a G-Gypsy-Phrygian pentachord, (F)–G–A♭–B–C; the second section, including the grace note, is converted to a G-Phrygian pentachord when B♭ replaces B (m. 7). The last section (mm. 9–12) is actually a G-Phrygian/Lydian hexachord, (F)–G–A♭–C/(F)–G–A–B–C. Restated in other terms, the G polymode is created by compression of a nondiatonic (Gypsy-Phrygian) pentachord to a G-Phrygian octave segment, and by extension of the latter configuration to a rotated octave segment of the F-Lydian mode (mm. 9–11). The aural effect of this remarkable folk song parallels that of the idiosyncratic Bartókian "neutral" tonality— neither minor nor major but simply a polymodal entity where the individual degrees are related only to a single principal tone.[20]

In 1910, increasing requests for Bartók to appear as a performer as well as to provide pianists with recital and teaching pieces led him to compose additional piano pieces that embodied the characteristic features of the Hungarian and Romanian folk music he had discovered in the rural villages of Transylvania. Bartók's previous transcriptions, including Slovak folk melodies, already manifested a new approach to exploring the levels of complexity in the compositional treatment of monophonic peasant music.

The basic level features the folk melody as a kind of musical jewel, with the accompaniment and other additions serving as the mounting. Because peasant song is for the most part monophonic, the accompaniments may be derived from the melodic structure, or freely invented (cf. Examples 3.1 and 3.13). In the second level, the folk melody and added material achieve parity, such as the interesting treatment given the combined Slovak folk tunes that form the *Rhapsody* (nos. 41–42) in Bartók's *For Children*. The third level employs the folk tune or its unique rhythm schema as a motto; the newly composed material is of primary importance (Example 3.20). The fourth level includes original compositions in which themes are invented in imitation of peasant music style (Example 3.17).

The highest level is reached when the work is essentially an abstract composition yet reflects the atmosphere or spirit of folk music by borrowing syllabic structure, rhythmic character, scalar configurations, or other peculiarities from folk music. Furthermore, when stylistic attributes of different ethnic origins are fused, such as those Bartók found among the Romanians, Slovaks, and Transylvanian-Hungarians, the outcome is music of magnetic quality (Example 3.22).

The first part of the binary form contains four thirteen-syllable melody

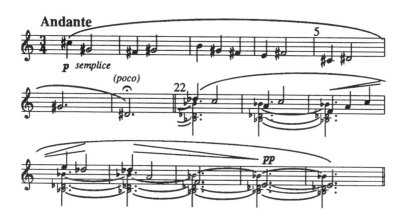

Example 3.22. Bartók, Four Dirges, op. 9a (1910), no. 2, first and third melody-sections.

sections, invented by Bartók in imitation of eastern European folk-song style. While the first two sections emphasize the characteristic old-style pentatonic intervals of the Transylvanian Hungarians (major seconds, minor thirds, and perfect fourths), the pitch collection is the C♯-Dorian mode. The thirteen-syllable section structure and triple meter, however, are Slovak characteristics (mm. 1–7). The third and fourth sections, chromatic compressions of the first two, feature octatonic scale segments similar to those in Romanian mourning songs. The leitmotiv, F–A–C–E (mm. 24–25), is also present.

THE TURN TOWARD
MUSICOLOGICAL ETHNOGRAPHY

Between 1909 and 1910, while Bartók was transcribing his growing collections of Hungarian, Romanian, and Slovak vocal and instrumental folk melodies—primarily as source material for future compositions—he noticed reciprocal relationships as well as marked differences between Hungarian and Slovak styles. The Transylvanian-Romanian material was for the most part unlike the Hungarian and Slovak melodies and, moreover, represented a compendium of unique musical dialects according to county or regional boundaries. In fact, the few foreign "contaminations" apparently resulted from contact with neighboring Székely villages. These findings prompted a change in Bartók's emphasis and approach. He was no longer using his ethnographic studies solely as inspiration for composing music

> but as a new field of creative endeavor. He found it as gratifying and pleasurable as composing, and without the agonies that inhabit the world of artistic creation. He had not yet discovered that this field would impose the agonies of its own thorns. He became like a priest of a second cult, devoted to preaching from both pulpits with equal fervor, relying on each creed to inspire the other.[21]

To determine and compare the typical forms and structures, Bartók developed a classification system based on the transposition of all melodies to G as the final tone and their subsequent analysis for the number of melody sections and related syllables, pitch class of section end tones, rhythm structure, content structure (that is, form), and scale. He also created special symbols to supplement music notation and dialectal pronunciation of the texts.

Example 3.23 shows certain diatonic and nondiatonic pitch collections, transposed to G as principal tone, that Bartók found in the melodies he had collected from 1907 to 1910. Although melodies with pentatonic turns occur elsewhere in eastern Europe, the symmetrical form of the pentatonic scale (a) is a unique feature of the Székely repertory (see Example

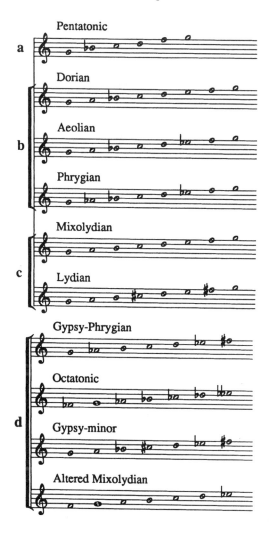

Example 3.23. Diatonic and nondiatonic pitch collections in Bartók's folk-music materials.

3.4). The minor modes (b) are found everywhere in the greatest frequency. The Mixolydian mode (c) is also frequently met, but the Lydian mode (d), a characteristic of the Slovak material and frequently found in Romanian melodies, is completely absent from the Hungarian fund. The nondiatonic folk modes are Romanian features, and some of them are based on Oriental (i.e., Gypsy) octave segments. As already mentioned, however, there is not a single example among the thousands in Bartók's folk-music collections where the complete (with two augmented seconds) Gypsy-minor or Gypsy-Phrygian scale occurs.

During the first half of 1910 Bartók wrote to the Turócszentmárton Printing Company in Czechoslovakia, publishers of the *Slovenské Spevy* (Slovak Songs) series, with a proposal for publication of his annotated Slovak collection of 400 folk songs, and to the Romanian Academy in Bucharest for a similar but slightly smaller collection of Transylvanian-Romanian folk songs gathered in Bihar County (now Bihor, Romania). The positive response to both projects was a timely godsend that helped to mitigate Bartók's despair over the inadequate performance and public rejection of his compositions, the illness of his young wife (Márta Ziegler married Bartók in the autumn of 1909), and his self-imposed isolation from hostile musical circles in Budapest: "I am very much alone here apart from my one friend Kodály; I have nobody to talk to. . . ."[22] Another, equally important project, which enabled him to express his feelings in a creative way, was the unexpected opportunity to compose an opera.

APPROACHING MUSICAL SYNTHESIS: *DUKE BLUEBEARD'S CASTLE*, OP. 11

In March 1911, the month Bartók reached his thirtieth birthday, he began setting the libretto to the one-act mystery play, *A kékszakállú herceg vara* (Duke Bluebeard's Castle), which had been written the previous year by the Hungarian poet, Béla Balázs (1884–1949). Although the Balázs play is based on Maeterlinck's tragedy, *Pelléas et Mélisande*, Bluebeard's castle perhaps symbolizes the impregnable human soul that Hungary's greatest poet, Endre Ady (1877–1919), has likened to "an ancient spell-bound castle, moss grown, impregnable and deserted."[23] On the other hand, if musical content is taken as the prime indicator, the opera is a psychodrama, with Bartók himself as the protagonist whose soul is tortured by memories of Stefi Geyer (represented by leitmotiv transformation) and the philistinic music public (represented by Straussian unresolved dissonances and orchestral forces, reminiscent of *Also sprach Zarathustra*).

When Bartók first read the Balázs libretto, which mainly consists of isometric eight-syllable text lines in the tradition of old Transylvanian-Hungarian folk poetry (see the Székely ballad in Example 3.4), he recalled his previous study of the Debussy-Maeterlinck opera, *Pelléas et Mélisande*, in 1907. The score had left him with an indelible impression of the pentatonic turns in Debussy's melodic style, to the point where they reminded him of similar peculiarities in the Székely folk songs he had collected that same year. He also recognized a distant relationship of Debussy's recitative-derived declamatory setting to the Székely parlando performance style.[24] He therefore decided to follow in Debussy's footsteps, whose stylistic aspects have been described as follows:

> For as Maeterlinck's drama moved in a realm outside ordinary time and space, so Debussy's music moved in a realm outside of the then known tonal system; lacking any strong formal associations within the field of music itself, his harmonies were irresistably attracted to the similarly free images of the poet. . . . Modal, whole-tone, or pentatonic melodies and harmonies suggest the far-off, dreamlike character of the play. The free enchainment of seventh and ninth chords, often in organum-like parallel movement, and the blurring of tonality by complex harmonic relationships are also typical.[25]

The action, limited throughout to dialogue between Bluebeard and his latest wife, Judith, takes place in the cavernous hall of Bluebeard's castle. Judith, searching for light to dispel the gloomy atmosphere, persuades her reluctant bridegroom to hand over the keys to the seven locked doors in the hall. The hall glows with light as she opens each door and discovers to her horror a torture chamber, an armory, a treasure chamber, a flower garden, and the landscape of Bluebeard's vast domain, all drenched with blood. When Judith opens the sixth door, the fading light reveals the motionless, white Lake of Tears. Bluebeard implores her not to open the last door, but when she disobeys, his three former wives emerge: the brides of the dawn, midday, and twilight. Bluebeard then places a crown on Judith's head, as the most beautiful wife, the midnight bride. She takes her place among the other wives, after they have passed through the seventh door, to be enclosed forever. Bluebeard avows: "There shall be darkness always . . . darkness . . . darkness."

Following the old-Hungarian peasant music tradition from the tonal point of view, the opera opens with a monodic quaternary in parlando style, constructed from the pitch collection F♯–A–B–C♯–E, that is, the symmetrical pentatonic scale that Bartók discovered in Székely villages (Example 3.24).

The first melody section of the quaternary is a direct borrowing from Dirge no. 2 (cf. Example 3.22). Next follows the "Castle" theme, which begins with an emphatic rendition of the minor second, E–D♯, within the octatonic pentachord, G–F♯–E–D♯–C. This intervallic distance, in melodic as well as harmonic form, is the basic, recurrent motif that invariably appears whenever there is an allusion to blood in the libretto.[26] When Judith opens the first door and sees the blood-encrusted torture instruments, two minor seconds are juxtaposed to form an X-cell (that is, a chromatic tetrachord), G♯–A–A♯–B. Bartók's opera thus marks the first emphatic rendition of X-cell motifs in his tonal language (Example 3.25).[27]

The high point of the opera is reached when the fifth door opens (R.N. 75), disclosing the vastness of Bluebeard's domain. The full orchestra, with the addition of an organ, plays a theme harmonized by chains of fortissimo major chords in root position, whose massive sonic effect parallels the so-called "Nature" motif that opens Strauss's *Also sprach Zarathustra*. Although the theme begins and ends in C major, and is based on the Chinese pentatonic scale C–D–E–G–A, the use of F♯ and G♯ (in the D- and E-major chords, respectively) reflects the infusion of the whole-tone pentachord C–D–E–F♯–G♯ in the sequence. The A-major

Example 3.24. Bartók, Duke Bluebeard's Castle, op. 11, mm. 1–17.

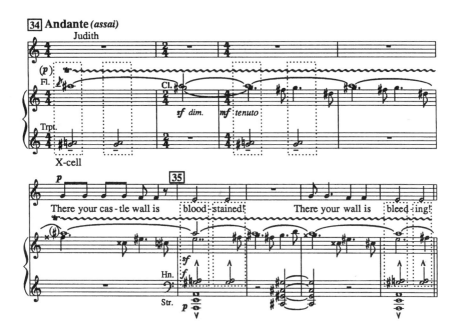

Example 3.25. Bartók, Duke Bluebeard's Castle, *R.N. 34–35.*

chord, with C♯ as its third degree, further disturbs tonal equilibrium. The expansiveness of Bluebeard's domain is also expressed by transposition of the theme to the subdominant (F), as component degrees of second-inversion chords (R.N. 76), to the altered submediant (A♭) as first-inversion chords (R.N. 77), and, finally, to the subdominant minor in root position (R.N. 78, m. 2).

When Judith opens the sixth door and sees the "still and dead waters" of the Lake of Tears, its motif is combined with the "Fate" (whole-tone) and "Blood" motifs in an orchestral interlude (R.N. 91–93). The Lake of Tears is represented by arpeggiated transformations of the leitmotiv seventh chord, A–C–E–(G)–G♯ (clarinet, harp), while the flute and celesta play arpeggiated whole-tone tetrachords, C–E–F♯–G♯, which terminate with a "Blood" motif trill, G♯–F♭♭. At rehearsal number 99, the "Blood" motif is highlighted as Z-cell nodes that alternate with the arpeggiated transformations (Example 3.26).

At rehearsal number 121, the chordal accompaniment begins with C-minor chords that harmonize the triadic "Seventh Door" motif. (It is indeed

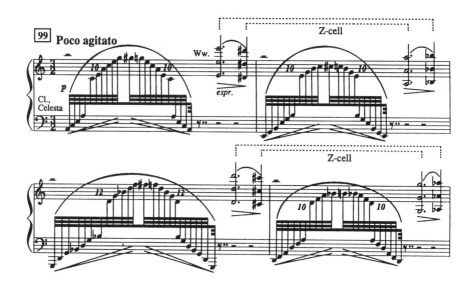

Example 3.26. Bartók, Duke Bluebeard's Castle, *R.N. 99.*

significant that a variant of this motif reappears as the second melody section of the fugue subject that closes Bartók's Concerto for Orchestra). When the English horn enters with the "Golgotha" motif, whose D♭ and F♯ degrees create the C Z-cell, the C-minor chord is transformed into scalar degrees of the octatonic pentachord, C–D♭–E♭–F♯–G (Example 3.27).

The motif designation "Golgotha" is suggested by Bartók's borrowing

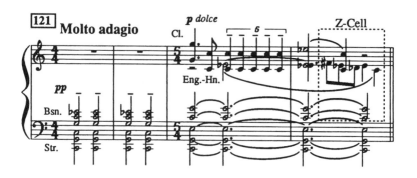

Example 3.27. Bartók, Duke Bluebeard's Castle, *R.N. 121.*

Example 3.28. Bach, St. Matthew Passion, *no. 69, mm. 1–2.*

of the opening ostinato accompaniment of "Ah, Golgotha!" from Bach's
St. Matthew Passion (Example 3.28). The music, a recitative in A♭ major
for alto solo, opens with a Mixolydian hexachord, A♭–B♭–C–D♭–E♭–G♭,
and contains tritones and minor-second or major-seventh dissonances.

Example 3.29 illustrates the unusual admixture of change of time,
motif blending, cellular construction, and the purposeful use of enhar-
mony. Bluebeard's text line is set to a portion of the modal "Seventh
Door" motif, while the English horn plays the cellular-oriented "Golgotha" motif. Judith's response begins with the "Blood" motif and leaps a
tritone, from E♭ to A, to form another Z-cell, A♯–A–E–E♭, while the strings
play sextuplet "Blood" motifs. Although the two Z-cells form the nodes of
the C-octatonic scale, C–D♭–E♭–E–F♯–G–A–A♯, Bartók's use of the Lydian F♯ rather than the Mixolydian G♭ of Bach, together with the insertion
of F♮ (m. 3), clearly point to a nine-tone C-Phrygian/Lydian polymode,
C–D♭–E♭–F–G–A–A♯/C–E–F♯–G–A, rather than an expanded octatonic
tonality.

During Judith's *Largo* passage through the seventh door (R.N.
136–137), she is accompanied by an orchestral interlude based on an alternation of the Gypsy-minor scale, B♭–C–D♭–E–F–G♭–A with whole-tone
("Fate" motif) pentachords. The opera closes with an epilogue (R.N.
138–140), consisting of a reprise of the pentatonic quaternary and
"Castle" motif that open the work. The final statement of the C Z-cell—
hitherto presented as minor seconds ("Blood" motif) a tritone apart—is
intoned by Bluebeard as tritones a minor second apart, thus creating the
"Darkness" motif (Example 3.30).

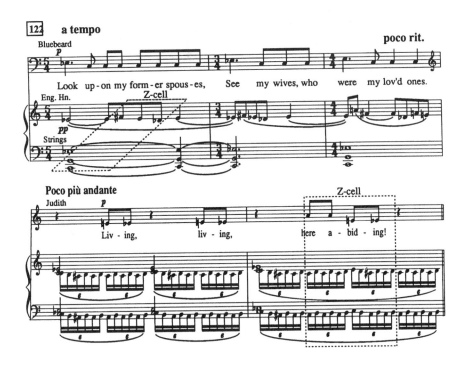

Example 3.29. Bartók, Duke Bluebeard's Castle, *R.N. 122.*

Duke Bluebeard's Castle represents the first stage in Bartók's quest to synthesize Western art music and eastern European folk music, beginning with Debussy's innovative tonal language, motif construction, and declamatory vocal style, together with related aspects Bartók discovered in Transylvanian-Hungarian, Romanian, and Slovak musical folklore. The single instance of integrating Bach's music heralds the distinctive polyphonic dimension yet to come.

Bartók temporarily interrupted work on his opera to collect folk music from Ruthenian peasants, because he wanted to acquire specimens of their *kolomyjka* (round-dance) music.[28] He was interested in tracing the connection between the Hungarian *kanásztánc* (hog-herder's dance) and the Romanian *Ardeleana* (Transylvanian) dance, with regard to the *kolomyjka* rhythm schema: 2/4 ♫♩|♫♩|♫♩|♩ ♩|. Example 3.31 is a *kolomyjka* dance-song melody in a nondiatonic folk mode, G–A–B–C–D–E♭–F.[29]

Example 3.30. Bartók, Duke Bluebeard's Castle, *R.N. 138–139.*

Example 3.31.

On September 20, *Duke Bluebeard's Castle* was completed, in time for entry in a Budapest opera competition. The committee of judges rejected the work as "impossible to perform," and Bartók decided to abandon public musical activities and concentrate on the collection and study of folk music, particularly with regard to other minority peoples of Hungary. He wrote:

> It is only when we had in that way systematically classified collections of Hungarian, Slovak, Rumanian, and Croatian folk songs that we could begin with the proper comparative folk song examination. And then we would be able to scientifically demonstrate which ones are the pure Hungarian types and which are borrowed melodies or reflect foreign influence.[30]

He began with the southernmost region of Hungary (the Bánát, now part of Romania), and in March 1912 recorded seven vocal melodies from Bulgarian peasants, including a Christmas song with an unusual 2/4 and 3/8 change of time. In 1910 and 1911, he had collected Romanian variants of the song, including several melodies with the same change of time (Example 3.32).[31]

Bartók was so impressed by the transmigration of the original Romanian melody (no. 62a) to a Bulgarian language area (no. 28), resulting in the additive rhythm in measures 1–2 (2/4+3/8=7/8) and the subsequent Romanian borrowing of the Bulgarian version (no. 62c), that he decided to study Bulgarian folk-music publications as well as augment his small collection of Romanian Christmas songs.

During the same month he collected Romanian folk music in Maramureș County, the northernmost region in Transylvania. He discovered another, hitherto unknown genre, *Cântec lung* ("long-drawn" melody), which has been described as

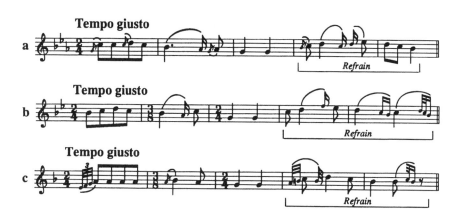

Example 3.32. (a) Bartók, Rumanian Folk Music, *vol. 4, no. 62a, mm. 1–5, (b) no. 62c, mm. 1–5, and (c) Bartók, "Musique paysanne bulgare du Banat," no. 28, mm.1–5.*

a single unmodulated melody of a manifestly instrumental character. It is freely improvised, somewhat in the manner of Eastern musical practice, particularly that of the Arabs, on the principle of the *"maqām,"* according to which each singer may, within certain limits, vary the given theme as he wishes.[32]

Bartók noted that its characteristic feature is an indeterminate structure, consisting of three parts: a sustained phrase opening of the fourth or fifth degree of a pentachord (usually G–A–Bb–C–D); an ornamented middle section; and a declamatory cadence on the first degree (Example 3.33).

In order to determine whether the *Cântec lung* is uniquely Romanian or of Oriental provenance, Bartók decided to investigate Arab peasant

Example 3.33. Bartók, Rumanian Folk Music, *vol. 5, no. 23a, mm. 1–8.*

music. In June 1913 he journeyed to northern Africa and collected vocal and instrumental melodies from informants in Arab villages in the Biskra District of Algeria:[33]

> In 1912 I discovered among the Maramureș Rumanians a certain kind of highly ornamented, orientally colored and improvisation-like melody. In 1913, in a village of Central Algeria bordering the Sahara Desert, I heard a similar melodic style. Although this similarity struck me at the first hearing, I did not dare to see in it anything but a fortuitous coincidence. Who would have thought that the distance between the two phenomena—more than 2,000 kilometres—could be bridged by a causal relationship![34]

The melody, a dance song with drum accompaniment and performed by men at weddings, is constructed from an octatonic tetrachord, F–A♭–C♭–D♭ (Example 3.34).

Another dance song by the same performers is assembled from motifs, similar to the indeterminate structure of certain Romanian instrumental pieces (cf. example 3.20, above). The pitch collection, moreover, is an altered octatonic scale, F–G–A♭–B♭–C♭–D♭–[E♭], thus providing additional evidence that octatonic configurations are found among the nondiatonic folk modes of rural peoples. Thus, they antedate the so-called artificial scales of Western art music, which have identical degrees (Example 3.35).[35]

From 1914 to 1915, Bartók composed piano pieces based on Roma-

Example 3.34. Bartók, "Die Volksmusik der Araber von Biskra und Umbegung," no. 34 (Tolga Oasis), mm. 1–11.

Example 3.35. Bartók, "Die Volksmusik der Araber von Biskra und Umbegung," no. 35 (Tolga Oasis), mm. 1–5.

nian folk-music sources, including twenty Christmas songs, in two volumes. In 1916 he wrote his Suite op. 14 for Piano, an abstract work whose third movement reflects the influence of an Arab peasant melody (Example 3.36).

The Suite's accompaniment consists of pentachords and heptachords

Example 3.36. (a) Bartók, "Die Volksmusik der Araber von Biskra und Umbegung" (El Kantara Oasis), and (b) Bartók, Suite op. 14 for Piano, third movement, mm. 5–12.

of the minor form of the D-octatonic scale, D–E–F–G–A♭–B♭–C♭ (mm. 7–8: L.H.). The melody, on the other hand, is a Z-cell tetrachord, D–E♭–G♯–A (mm. 11–12: R.H.), of the Phrygian form of the D-octatonic scale (D–E♭–F–F♯–G♯–A–B–C). The enharmonic change of A♭ to G♯ (m. 9: L.H.) signifies a conceptual shift from octatonicism to Bartókian polymodality, that is, to a nine-tone D-Phrygian/Lydian polymode, D–E♭–F–G–A–B♭/D–E–G♯–A–C♭.

In 1917, an outstanding performance of Bartók's ballet, *The Wooden Prince*, followed a year later by the premiere of *Duke Bluebeard's Castle*, changed the attitude of the Budapest public toward his compositions. Following the end of World War I that year, however, the political upheaval and depressed economic conditions in Hungary "were not conducive to serious work."[36] A short-lived communist dictatorship replaced the Habsburg monarchy but was overthrown by the repressive Horthy regency on March 1, 1920. On June 4, the Treaty of Trianon separated Slovakia, Ruthenia, Transylvania, and Croatia, including their enclaves of Hungarian inhabitants, from Hungary. So far as Bartók was concerned, the resultant creation of Czechoslovakia, Yugoslavia, and the attachment of Transylvania to Romania meant that he would no longer have free access to those territories for collecting folk music. Bartók apparently memorialized the forceful dismemberment of his country with the Improvisations on Hungarian Peasant Songs op. 20, for Piano. This masterpiece of twentieth-century piano literature contains eight old-style folk-song melodies, one from a Hungarian village in Transylvania and the others from Hungary proper. Nos. 1 and 8 are Dorian, and 4–6 are pentatonic. Nos. 2, 3, and 7 are modal combinations: the first half of 2 is Mixolydian, the second half is Dorian; the first half of 3 is Aeolian, the second half is Mixolydian; the first half of 7 is Aeolian, the second half is Phrygian. So far as the composed parts are concerned, Bartók indicates that a well-chosen folk melody can be treated as an invented theme for the creation of an original work:

> I myself have tried various procedures in the transcription of folk music, ranging from the most simple to rather complicated procedures. In my Eight Improvisations for Piano I reached, I believe, the extreme limit in adding the most daring accompaniments to simple folk tunes.[37]

Bartók's "daring accompaniments" consist for the most part of Z-cells as intermediary configurations in the fusion of diatonic and octatonic entities, and thus represent an unusual application of his innovative poly-modal chromaticism.[38]

Following the closing of the newly drawn international borders during the first few postwar years, Bartók devoted much of his time to the transcription, classification, and preparation for publication of his Hungarian folk-song collection. The increasing interest in his compositions abroad brought a request for a London recital of his piano pieces. Because the offer resulted from the efforts of the d'Arányi sisters (both violinists, who had moved to London from Budapest), Bartók decided to include a piece for violin and piano, which he would write for Jelly d'Arányi, his one-time pupil. On December 12, 1921, he completed the Sonata no. 1 for Violin and Piano, a work that marks his turn toward Beethoven with regard to formal construction. One commentator has described the inclination this way:

> Naturally this does not mean a revival of the classical scheme, for it was never the complete forms as such he took over but the principles lying behind them. The key to his sonata form is therefore not the particularly determined order of themes and modulations, but the sonata principle stripped to its roots, in the free yet regular sense in which Beethoven uses it.[39]

Although the construction of the first movement has the traditional exposition, development, recapitulation, and coda, the Beethoven model is expanded to improvisation-like treatment of thematic material. Each instrument, moreover, is given more or less independent material suitable to its character. Thus, the violin plays sustained melodic lines for the most part, and the piano, except for a few arpeggios, has octave and chord passages in accordance with Bartók's innovative concept that the piano is essentially a percussion instrument.

The second movement is an adagio in ternary (ABA) form, which opens with the solo violin and is followed by piano chords in C Y-cell (whole-tone tetrachord) sequences, C–D–E–F♯, that culminate in a C Z-cell, C–C♯–F♯–G (R.N. 1). The whole-tone and other configurations, together with the contrasting treatment of the piano as a string instrument, recall Debussy's piano writing, particularly *La Cathédrale engloutie* (The Sunken Cathedral; no. 10 from *Douze Préludes*, book 1). The last eight measures of the reprise reverse the procedure: the piano chords form an F Z-cell, F–F♯–B–C, followed by an A Y-cell, A–B–C♯–D♯. The movement ends on an altered octatonic pentachord, C–C♯–[]–(E♯)–F♯–[]–A.

A	B: m. 127	A: m. 222	C: m.259	A: m. 372	B: m. 445	A: m. 515
Prelude	Theme 4 (Piano)	Theme 1	Theme 6a (Piano)	Theme 1	Theme 4 (Piano)	Theme 6a (Piano)
Theme 1	Theme 5		Theme 6b	Interlude	Theme 7	Theme 1
Theme 2	Interlude		Theme 6a		Interlude	Theme 2
Interlude			Theme 6b			Interlude
Theme 3			Interlude		Codetta	
Interlude						

Example 3.37. Bartók, Sonata no. 1 for violin and piano (1921): structure of the third movement.

The third movement is a large rondo form, ABACABA-codetta, in which the violin and piano alternate thematic renditions (Example 3.37).

The thematic material and its permutations stem from Romanian source material, specifically from instrumental music Bartók collected in the Maramureș (northern) region of Transylvania, including a number of pieces played by village Gypsy performers on the violin and guitar. The indeterminate structure of the violin part usually consists of twin-bar motifs featuring eighth- and sixteenth-note values (see Example 3.20); the guitar accompaniment is invariably an ostinato of perfect fifths (Example 3.38).

The first theme of the Sonata is compiled from such twin-bar motifs, but as octatonic hexachords—such as B–C♯–D–E–F–G, and smaller seg-

Example 3.38. Bartók, Rumanian Folk Music, vol. 5, no. 173h, mm. 1–4.

ments—rather than modal configurations. Furthermore, the piano accompaniment is an ostinato of fifth chords that are added-note C♯ Z-cells, C♯–D–(F♯)–G–G♯ (Example 3.39).

The second theme opens with whole-tone violin motifs, A♯–G♯–F♯–E–D–C and C♭–D♭–E♭–G, which are also accompanied by an extended Z-cell ostinato, G♯–A–D–D♯ (mm. 48–49). The E-Dorian violin motifs in the third theme feature Hungarian dotted-rhythm schemata, ♫. ♫., and are accompanied by an X-cell ostinato, E–F–F♯–D♯, (mm. 99–101, b.1). The fourth and sixth themes, played by the piano, contain octatonic configurations, and the fifth theme (violin) again begins with whole-tone passages. The final return of Theme 1 (mm. 374–76) is accompanied by an ostinato of B half-diminished seventh chords, B–D–F–A (piano, L.H.), and major seconds, A♭–B♭ (R.H.), where the resultant combination of major seconds forms another X-cell, A–B/A♭–B♭. The movement ends with a Bartókian consonant seventh chord, C♯–E–G♯–B.

The Bartók-d'Arányi performances of the work in London during March 1922 were attended by more than twenty music critics. The reviews established Bartók's international reputation by referring to him as either a master composer or one of the greatest geniuses of modern music. Exhilarated by this long-awaited recognition, together with requests to return to England and give concerts in Paris and elsewhere in Europe, Bartók composed his Sonata no. 2 for Violin and Piano from July to November that year. Because the two-movement work represents the fusion of Romanian instrumental folk music and rondo form, an overview of the sources will help clarify its related structural attributes.

Example 3.39. Bartók, Sonata no. 1 for violin and piano, third movement, mm. 5–8.

The *Cântec lung* ("long-drawn" melody) Bartók discovered in Mara-
mureş County (see Example 3.33) has its instrumental variants played on
the peasant flute, violin, or bagpipe. It is frequently performed as a composite piece beginning with the designation "When the shepherd lost his
sheep" followed by a dance melody designated by the words "When the
shepherd found his [lost] sheep." Bartók wrote,

> This genre is spread well over all the Rumanian territory. The two kinds,
> in fact, belong together, forming a double piece. First comes the slow
> one, expressing the sorrow of the shepherd, then follows, without any in-
> terruption, the fast one, expressing his joy. Such a double piece—almost
> a suite—is repeated as long as the player or listeners like it.[40]

The double piece illustrated in Example 3.40, played on a *trişca* (a
recorder-like peasant flute), is significant from tonal as well as formal
viewpoints. The pitch collection in the *Cântec lung* (melody no. 747) is a
Lydian-related octatonic hexachord, G–[]–A♯–B–C♯–D–E–(F♯), and its
structure is essentially indeterminate, notwithstanding the ternary orientation of long-drawn tones preceding and following a series of variations on
the melody. The dance tune (no. 293bis) is Dorian but with a variable

Example 3.40. Bartók, Rumanian Folk Music, *vol. 1, (a) no. 747, mm. 1–6, and (b)
no. 293bis, mm. 1–8.*

seventh-degree, F or F♯; the complete piece is an *Ardeleana*-type quaternary, based on the Ukrainian *kolomyjka* rhythm (see Example 3.31).

The Hungarian instrumental material also contains many examples of composite pieces, consisting of an extended, slow dance melody as the main part and a shorter, fast dance as the added part. When city Gypsy bands adopted this genre, one outcome was the innovative *lassan-friss* (slow-fast) binary form used in Liszt's Hungarian Rhapsodies. In addition, Bartók, who had previously edited teaching editions of Beethoven piano sonatas for the Budapest publisher Rózsavölgyi, was quite familiar with Beethoven's two-movement piano sonatas (opp. 53, 54, 78, and 111). In fact, in op. 111 (Beethoven's last piano sonata), the skeletonized melodic contour of the adagio theme in the first movement is strikingly similar to the allegro theme in the second movement.[41]

Thus, the large binary design of Bartók's second violin sonata represents a synthesis of Beethovenian rondo-variation form and Romanian shepherd double-piece structure that combines the *Cântec lung* and a dance tune such as the *Ardeleana*. The first movement, in ABACADA-codetta form, opens with sustained tones (E), in typical *Cântec lung* style, while the piano sounds the principal tone, F♯ (mm. 1–4). The violin continues with the first theme, whose first melody-section (mm. 5–8) consists of two motifs: the first one a whole-tone pentachord, G♯–F♯–E–D–C, and the second a whole-tone tetrachord, E–D–C–B♭ (Example 3.41).

The form of the second movement is ABCBDABA-coda. Its first theme, perhaps symbolic of the happy shepherd who has found his lost sheep, is the retrograde form, in augmented values, of the whole-tone pentachord in the first theme of the first movement. The accented repetitions of the note A are an imitation of the "shifted" rhythm that occurs in some Romanian instrumental pieces, where a strong beat loses its accent and a weak beat gains one (Example 3.42).[42]

The fourth theme is based on the *kolomyjka* rhythm that identifies the

Example 3.41. Bartók, Sonata no. 2 for Violin and Piano, first movement, mm. 5–8.

Example 3.42. Bartók, Sonata no. 2 for Violin and Piano, second movement, mm. 1–5.

Romanian *Ardeleana* dance form. The unusual piano accompaniment consists of whole-tone chord clusters and scalar configurations (mm. 189–212, 228–253). The coda, a reprise of the first theme from the first movement, provides an architectonic or rounded shape to the work.[43]

When in 1923 Bartók accepted a commission to compose a work in celebration of the fiftieth anniversary of the merging of Buda and Pest, he realized that he could personally memorialize the event by integrating Hungarian and other national folk-music styles. The outcome was the Dance Suite for Orchestra (1923), which he subsequently transcribed for piano, consisting of five dances connected by a ritornello (small repetition). The first dance marks Bartók's earliest invention of a "chromatic" theme, which "has some resemblance" to Arab chromatic folk melodies (Example 3.43).[44]

The 2/4 rhythm schema of three quaternate eighth-notes ending with a bar of two quarter notes is typical of Ukrainian *kolomyjka* dance tunes, and was taken over by Transylvanian Hungarians for their *kanásztánc* (hog-herder's dance) melodies (cf. Example 3.31).[45] The arrangement of slurs is an ingenious adaptation of Romanian "shifted" rhythm, resulting in emphatic rendition of melodic intervals of a minor third, major second, and minor second. So far as tonality is concerned, the melody begins with

Example 3.43. Bartók, Dance Suite for Piano (1925), first dance, mm. 1–5.

a glissando from F to A, followed by repetitions of the X-cell (chromatic tetrachord) motif, A♭–A–B♭–C♭. The complete melody (mm. 1–14) and its simple intervallic accompaniment, G–D and F♯–E♭, identify the tonality of the first dance as a G Phrygian/Lydian twelve-tone polymode, G–A♭–B♭–C–D–E♭–F/G–A–B–C♯–D–E–F♯.

The Five Village Scenes for Voice and Piano (1924), a transcription of Slovak folk songs, is the only work Bartók composed during the last two years of this stage in his development. The events leading to his creative stagnation began when he was no longer able to continue the large-scale collection of musical folklore:

> The politically and financially chaotic conditions prevailing after the war put an end to any endeavor of that kind . . . The result of our activity up to the autumn of 1918 has been the following number of melodies: 8,000 Hungarians, 2,800 Slovak, 3,500 Rumanian, and 150 from other nationalities (Ruthenians, Serbians, Bulgarians, Gipsies).[46]

Bartók thereafter concentrated his efforts on the analysis and classification of the collected melodies, including a vast number of others, such as the related Czech and Moravian material, that had appeared in various publications. He published the results of his findings in scholarly essays and negotiated contracts to write studies on Hungarian, Romanian, and Slovak folk music. His growing fame as composer and pianist brought many offers for concert engagements at home and on tour abroad; their preparation and his obligations as professor of piano at the Budapest Academy of Music continually interrupted his ethnomusicological research.

In the summer of 1923, his marriage to Márta Ziegler ended in divorce by mutual agreement; in August he married his pupil Ditta Pásztory. In 1925, Bartók's first concert tour in Italy began with recitals in Milan on March 10 and Rome on March 12, and ended with Naples and Palermo on March 14 and 15. He returned to northern Italy on holiday during July and gave a concert in Trieste on December 7.

Although the Dance Suite is the epitome of Bartók's fusion of national styles, an equally significant achievement in this second stage in his development is the remarkable articulation of Beethovenian progressive form and structural aspects of Romanian instrumental folk music that is so prominent in the Sonata no. 2 for Violin and Piano. Another, equally significant achievement was his discovery of seventeenth- and eighteenth-century Italian keyboard music during one or another of his visits to Italy.

Just as Liszt had been inspired by Italian Baroque keyboard music to create his "new music" tonality and form that are embodied in the Piano Sonata in B Minor, so Bartok, perhaps following in Liszt's footsteps, discovered in such keyboard music the contrapuntal techniques that are embodied in the works composed in 1926, the year that inaugurates the highest stage in his artistic career.[47]

Chapter 4

SYNTHESIS OF EAST AND WEST: 1926–1945

$\mathscr{A}$t an interview in Paris during the first week in March 1939, Bartók paid tribute to the role played by Debussy in shaping his music:

> Debussy's great service to music was to awaken among all musicians an awareness of harmony and its possibilities. In that, he was just as important as Beethoven, who revealed to us the meaning of progressive form, and as Bach, who showed us the transcendent significance of counterpoint. Now, what I am always asking myself is this: is it possible to make a synthesis of these three great masters, a living synthesis that will be valid for our own time?[1]

Bartók, noted for his great reserve and modesty, apparently was unable to state simply that he had already achieved such a synthesis in the piano works composed in 1926: Sonata for Piano (June), *Out of Doors* for Piano (June and August), Nine Little Piano Pieces (June and August/September), *Mikrokosmos*,[2] and Concerto no. 1 for Piano and Orchestra (August–November). The generative factors in this sudden flood of works can be attributed to his personal need for new concert pieces, the influence of Stravinsky's new music, and the discovery of Baroque source materials during his tours of Italy in 1925, which enabled him to create a distinctive contrapuntal style in his compositions.

In 1924, Stravinsky composed his Concerto for Piano and Wind Instruments and Sonata for Piano, and performed them on tours of Europe and the United States. Bartók, on the other hand, had only his early Rhapsody for Piano and Orchestra, op. 1, (1904) to offer Amsterdam and Budapest audiences during the fall of 1925. "I must compose a piano concerto," he said at an interview on November 22. "This is sadly lacking. This will be my next work."[3] When Stravinsky appeared in Budapest on March 15, 1926, Bartók attended the concert. He was so impressed with the Concerto that he studied the score of *Histoire du soldat* (1918), Stravinsky's first neoclassical work, which includes Bachian preludes.[4]

The problem of counterpoint was solved after Bartók had acquired organ and clavicembalo works of Italian Baroque composers while he toured Italy. As he states in a later communication:

> Why have I made so little use of counterpoint? . . . In my youth my ideal of beauty was not so much the style of Bach or Mozart but of Beethoven. Recently it has changed somewhat; of late I have been much occupied with pre-Bachian music, and I believe that traces of this can be observed in the Piano Concerto and Nine Little Piano Pieces.[5]

An obvious trace stems from Bartók's transcription of the Sonata in G Major by Azzolino Bernardino della Ciaia (1671–1755). Bartók played the four-movement work during a Budapest radio broadcast on November 10, 1926, after he had completed the Concerto no. 1 for Piano and Orchestra. The first movement of the Concerto begins with a quotation from the fugue subject that opens the second movement of della Ciaia's composition (Example 4.1).

The unique second movement features introductory and closing dialogues between the percussion ensemble (timpani, two side-drums, bass drum, four cymbals, and gong) and the piano as a pitched percussion instrument (mm. 1–20, R.N. 15–18). Another dialogue occurs between the percussive piano and the lyrical woodwind ensemble (Example 4.2).

The piano plays an ostinato of paired major sevenths in each hand, D♭–C to E♭–D and B♭–A to A♭–G, which are reconfigured X-cells, C–D♭–D–E♭ and G–A♭–A–B♭ (R.N. 8). The ostinato serves as the accompaniment while the clarinet plays the pentatonic second theme. During the reprise of the theme by the English horn—followed by successive entries of the bassoon, oboe, and clarinet in free chromatic counterpoint—the piano ostinato is expanded to quartal sonorities that are constructed

Example 4.1. (a) della Ciaia, Sonata in G major, second movement, mm. 1–5, and (b), Bartók, Concerto no. 1 for Piano and Orchestra, first movement, mm. 38–44.

from an octatonic hexachord, C–D♭–E♭–[]–G♭–[]–A–B♭, in the first two beats of the bar, and an added-note Z-cell, D♭-D-(E♭)-G-A♭, on the third beat (R.N. 9).

Bartók's ingenious use of pentatonicism in the folk-like clarinet theme and abstract cellular constructions in the piano accompaniment are derived from partition of the octatonic scale into two symmetrical pentachords a tritone apart, A–C–D–E–G and E♭–G♭–A♭–B♭–D♭, respectively.

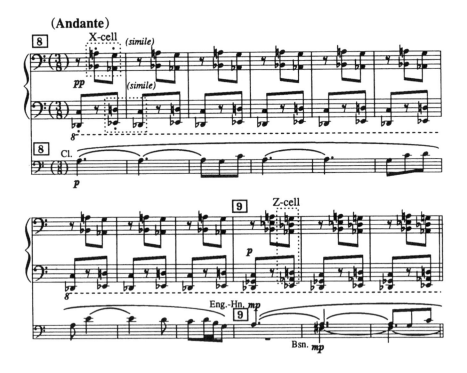

Example 4.2. Bartók, Concerto no. 1 for Piano and Orchestra, second movement, mm. 91–102.

When the passing tone, B, appears in the theme, its pitch collection is extended to a modal hexachord. This interaction of octatonic, pentatonic, and modal formations produces the A-Lydian/Phrygian eleven-tone polymode, A–B–D♭–E♭–E–G♭–A♭/A–B♭–C–D–E–G.

At rehearsal number 10, the entry of the flute increases the texture to four- and five-voice counterpoint, while the homophonic texture of the ostinato is also expanded to five-note cluster chords. The woodwind ensemble continues with rhythm schemata in the style of Romanian bagpipe motifs, together with the increasingly dense piano ostinato with hexachordal clusters (mm. 126–132).

In sharp contrast to the structural classicism of the Concerto is the impressionism of *Out of Doors*, five piano pieces titled *With Drums and Pipes, Barcarolla, Musettes, Musiques Nocturnes,* and *The Chase.* The fourth piece, reminiscent of Debussy's *Préludes* for piano, is not only a memento of visits to his sister's family in Békés County (Hungary) and

Un poco più andante

Example 4.3. Bartók, Out of Doors, *"Musiques Nocturnes," mm. 17–25.*

nearby Transylvanian villages to collect Hungarian and Romanian folk music, but also marks the first appearance of the "Night's music" genre that recurs in various transformations in later Bartók works.

The piece begins with "the concert of frogs heard in peaceful nights on the [Hungarian] Great Plain" and other sounds of mysterious nocturnal creatures, which are represented by X-cell motifs, minor seconds, major sevenths, and arpeggiated chromatic cluster-chords (mm. 1–16).[6] The first theme, a four-section heterometric melody, seems to be in imitation of a Transylvanian-Romanian folk song. The skeleton form of the chromatic melody is an octatonic hexachord, G–F♯–E–E♭–C♯–C (Example 4.3).

The "Night's music" returns as an interlude (mm. 34–37). The second theme, a four-section melody that ends on the second degree (C♯) of the B-major scale, imitates the characteristic Transylvanian-Romanian *fluer* (peasant flute) performance style (Example 4.4).

The accompaniment (not shown) consists of descending white-key

(Lento)

Example 4.4. Bartók, Out of Doors, *"Musiques Nocturnes," mm. 48–57.*

triads and cluster chords, from E to A, which ends with a Bartókian neutral (major/minor) cadence, A–C–C♯–E (m. 57). The juxtaposed pitch collections, however, represent discrete partitions of the E-Phrygian/Lydian twelve-tone polymode, E–F–G–A–B–C–D/E–F♯–G♯–A♯–B–C♯–D♯. The reprise of the first theme includes the second theme as an obbligato (mm. 58–66). The piece ends with the "Night's music" as a postlude, together with an attenuated variant of the second theme.

In Nine Little Piano Pieces (1926), Bartók returns to his earlier (1908–1913) practice of writing pedagogical music for the keyboard. The collection begins with Four Dialogues, contrapuntal pieces that at first sight appear to be in the style of Bach's two-part inventions. While there are contrapuntal devices such as imitation, inversion, and more-or-less strict canonic writing, the polyphonic orientation is free development of motifs in the style of Baroque Italian composers. The motivic construction, however, reflects the interaction of diatonic and nondiatonic formations within the context of Bartókian polymodal chromaticism.

The Third Dialogue (Example 4.5) is a particularly representative example of such polymodal chromaticism, in which the tonality is a C-Phrygian/Lydian twelve-tone polymode (m. 30). According to the organization of phrases in the treble staff, the melody has a folkloric structure of four sections, ending on the second degree, D, as its final tone (m. 8). This type of cadence is a characteristic of Romanian folk melodies. The

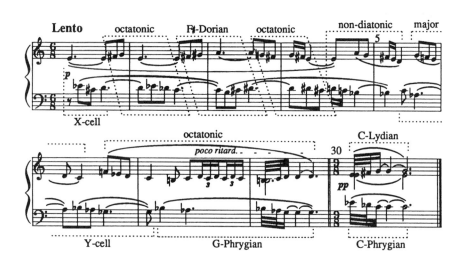

Example 4.5. Bartók, Nine Little Piano Pieces, "Third Dialogue," mm. 1–8, 30.

nondiatonic formation (mm. 4–5) is the D-Mixolydian mode with lowered sixth degree, D–E–F♯–G–A–B♭–C, and the polymodal cadence (m. 30) is derived from contrary-motion partitions of the C-octatonic hexachord, C–D♭–E♭–E–F♯–G.

The melodic contour is Bartók's invention, which is contrapuntally interwoven with the likewise folkloric construction in the bass clef. The outcome is a uniquely wrought yet technically facile example of polyphonic texture that points ahead to such masterpieces as the String Quartet no. 4 and the Music for Strings, Percussion, and Celesta.

Bartók's first concert tour of the United States began with his arrival in New York on December 18, 1927, and continued in various cities from coast to coast. There was great interest in his appearances; many press releases, reviews, and interviews appeared in the media until his departure March 1, 1928. A number of successful recitals, which included the Sonata no. 2 for Violin and Piano, were given with the violinist, József Szigeti. Early that autumn, perhaps inspired by the positive American reception of his works, Bartók decided to write similar chamber music, based for the most part on instrumental pieces in his Romanian folk-music collection. The first composition, dedicated to Szigeti, is the two-movement Rhapsody no. 1 for Violin and Piano. The first theme of the second movement is a *judecata* (judgment), a dance piece based on a Romanian folk song as played by a peasant violinist.[7] It is interesting that a variant of this melody, titled *The Gift to Be Simple*, was brought to New York in 1774 by the Shakers (an English Quaker sect) and subsequently transcribed by Aaron Copland as the source melody for a set of dance variations in his ballet, *Appalachian Spring* (1944).[8]

In sharp contrast to the ebullient duet is the cerebral, much-celebrated String Quartet no. 4, which Bartók composed between July and September 1928. His structural analysis states that the character of the five movements corresponds to classical sonata form, where the third, slow movement is the kernel and the other, fast movements are arranged in layers around it. He describes the third movement as a three-part form:

measures   1–34: Part 1 (melody in the cello);
           34–54: Part 2 (melody begins in the first violin, then in the
                  second violin, finally in the second violin and viola);
           55–63: Part 3 (free recapitulation: the melody is inverted
                  and divided between the cello and the first violin);
           64–71: Coda.[9]

On the other hand, however, the ternary structure of the movement corresponds to the improvisatory style of Romanian *Cântec lung* music, particularly the programmatic instrumental pieces designated *Când păcurarul perdut oile* ("When the shepherd lost his sheep"), which Bartók first introduced in the slow movement of his Sonata no. 2 for Violin and Piano.[10] Example 4.6 further subdivides Bartók's tripartite form in terms of the basic recitation-improvisation-declamation Romanian instrumental style.

Another structural attribute of the movement is its adherance to the proportions of the golden section, or its arithmetical mean—the Fibonacci series—where the three parts and certain subdivisions correspond to the ratio $5 : 8 : 13 : 21 : 34 : 55$, and so on. Similar calculations made of various works—particularly the first movements of Haydn, Mozart, Beethoven, Schoenberg, and Bartók quartets—show the same formal basis.[11] There is

PART	Measures	Instruments	Structural Subdivisions
One			
	1–6	Vlns., Vla.	Introduction
	6–10	Vlc.	Recitation on D
	11–13		Improvisation 1
	14–17		Recitation on F
	17–21		Improvisation 2
	22–25		Recitation on B
	26–30		Improvisation 3
	31–34		Declamation on A
Two			
	34–41	Vln. 1	Recitation on E♭
	42–46	Vln. 2	Improvisation 4
	47–55	Vln. 2, Vla.	Declamation on C
Three			
	55–63	Vln. 1, Vlc.	Improvisation 5
Coda			
	64–68	tutti	Interlude
	69–71	Vln. 1	Declamation on D

Example 4.6. Bartók, String Quartet no. 4, third movement, structural subdivisions.

no evidence, however, that Bartók deliberately composed any of his works according to the golden section.

As regards tonal organization, the movement is replete with cellular tetrachords (X, Y, and Z) and diatonic, octatonic, and whole-tone formations.[12] The twelve-tone Lydian/Phrygian polymode, with D as the principal tone, is most frequently partitioned into whole-tone configurations. In Part 2, while the second violin and viola are playing the declamation, the accompanying double-stops in the first violin and the cello form the Hungarian (symmetrical) pentatonic scale, E♭–G♭–A♭–B♭–D♭ (mm. 47–52). Part 3 continues the Hungarian orientation in the dialogue between the cello and the first violin, where the prevalence of perfect fourths reflects the influence of old-Hungarian melodic style (mm. 55–63). In the coda, moreover, Slovak influence is manifest when the declamation ends with the Lydian mode, D–E–F♯–G♯–A–B–C♯, projected as a vertical sonority (mm. 70–71).

MIKROKOSMOS: AN INTRODUCTION TO BARTÓK'S SYSTEM OF COMPOSITION

In 1929, Bartók selected eighteen of the illustrative pieces he had composed in 1913 for *Zongora Iskola* (Piano School) for reprinting as *The First Term at the Piano*.[13] Two years later, when Bartók moved to another Budapest residence, he was so dissatisfied with the mandatory singing classes in the new school attended by his younger son, Peter (then eight years old), that the authorities permitted the father to attend to the son's music education. Then, on October 12, 1932, in response to the request of his Vienna publisher, Universal Edition, that he write some easy piano pieces, Bartók replied:

> It coincides very well with my own plans that you are just now asking for some very easy piano pieces from me: during this past summer I wrote several—about 35—beginning with the easiest (like the pieces that Rózsavölgyi published in the "First Term") and progressing in difficulty. But because I have a many-sided project in mind, it will be a long time before I can complete it.[14]

The "many-sided project" eventually became *Mikrokosmos*, a six-volume compilation (153 pieces and 33 exercises) completed in 1939.

Bartók's interpretation of the work is only partially given in the Preface and Notes to the *Mikrokosmos* publication, where most emphasis is on general directions for the teaching of the first four volumes:

> In a 1944 interview broadcast by WNYC (New York City radio), Bartók also referred to *Mikrokosmos* as "a series of pieces in all of different styles to represent a small world." And in his last comment about the work, he states that it "appears as a *synthesis* [emphasis added] of all the musical and technical problems which were treated and in some cases only partially solved in the previous piano works," particularly with regard to his new trend of piano writing in which "the percussive character of the piano" is accentuated.[15]

The following *Mikrokosmos* pieces have been selected as exemplars of the composer's stated lifework objective: the synthesis of eastern European folk music—that is, Bartók's fusion of rural (peasant) music styles—and Western art music.

VOLUME 1

Contrary Motion (no. 17). This miniature has a rounded AA^5A^5vA structure and a nine-syllable, dotted-rhythm schema, which are borrowings from new-Hungarian folk-song style.[16] Also notable is the polymodal counterpoint based on the G-Lydian/Mixolydian nine-tone polymode, G–A–B–C♯–D–E–F♯/G–A–B–C–D–E–F, which is similar to the opening measures in Frescobaldi's Toccata in G Major.[17]

Syncopation (no. 27). The polymodal counterpoint illustrates the interaction of diatonic (R.H.: C–D–E–F–G) and octatonic (L.H.: G♯–A–B–C–D) pentachords.

Imitation Reflected (no. 29).The partition of the ascending form of the A-melodic minor scale into symmetrical pentachords, with E as the dual axis, serves a higher structural purpose in measures 1–5, in which C–D–E/E–F♯–G♯ comprise the first five degrees of the whole-tone scale.

VOLUME 2

Minuetto (no. 50). This piece is in the *menuet* style of J. S. Bach, including the rhythm schemata, with A as the principal tone. The juxtaposition of D♯ and D♮ (mm. 1, 5, 15, and 17) results in the A-Lydian/major hexa-chordal polymode, A–B–C♯–D♯–E/A–B–C♯–D–E.[18]

Minor Sixths in Parallel Motion (no. 62). The rhythm schema is based on an extended version of the Ruthenian *kolomyjka* (i.e., Ukrainian round dance: 2/4 ♫♩|♫♫|♫♫|♩ ♩ |), and the melodic contour resembles the first theme of Bartók's Dance Suite for Orchestra.[19] The tonality is the A-Phrygian/Lydian twelve-tone polymode, A–B♭–C–D–E–F–G/A–B–C♯–D♯–E–F♯–G♯, ending in A major. The first section (mm. 1–12) consists of a "neutral" (i.e., minor/Lydian) hexachord, G–A–B♭–B–C♯–D. The second and third sections (mm. 13–28, 29–40) feature octatonic pentachords in each hand (L.H.: A–B♭–C–D♭–E♭; R.H.: E♯–F♯–G♯–A–B).

Melody Divided (no. 66). This piece is a remarkable example of Bartókian fusion of national folk-music styles of eastern Europe and their synthesis with Western art-music techniques. The melodic structure, A^5AA^5vAv, is derived from the old-style Hungarian quaternary, with its characteristic fifth transposition and pentatonic scale construction (mm. 1–12). The addition of nonaccented degrees in the second half of the melody (R.H. C♯, m. 16; L.H. F♯, m. 22) transforms the pentatonic tetra-chords into major pentachords. The ostinato dyads in the accompaniment are organized as Lydian (L.H., m. 2–6) or minor (mm. 8–12) tetrachords of the E-Phrygian/Lydian twelve-tone polymode, E–F–G–A–B–C–D/E–F♯–G♯–A♯–B–C♯–D♯. The pentatonic tetrachords and major penta-chords in the melody are, of course, other segments of the same poly-mode. The fourth melody section ends in Romanian style on the second degree, F♯ (L.H., m. 24). The F♯ reappears in the postlude, however, as the principal tone of an inverted supertonic seventh chord (m. 29). This dissonance is treated as a functional chord that ostensibly resolves by way of a plagal cadence to the tonic. Because the latter is a dissonant, inverted seventh chord, E–G–B–D, it is therefore an extrafunctional consonance whose exclusively pentatonic degrees are equal in importance.[20]

VOLUME 3

Hommage à R. Sch. (no. 80). The architectonic form (AABAv) is extended by a postlude (mm. 16–22), and the tonality is the C-Phrygian/Lydian twelve-tone polymode, C–D♭–E♭–F–G–A♭–B♭/C–D–E–F♯–G–A–B. The accompaniment consists of a twin-bar ostinato whose pitch content is a chromatic scale from B to F♯ but structured as ascending and descending tetrachords that outline the C Z-cell, B–F–F♯–C (L.H., mm. 1–8; R.H.,

mm. 9–12). The neutral (major/minor) melody, G–A–B♭–B–C–D–E♭
(R.H., mm. 1–8) is reconstructed in Part B to incorporate the G Z-cell,
G–A♭–C♯–D (L.H., mm. 9–10). The melodic structure and the accompaniment of the postlude contrast three cadence formulas: C-harmonic/
melodic minor (mm. 15–17); C-octatonic (R.H.: C Z-cell in mm.
18–19); and C-Aeolian mode (mm. 20–22).

Two Major Pentachords (no. 86). This piece is an invention in free
counterpoint, which Bartók describes as "one voice in C, the other in F♯ in
juxtaposition. Often employed in modern music and when understood
would solve many of its mysteries."[21] Although the illustrative small-head
notation above the piece illustrates the two pentachords as discrete scalar
pitch collections, they are juxtaposed in the composition as heptatonic
partitions of complementary C-octatonic scales, C–C♯–[]–E–F♯–G–A–A♯/
C–D–[]–F–F♯–G♯–A–B. Thus, complementary octatonic partitions of the
chromatic scale provide an alternate, nondiatonic approach in the
Bartókian system of polymodal chromaticism (Example 4.7).

The first section begins with the C Z-cell, F♯–C♯–C–G (mm. 1–4); the
second section (mm. 5–8) has the retrograde construction of the cell,
G–C–C♯–F♯. The fifth section (mm. 19–26) contains held notes that ex-
tend the texture to three parts, and the four-part sixth section (mm.
27–32) introduces the G X-cell, F♯–G♯–F–G, as harmonic major seconds.
The seventh section (mm. 33–36) features a reprise of the C Z-cell as the
emphatic tones of a heptachordal C-Lydian/Phrygian polymode, C–D–
E–F♯–G–B/C–C♯–G, and ends with the juxtaposition of F♯ (L.H.) and the
C-major triad (R.H.) as a Bartókian consonant chord.

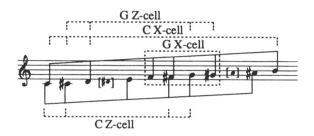

*Example 4.7. Hexachordal partitions of complementary octatonic scales and interre-
lated cells.*

VOLUME 4

Diminished Fifth (no. 101). This piece is a folk-style companion to the abstract *Two Major Pentachords* (no. 86), which could have been designated *Two Minor Tetrachords*. Both compositions feature part-writing at the interval of a tritone, Z-cell contructions, and octatonic partitions that are "*Probably* [emphasis added] in the key of D minor."[22] *Diminished Fifth*, however, based on the D-Phrygian/Lydian twelve-tone polymode, D–E♭–F–G–A–B♭–C/D–E–F♯–G♯–A–B–C♯, begins with partitions of the minor form of the D-octatonic scale into constituent minor tetrachords (R.H.: D–C–B–A; L.H.: A♭–G♭–F–E♭). The juxtaposed tetrachords, moreover, are linked by means of the D Z-cell, D–E♭–A♭–A (mm. 1–11). The same procedure is followed in the third section (mm. 12–19), which, transposed to G, provides the remaining degrees of the chromatic scale (Example 4.8).

The fifth section consists of juxtaposed F- (R.H.) and B- (L.H.) Aeolian modes, and its pitch content provides the twelve degrees of the chromatic scale. Here, too, the modes are linked by B, A, G, and E Z-cells (mm. 27–29, 30–31, 31–31, and 33–34, respectively). Following a reprise of the opening bars in the sixth section (mm. 36–42) and the reordered G Z-cell, C–D♭–G♭–G (mm. 43–44), the piece ends on a semicadence, E♭–A (m. 45), the same tritone with which it began.

Bulgarian Rhythm (no. 115). Bartók made his first contact with Bulgarian peasant music during March 1912 in the Banat region of Hungary (southwestern Transylvania, now part of Romania). Although he made preliminary transcriptions of the eight vocal melodies he had collected, it was not until 1935 that he revised them, together with twenty-one Serbian instrumental and vocal melodies collected in November 1912. The revisions were a necessary adjunct to his preparation for publication, beginning in 1932, of his Romanian folk-music material: he discovered that about 5 percent of the latter had a peculiar, 9/16 asymmetrical rhythm that he suspected were in "the so-called 'Bulgarian' type of rhythm."[23] He

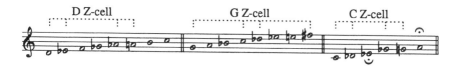

Example 4.8. The minor form of the D and G octatonic scales, and their Z-cell nodes.

printed the revised melodies in pamphlet format, mailed them to Yugoslav
and Bulgarian ethnomusicologists for evaluation, and about the same time
began the study and analysis of multiple thousands of Bulgarian folk
melodies and the lists of rhythm types in Wassil Stoin's published collections.[24] In 1938 he published his essay, "The So-called Bulgarian
Rhythm,"stating that

> Bulgarian rhythm is that in which the quantities indicated in the irregular
> time-signatures are exceptionally short (M.M. = 300–400), and in which
> these very short, basic quantities [indicated as sixteenth or eighth notes]
> are not evenly—that is to say not symmetrically—grouped within larger
> quantities. . . . It appears that the most frequent Bulgarian rhythms are
> as follows: 5/16 (subdivided into 3 + 2 or 2 + 3); 7/16 (2 + 2 + 3)—
> the rhythm of the well-known *Ruchenitza* dance); 8/16 (3 + 2 + 3);
> 9/16 (2 + 2 + 2 + 3); . . . [25]

Although Bartók was aware that this kind of asymmetrical rhythm exists in Turkish folk music, where it is known as *aksak* ("limping" rhythm),
he found it to be best known and most widespread in Bulgaria; he therefore designated the phenomenon as "Bulgarian rhythm." *Mikrokosmos* no.
115 is "an original Bulgarian theme. Altered key of G."[26] The irregular
5/8 time signature, organized as asymmetrical 3 + 2 and 2 + 3 eighths,
represents Bulgarian *pajdushko* dance rhythm.

Each part of the rounded form has a nonarchitectonic substructure:

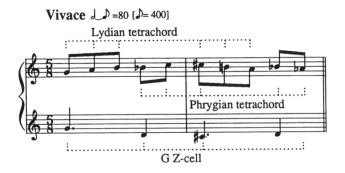

Example 4.9. Bartók, Mikrokosmos *no. 115, "Bulgarian Rhythm," mm. 1–2.*

Example 4.10. Bartók, String Quartet no. 5, third movement: Scherzo, mm. 3-4, 24; Trio, mm. 1, 17–18.

A = a b c d (mm. 1–8); B = a b c (mm. 9–22); and Av = a b c d (mm. 22–32). The melodic construction is based on partitions of the chromatic scale into G-Lydian and Phrygian tetrachords in Part A (Example 4.9) and their transposition to D in Part Av, thus forming the G-Lydian/Phrygian twelve-tone polymode, G–A–B–C♯–D–E–F♯/G–A♭–B♭–C–D–E♭–F.

The emphatic rendition of D in the accompaniment of Part A creates the G Z-cell, G–A♭–C♯–D, an octatonic substructure that serves to articulate the modal tetrachords. Part B reverses the 3 + 2 rhythm schema into 2 + 3 eighths, Part Av begins with a two-part canon at the octave, and the work closes with a v^7–I modal cadence.

It is noteworthy that when Bartók began his investigation of Bulgarian folk music he had already understood the significance of its dynamic additive rhythms as a new source for composition.[27] Thus, when he composed the third movement of the String Quartet no. 5 during the summer of 1934, he created original themes based on Bulgarian rhythm schemata. Moreover, an ingenious Bulgarian cross rhythm is created in the Trio by juxtaposition of the theme (Vln. 1: m. 1) and the twin-bar ostinato (Vcl.: mm. 17–18), where the latter is restructured as 2 + 3 + 3 + 2 eighths (Example 4.10).

In 1936, Paul Sacher, founder and director of the Basel (Switzerland) Chamber Orchestra, commissioned Bartók to write a new work in celebration of the tenth anniversary of the founding of the orchestra. Because of financial and technical difficulties, Sacher asked for elimination of wind players and their substitution by a piano, cembalo, or some other kind of percussion instrument. The work—Music for Strings, Percussion, and Celesta—was completed the same year and represents the ultimate in Bartókian thematic transformation by way of a new device: changing chromatic degrees into diatonic ones. He invented this procedure in 1926, and it appears for the first time in the *Menuetto* (no. 5) from Nine Little Piano Pieces (Example 4.11).

The theme in the first section (mm. 1–8) is a gapped chromatic pentachord from B to E. The second section (mm. 9–20) is a transformation of the first section but similar in melodic contour. Bartók explains this way:

> What characterizes a melody as a variant of another? I should say that variants are melodies in which the pitch relation of the various principal tones to each other shows a certain similarity; or, in other words, in which the contour line is entirely or partly similar.[28]

The transformation is an extension in range from chromatic degrees, B–C♯–D♯–E, into modal ones, that is, into a gapped segment of the A-Mixolydian mode, A–B–D–E–F♯–G. Additionally, the part writing in the accompaniment shows emphatic rendition of C♯ (the modal third degree) as an ostinato.

Bartók further explains:

> In other words, the succession of chromatic degrees is extended by levelling them over a diatonic terrain. You know very well the extension of

Example 4.11. Bartók, Nine Little Piano Pieces, "Menuetto," mm. 1–7, 9–15.

themes in their value called augmentation, and their compression in value called diminution. These devices are very well known, especially from the art music of the seventeenth and eighteenth centuries. Now, this device could be called "extension in range" of a theme. For the extension we have the liberty to choose any diatonic scale or mode. We will choose one of them which will best suit our actual purposes.[29]

With regard to Music for Strings, Percussion, and Celesta, the first movement is a fugue whose chromatic subject is derived from juxtaposed partitions of the A-Phrygian mode, A-B♭-C-D-E, and the A-Lydian mode, A–B–C♯–E♭/D♯–E (mm. 1–4). The arrangement of these individual modal degrees, however, is in accordance with symmetrical partitions: the A Z-cell, A–B♭–E♭–E, and permutations of its subsumed X-cell, B–C–C♯–D (Example 4.12). Transposition of the subject to E (mm. 5–8) completes the A-Phrygian/Lydian twelve-tone polymode.[30]

According to Jószef Ujfalussy, "The theme of the fugue permeates the entire work with all the stubborn persistence of a Berlioz *'idée fixe.'* In the second movement, the material of the fugue is used to form a scherzo. . . ."[31] In further explanation of the outcome when chromatic degrees are extended in range, Bartók states:

Andante tranquillo

Example 4.12. Bartók, Music for String Instruments, Percussion and Celesta, first movement, mm. 1–4.

As you will see, such an extension will considerably change the character of the melody, sometimes to such a degree that its relation to the original, non-extended form will be scarcely recognizable. *We will have mostly the impression that we are dealing with an entirely new melody* [emphasis added]. And this circumstance is very good indeed, because we will get variety on the one hand, but the unity will remain undestroyed, because of the hidden relation between the two forms.[32]

The melodic contour of the first theme in the second movement parallels the first half of the fugue subject, and its pitch content likewise consists of juxtaposed Phrygian and Lydian partitions transposed to C as the principal tone, C–D♭–E♭–F–G/C–D–E–F♯–G–A. The hidden relation between the fugue subject and the theme of the second movement is found in the cellular construction: the predecessor X-cells are extended in range to Y-cells (whole-tone tetrachords) that are interlocked as subsumed entities of the C Z-cell (Example 4.13).

In the third movement, the fugue subject returns in its original pitch configuration, in augmentation of note values, but with its four motifs (mm. 18–19, 33–35, 46–48, 60–63) separated by a prelude, interludes, and a postlude. The prelude features a B Z-cell dialogue between the xylophone and timpani, B–C–F–F♯ (mm. 1–4), that is followed by another one, based on the C Z-cell, C–C♯–F–F× , between the tremolos in the violoncello and contrabass (F♯, C) and the basically octatonic principal tones of the viola melody, C♯–D♯–E(E♯)–F×–[]–A♯ (mm. 5–9). The first interlude contains permutations of the first motif by the celesta and first violin

Example 4.13. Bartók, Music for String Instruments, Percussion, and Celesta, second movement, mm. 1–5.

(mm. 23–31), and the second interlude features celesta arpeggios that alternate pentatonic partitions of the chromatic scale, E♭–G♭–A♭–B♭–D♭ and E–G–A–B–D (mm. 34–41).

The third motif also shows extension in range from the original chromatic hexachord to a pentachordal configuration and its retrograde form, C–A–B♭–E♭–D/D–E♭–B♭–C. The third interlude follows with transformations of the extended motives (mm. 49–59), and the fourth motif is a chromatically compressed transformation, in augmented values (mm. 6–64). The fourth interlude, also in augmented values, is a variant of the first interlude (mm. 64–74). The postlude (mm. 75–82) is a varied reprise of the prelude, thus providing the movement with an architectonic form.

The fourth movement "shows the main theme of Movement I, which is extended, however, by diatonic expansion of the original chromatic form"[33] (Example 4.14).

The extension results in a nondiatonic Slovak folk mode, C–D–E–F♯–G–A–B♭, which Bartók discovered in 1907 and was verified by Kodály in 1911 (Example 4.15). As the folk song shows, the configured degrees represent the Lydian mode with a lowered (i.e., Mixolydian) seventh degree or, in other words, a Lydian/Mixolydian heptachordal polymode.[34]

The converse of diatonic extension is "chromatic compression," illustrated for the first time in *Mikrokosmos* no. 64b.[35] This procedure also appears as a transitional device in the fourth movement of Music for Strings, Percussion, and Celesta, where the diatonically extended theme "is gradually compressed into chromatic phrases associated with the original fugue subject" (mm. 214ff.).[36]

Molto moderato

Example 4.14. Bartók, Music for String Instruments, Percussion, and Celesta, fourth movement, mm. 203–209.

Example 4.15. Bartók, Slowakische Volkslieder, *vol. 2, no. 870.*

Bartók's last trip to collect folk music occurred in November, as part of an official invitation to visit Ankara, the capital city of Turkey. He gave lectures on musical folklore and participated in an orchestral concert of Hungarian music. During an excursion to a village in South Anatolia, close to the Syrian border, he listened to the singing of an old man, Ali Bekir, who sang an old narrative "about some war of the old days. I could hardly believe my ears, for it sounded just like a variant of an old Hungarian tune. In great joy I recorded the old Bekir's song. . . .The second tune I heard from the old Bekir was again a variant of a Hungarian song" (Example 4.16).[37]

In another village, Bartók recorded six instrumental pieces played by

Example 4.16. Bartók, Turkish Folk Music from Asia Minor. *Melody no. 8a (skeleton form) and its Hungarian variant (Appendix 2).*

two illiterate musicians of the nomadic Abdal tribe. Sometimes during the performance, the players walked to and fro in dance steps:

> The music itself was bewildering. One of the musicians played on an instrument something like an oboe, the *zurna*, the other on a *davul* (bass drum) tied in front of him. He beat that drum with terrific energy with a wooden drumstick, and I really thought at times that either his big drum or my eardrum would break. Even the flames of three flickering kerosene lamps jumped at every beat.[38]

Bartók's later note to the melody describes the bass drum as an instrument with two heads, which is struck with a regular (unfelted) wooden drumstick in the right hand and a flexible wooden rod in the left.[39] Most of the Turkish recordings had been transcribed before the end of May 1937, when he initiated steps to obtain a joint Turkish-Hungarian publication. But this venture had to be interrupted by his acceptance, the same month, of a second commission from Paul Sacher and the Basel section of the International Society for Contemporary Music (ISCM), for another chamber music piece. Bartók decided on a quartet for two pianos and two groups of percussion instruments. He composed the Sonata for Two Pianos and Percussion during July and August and, in the third movement, apparently commemorated his timbral impression of the Turkish *davul* (Example 4.17).

Toward the end of August, Bartók began the composition of the Concerto no. 2 for Violin and Orchestra, which had been commissioned in 1936 by the Hungarian violinist Zoltán Székely, and completed it on December 31, 1938. This masterpiece—today a part of the standard repertory and acclaimed repeatedly as the best violin concerto since Brahms—is another exemplar of Bartók's successful achievement of his goal as a

(Allegro non troppo)

Example 4.17. Bartók, Sonata for Two Pianos and Percussion (1937), third movement, mm. 116–122.

composer: the synthesis of eastern European folk-music elements and Western art-music techniques. It is interesting indeed that in one of the preliminary sketches Bartók's tempo designation for the first movement is *Tempo di Verbunkos*, which was subsequently changed to *Allegro non troppo*. However, there is no return to the Gypsy-oriented musical language of the nineteenth century: the *verbunkos* (recruiting dance) style relates only to the alternation of fast and slow sections and the bravura of the solo violin.[40]

The first movement, in sonata form, opens with a short introduction by the harp (triads) and lower strings (pizzicato motif) in the B-Mixolydian/Aeolian heptachordal polymode, B–C♯–D♯–E–F♯–G–A (mm. 1–7). The entry of the solo violin with the main theme, however, shows emphatic rendition of the B-pentatonic scale, B–D–E–F♯–A (mm. 6–10), followed by fifth transposition to F♯–A–B–C♯–E (mm. 11–14). The rhythm schema of the theme is 4/4 ♫|♩. ♪♪♩♩ |♪♩ ♫♫|♪♩♩♩. ♪|♫♩. |. The pentatonicism, fifth transposition, predominant fourths in the melodic contour, and dotted-rhythm schema are characteristic features of old-Hungarian folk music; on the other hand, the tonality of the theme and its accompaniment in these opening bars is the Bartókian B-Lydian/Phrygian twelve-tone polymode, B–C♯–D♯–E♯–F♯–G♯–A♯/B–C–D–E–F♯–G–A.

The contrasting (i.e., second) theme, also introduced by the violin solo, is constructed in the guise of a twelve-tone row, that is, as if the composer had embraced Arnold Schoenberg's method of composition: the construction of a strict twelve-tone row (the prime) whose degrees are thereafter transformed by inversion, retrograde, retrograde-inversion, and transposition. Bartók's "row," however, is predictably a polymodal construction—note the assignment of accidentals!—in which the juxtaposition of the Phrygian and Lydian modal partitions of the chromatic scale, A–B♭–C–D–E–F–G and A–B–C♯–D♯–E–F♯–G♯, respectively, is based on A as the principal tone (Example 4.18).

In the subsequent permutations of the theme by the violin solo or the orchestra, in A or transposed to D, all twelve tones are present but within a tonal context (mm. 76–92). In this way Bartók fulfilled a long-held objective: "to show Schoenberg that one can use all twelve tones and still remain tonal."[41] While it is true that in the 1920s Bartók thought he was approaching a species of twelve-tone music, even in that period "the absolute tonal foundation is unmistakable." Indeed, he found it necessary to

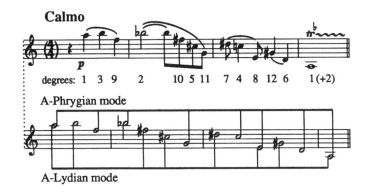

Example 4.18. Bartók, Concerto no. 2 for Violin and Orchestra, first movement, mm. 73–76.

restate his credo in a later essay, in which he asserts that it is impossible to reconcile music based on folk music with atonality or with twelve-tone music because folk melodies are always tonal:

> The fact that some twentieth-century composers went back for inspiration to old folk music acted as an impediment to the development of twelve-tone music. Far be it from me to maintain that to base his music on folk music is the only way to salvation for a composer in our days. But I wish that our opponents had an equally liberal opinion of the significance of folk music.[42]

The remainder of the first movement includes programmatic passages that in no uncertain musical terms confirm Bartók's opinion of atonality in general and the Vienna Schoenberg circle in particular. Following the first statement of the contrasting theme,

> [t]he ensuing conversation between solo and orchestral choirs is a parody of the 12-tone technique of composition. Instead of treating the theme in accordance with rigid procedural rules, Bartók varies the material so that all 12 tones are present but within a tonal context. When the orchestra breaks into three loud guffaws [mm. 92–95], the solo tries to camouflage its "atonality" with Romanian *Ardeleana* (round dance) rhythm patterns

[mm. 94ff.]. But the string section insists on a traditional accompaniment in tonally based triads until the trombones end this sorry state of chromatic affairs with a snort of derision [mm. 113-14: "flutter tongue"].[43]

At the end of July 1939, Bartók arrived in Switzerland to compose a new work for the Basel Chamber Orchestra. He completed the Divertimento for String Orchestra on August 17 and, a day or two later, began work on another commission, the String Quartet no. 6, for the New Hungarian String Quartet. The manuscripts indicate that his original intention apparently was a four-movement quartet, introspective in character, which would reflect the preparations for war that threatened to engulf western and eastern Europe, but would close with a folk-styled dance movement to represent his longing for a peaceful solution among the contentious nations. Later that month, however, when the nonaggression pact between National Socialist Germany and the Soviet Union was signed, Bartók realized that his world was coming to an end. Thus, when he returned to Budapest and began making preparations to leave Hungary, he discarded the unfinished dance piece and replaced it with a brief, poignant farewell of infinite sadness.[44]

The first movement sketch begins at measure 24 of the printed score, is in sonata form, and ends on a D-major triad. The second movement, a grotesque parody of a German military march, immediately follows, but in the printed score begins at measure 17. When on August 24 a radio broadcast announced the signing of the Hitler-Stalin treaty, the disillusioned composer momentarily interrupted his work to mark the unholy event with the creation of the *Mesto* (mournful) theme that would eventually precede each movement in the first draft.

Turning to the first movement of the printed score, the contrasting theme consists of three motifs, in which the first one is a remarkable transformation of a Hungarian *nóta* (national melody). This nineteenth-century urban folk song (Example 4.19) also appears in Liszt's Hungarian Rhapsody no. 14.

The dotted-rhythm schema, 2/4 ♪. ♪ ♪♪. | ♪. ♪ ♪♪. |, is a unique characteristic of new-style Hungarian folk song. Bartók was convinced that the new style "was born in Hungary and was known throughout the country, even at the beginning of the nineteenth century. . . . It exercised a considerable influence upon the more recent Slovak and Ruthenian peasant

Andante

Example 4.19. István Bartalus, 101 Magyar népdal *(Hungarian Folk Songs), no. 22.*

music, but hardly any upon the Romanian."[45] A softer variety of this rhythm, 6/8 ♩♪♪♩|♩♪♪♩|, is a feature of the contrasting theme (Example 4.20).[46]

Note, too, the contour reversal between the first motif and the opening bars of the *nóta*, and the use of an alternate Hungarian dotted-rhythm schema, ♪♩♩♪|♪♩♩♪|, for the second motif (mm. 83–84). The transformation also illustrates Bartók's art of thematic construction through articulation of symmetrical configurations. The whole-tone Y-cells are followed by seemingly pentatonic progressions of minor thirds and perfect fourths in the second motif, but these intervals stem from a hexachord of the minor form of the C-octatonic scale, C–D–E♭–F–G♭–A♭–(B♭).[47] The

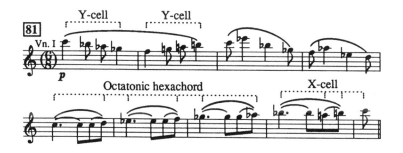

Example 4.20. Bartók, String Quartet no. 6, first movement, mm. 81–89.

same hexachord appears in scalar form in the third motif (mm. 85–87) and is linked to a closing X-cell, C–B–B♭–A, whose degrees are essential components of the opening Y-cells, thus providing a rounded tonal organization of the theme (mm. 87–89).

In the episodic material that follows, the upper and lower strings are engaged in an unusual, two-part imitative counterpoint, where X-cells and Z-cells are juxtaposed as well as articulated in a twelve-tone environment (Example 4.21). It is indeed worthy of note that Bartók's original concept was the articulation of the X-cells with four whole-tone tetrachords structured as arpeggiated French sixth chords, C–E–F♯–B♭, C♯–F–G–B, D–F♯–G♯–C, and E♭–G–A–C♯ (mm. 127–130).

The subsequently discarded dance piece, intended as the fourth movement and preceded by the first half of the *Mesto* theme (mm. 1–45 in the printed score), has features that are in near relation to Romanian instrumental melodies. The second half of the first theme (mm. 4–16 in the sketch) has the character of bagpipe motifs played on the violin or peasant

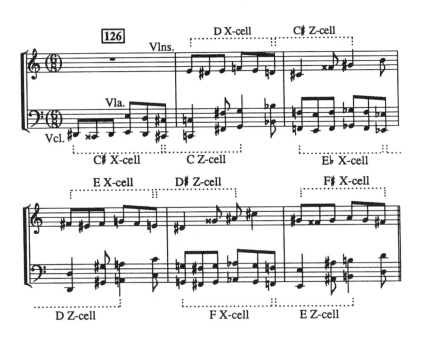

Example 4.21. Bartók, String Quartet no. 6, first movement, mm. 126–31.

flute, and is somewhat similar to the motifs that open the fifth movement of the Concerto for Orchestra. The syncopated contrasting theme (mm. 66ff.), in twin-bar alternation of 8/4 and 9/4 time that shows permutations of the 8/4 rhythm schema as ♩ ♩ ♩ ♩. and ♩ ♩ ♩ ♩ ♩, carries out Bartók's innovative concept of Hungarian dotted rhythm in flattened form. The accompaniment is an ingenious emulation of a Romanian bagpiper: the sustained trills in the second violin represent the dominant pipe of the instrument, and the tied notes in the cello serve as the tonic pipe. At the same time, the viola strums pizzicato triads in imitation of a peasant violinist who accompanies the violin solo on a three-stringed instrument: "The bridge is completely flat, the tones of the accompanying chords, therefore, will sound together. The chords themselves will be various kinds of triads in close position" (Example 4.22).[48]

The ominous turn in political events impelled Bartók to interrupt his work on the quartet and return home to complete the fair copy of the Violin Concerto no. 2, *Mikrokosmos,* and other works in progress. Perhaps in October, soon after Germany and Russia had conquered Poland and carved up its territory between them, Bartók abandoned the dance format and replaced it with the extended *Mesto* as the finale but included a fleeting reprise of the first and contrasting themes from the first movement (vol. 4: mm. 46, 54, and 55–63, respectively), thus providing the semblance of an architectonic structure to the quartet.[49]

In November, arrangements had been made for concerts with József Szigeti during the spring of 1940, at the Coolidge Festival (Washington, D.C.) and in New York, and personal appearances as pianist and lecturer in other American locales. But the precarious health of his mother forced Bartok to reconsider his plans: ". . . when the war broke out, I was at a loss, whether to go to America or not to go. In Nov., I decided not to go and have written a letter to the Library of Congress. Finally, in Dec., I changed again my standpoint (owing to Mr. Szigeti's persuasion), so I will go."[50] It should be noted, however, that Bartók's mother died in December—a grievous loss that severed the strongest tie binding him to Hungary. He decided to explore the possibilities of emigrating to America, specifically with the view toward continuing his folk-music research and publishing the results of his monumental studies of Romanian and Turkish musical folklore. Thus, when the String Quartet no. 6 was brought to a close in Budapest during November, it became the last composition Bartók would create in his native land.

Example 4.22. Bartók, String Quartet no. 6, discarded fourth movement, mm. 126–31.

BARTÓK IN AMERICA

In September 1934, when Bartók left his teaching position at the Budapest Academy of Music for a research appointment at the Budapest Academy of Sciences, his primary task was the classification and eventual publication of the vast Hungarian folk-music materials that he, Kodály, and other collectors had assembled. An important concomitant problem, however, was the differentiation of indigenous melodies and those reflecting foreign influence, particularly the specimens gathered in former Hungarian territories. A substantial part of such investigation had already been achieved by Bartók in more than a decade of collecting, transcribing, and classifying Slovak and Romanian folk music. The major lacuna was the absence of reliable Yugoslav material, for reasons elaborated by Bartók at Harvard University on April 22, 1940, as part of his lecture on some problems of folk-music research in eastern Europe:

> If we want to examine the Serbo-Croatian material we find ourselves up against a few obstacles. The material consists of about 4,000 tunes, for the most part in pre-war [World War I] transcription and collected without the Edison phonograph. Subtleties of execution and grace-notes can scarcely be studied at all, since they are lacking in these rather amateurish transcriptions, but at least types and classes can be established.[51]

A few days later, a letter arrived from Harvard professor Albert B. Lord, who had attended the lecture, advising Bartók that, contrary to the latter's assumption that there are no recorded collections of Yugoslav folk music, a fairly large collection of recordings had been made in Yugoslavia from 1934 to 1935 by the late Harvard professor Milman Parry. Lord also stated that the recordings were on hand, a description of them would be mailed to Bartók, and that a meeting should be arranged with several New York scholars who were interested in musicological aspects of the Parry Collection. Bartók's concert at Columbia University on May 1 provided him with the opportunity to confer with them and other faculty members of Columbia University, and it was mutually agreed that a position at Columbia would be sought for Bartók. It was also decided that the appointment would include the transcription of Parry Collection heroic songs, as illustrative music material for Lord's planned book on the textual aspects of those songs.[52]

Also at this time the New York office of Boosey & Hawkes, Bartók's new publisher, initiated contractual arrangements for a coast-to-coast concert tour for him in the fall. He therefore returned to Budapest to make his preparations for emigrating to the United States. The unparalleled opportunity of working with recorded Yugoslav material provided Bartók, now fifty-nine years old, with the incentive to take this bold step:

> The reason for inviting me here (apart from the fact that it would help me personally) was so that I could accomplish certain research work, that is, to study and transcribe this incomparable material on Yugoslav folk music. It

is, in fact, this work which brought me here (as far as work is concerned, without taking into consideration my own feelings); material such as this can be found no where else in the world, and (apart from some Bulgarian material) this is what was so badly lacking to me over in Europe.[53]

On October 30, Bartók and his wife disembarked in New York and set out on a recital and lecture tour of the United States. In February 1941, Bartók received word of his temporary appointment as visiting associate in music in Columbia University. Then, on March 27, he began the transcription of Parry Collection recordings that had been sent down from Harvard. Because the recordings included seventy-five lyric songs, he realized that their transcriptions could be compared with the 3,500 melodies in his annotated compilation of printed material, which had been collected by Slavic ethnomusicologists, and the results published in what eventually became the first definitive study of Yugoslav folk music in the English language. In 1942 Columbia's Ditson Fund allocated funds for publication by Columbia University Press, and Albert B. Lord agreed to collaborate with regard to preparation of the texts and their translations.[54]

Bartók found that Yugoslav folk songs are for the most part comprised of the first four, five, or six degrees of a diatonic major, minor, or some other "very peculiar scale formations," ending on the second degree as the fundamental. This unique imperfect (that is, half-) cadence infiltrated the folk-music material of neighboring Romanian and Bulgarian territories to such an extent that Bartók designated the phenomenon as the "Yugoslav cadence."[55] The other scales, "intermediate" between the Yugoslav diatonic and so-called chromatic melodies, are currently designated as octatonic formations, such as F–G–A♭–B♭–C♭ and G–A–B♭–C–D♭–[]–E.[56]

Bartók's transcriptions of recorded Dalmatian folk melodies include a remarkable type of part song that is preceded by an instrumental prelude performed on a pair of oboe-like *sopila* (sopels). The instrumentalists play minor sevenths; the inverted voice parts generally are major seconds (Example 4.23).

Bartok adds this remark about the transcription: "Listening to these records, one may hear the major seconds sometimes 'degenerate' into minor thirds. Nevertheless, since these deviations seem to be more or less due to chance, this kind of performance may be called 'part-singing in major seconds.' . . . [The *sopila*] minor sevenths are never changed into any other interval."[57]

Although he completed the first draft of his portion of the work early in 1943, a combination of frustrating circumstances continually delayed

Example 4.23. Bartók, Yugoslav Folk Music, *vol. 1, 63.*

the attempt to achieve the final form of the book. Collaboration with Lord by means of correspondence; multilingual text matter, including many special symbols devised by Bartók, that presented special problems for solution by the printer; and, above all, Bartók's struggle with the English language as well as the difficulties he had with the autographer of the exceedingly complex music examples—all contributed to one postponement after another. It was not until 1951, six years after Bartók's death, that the book, *Serbo-Croatian Folk Songs*, finally appeared in published form.

Concomitant with his work on Yugoslav folk music, Bartók resumed the preparation of fair copy for projected books on Romanian and Turkish folk music, editing, classifying, and annotating the huge manuscript collections he had brought with him from Hungary. When he had completed the first two volumes of *Rumanian Folk Music*, he opened negotiations with the New York Public Library for publication of the work. That institution's initial enthusiasm for the undertaking quickly waned when the cost estimates were presented by the printer, and in June 1943 they withdrew their offer of publication. Bartók offered the much smaller *Turkish Folk Music from Asia Minor* study as a replacement, and prepared the final copy during a summer convalescence at Saranac Lake, New York. When the library rejected the book in October, and Boosey and Hawkes indicated that they might publish the Romanian volumes after the war ended, Bartok decided to complete his monumental task in Romanian musical folklore by adding a third volume of song texts, including a unique approach to their classification. After he completed the fair copy during the spring of 1945, he deposited the Romanian and Turkish drafts "at the Columbia University Music Library—there they are available to those few persons (very few indeed) who may be interested in them."[58]

It was in April 1942 that Bartók experienced the first symptoms of the incurable leukemia that would end his life in September 1945. In a letter written on December 31 he indicates that the state of his health

> is impaired since the beginning of April: since that time I have every day temparature elevation (of about 100°) in the evening, quite regularly and relentlessly! The doctors cann't [sic] find out the cause, and as a consequence, cann't [sic] even try a treatment. Is that not rather strange?"[59]

Bartók was nevertheless able to continue his research work and, in addition, present a lecture at the October meeting of the American Musicological Society. When he returned home, his temperature was elevated another two degrees. Nevertheless, in January he and his wife gave the first performance of the Concerto for Two Pianos and Percussion, basically an orchestral accompaniment to the original Sonata for Two Pianos and Percussion, which Bartók had reluctantly composed and agreed to perform as a means for augmenting his inadequate income. In February he took up residence in Cambridge, Massachusetts, in connection with his temporary appointment as visiting lecturer at Harvard University. His jottings indicate his intention to give the following lectures:

1. Revolution, evolution [in music].
2. Modes, polymodality (polytonality, atonality (twelve-tone music))
3. Chromaticism (very rare in folk music)
4. Rhythm, percussion effect
5. Form (every piece creates it own form)
6. Scoring (new effects on music), piano, violin as percussive instruments (Cowell)
7. Trend toward simplicity
8. Educational works
9. General spirit (connected with folk music)

In March, after Bartók had given the first three lectures and completed his notes for the fourth,[60] a sudden breakdown forced cancellation of the series. A number of medical examinations ended with the opinion that "at last we have the real cause—tuberculosis." He returned to New York and was soon thereafter hospitalized for additional X-rays that conclusively eliminated tuberculosis as the probable cause of his illness.

It [a very slight degree of lung trouble] *does not account for the high temperatures*. So we have the same story again, doctors don't know the real cause of my illness—and, consequently, can't treat and cure it! They are groping about as in a darkness, try desperately to invent the most extraordinary hypotheses. But all that is of no avail.[61]

In addition to subsidizing Bartók's medical bills, the American Society of Composers, Authors, and Publishers provided a special grant that would enable him to convalesce in a small cottage at Saranac Lake during the summer. Before Bartók left the city, Serge Koussevitzky, conductor of the Boston Symphony Orchestra, visited him in the hospital and offered a thousand-dollar commission for an orchestral composition:

They agreed on a purely orchestral work; it was Béla's idea to combine chorus and orchestra. I am so glad that plans, musical ambitions, compositions are stirring in Béla's mind—a new hope, discovered in this way quite by chance, as if it were incidentally. One thing is sure: Béla's "under no circumstance will I ever write any new work—" attitude has gone. It's more than three years now—[62]

On July 20, Ralph Hawkes wrote to Bartók, asking whether any new compositions were under way. The July 31 response included a long description of the illness and the various medical diagnoses: "I feel better [when I have periods of lower fever]. But on the whole there is no perceptible change! Now about the doctors . . . they are groping about in the darkness."[63] On August 15 Bartók began composing the Concerto for Orchestra, beginning with the third movement (*Elegia*) and its opening quotation of the "darkness" theme from his opera *Duke Bluebeard's Castle*. The fourth and fifth movements, then the second, and finally the first movement were composed. The work was completed October 15.

Another work, the Sonata for Solo Violin, a commission from Yehudi Menuhin, was completed on March 14, 1944, and given its first performance by Menuhin at his New York recital in November. Then, on December 1 and 2, Koussevitzky and the Boston Symphony played the first two performances of the Concerto for Orchestra. "We went there [Boston]," Bartók wrote to a former pupil on December 17, "for the rehearsals and performances. . . . Koussevitzky is very enthusiastic about the piece, and says it is 'the best orchestra piece of the last 25 years' (including the works of his idol, Shostakovich!)."[64] In another letter to the same correspondent, on December 25, Bartók said:

Example 4.24a. Commonality of second-movement construction: Beethoven, Fourth Piano Concerto op. 58.

I received your Four B's program this morning. Was this a deliberate act of yours? This reminds me of a criticism appearing in Jan. 1944 in the San Francisco Chronicle and saying: "the sonata (1st violin piano sonata, played there by Menuhin) emphasizes again what has often (?!?) been suggested in these columns—that Bartók is the fourth in the procession of the great B's in music." This is, by the way, an amplification of the "jeu de lettres" invented by Bülow—if I remember well—at the occasion of the 1st performance of Brahm's [sic] 1st symphony.[65]

In January 1945, Bartók agreed to compose a viola concerto for William Primrose, and in February his publisher not only asked for new choral works but also sent an advance payment for a seventh string quartet. He refused other offers for a piano concerto and a concerto for two pianos. "I should like to write a concerto for Mother," he wrote to his younger son, Peter, on February 21. "This plan has long been in the air.

Example 4.24b. Commonality of second-movement construction: Bartók, Concerto no. 3 for Piano and Orchestra.

If she could play it in 3 or 4 places then it would bring in about as much money as the one of the commissioned works I refused. . . ."[66] Following the advice of his doctors and his own wishes, Bartók returned to Saranac Lake in June and worked simultaneously on the Concerto no. 3 for Piano and Orchestra and the Concerto for Viola and Orchestra.

Bartók once again returned to Beethoven as the wellspring for the piano concerto. He followed the classical three-movement construction: the first movement is in sonata form but with a short development before the recapitulation of the first theme; the third movement is in rondo form; and the second movement, a large ternary form, has significant common-alities with the slow movements in Beethoven's Fourth Piano Concerto op. 58 and Quartet op. 132. The most obvious parallel in both concertos is the dialogue between the strings and piano solo (Example 4.24).

Molto adagio

Example 4.25. Beethoven, Quartet op. 132, mm. 1–3.

The second relationship is the tetrachordal motif in the Bartók concerto (Example 4.24b: C–F–E–A) and the Beethoven Quartet op. 132 (Example 4.25: C–A–G–C). Bartók's transformation of Beethoven's motif also represents the reordering (F–A–C–E) of the fateful "declaration of love" leitmotiv in his Violin Concerto no. 1 and first Elegy (cf. Examples 3.5 and 3.7, respectively).

It is also interesting that Beethoven wrote "Heiliger Dankgesang eines Genesenen an die Gottheit, in der lydischen Tonart" ("Holy song of thanksgiving to the Godhead, by one recovered from sickness, in the Lydian mode") above the tempo mark at the beginning of the movement.[67]

The third connection—imitations of birdsong—is shown in Example 4.26. In (a), the second movement of Beethoven's Symphony no. 6, op. 68, the woodwind instruments are assigned the degrees of an added-note major chord, B♭–D–F–G, to imitate the nightingale, quail, and cuckoo. In (b), Bartók's concerto, the same instrumentation is used, but the degrees are those of the anhemitone-pentatonic scale, B♭–C♯–D♯–F♯–G♯.

In August, however, Bartók's health began to deteriorate, and he returned to New York at the end of the month. Although he was depressed by his illness, he found the strength to complete the fair copy of the third piano concerto, except for the last seventeen bars, and continue work on the viola concerto sketches.[68] The latter manuscript, his last creative impulse, is an epitaphic memoir of the Bartók system of composition. The first movement, in the C-Lydian/Phrygian twelve-tone polymode, C–D–E–F♯–G–A–B/C–D♭–E♭–F–G–A♭–B♭, opens with a dialogue between the theme in the viola solo and the accompaniment in the cellos and basses (Example 4.27).

Example 4.26. Birdsong imitations in (a) Beethoven, Symphony no. 6, op. 68, second movement, mm. 134–36; and (b) Bartók, Concerto no. 3 for Piano and Orchestra, second movement, mm. 63–65.

Example 4.27. Bartók, Concerto for Viola and Orchestra, first movement, mm. 1–5, 14–17.

The theme is an extended pitch collection of the C-minor-octatonic scale, C–[]–E♭–(E)–F–[]–A♭–A–B, and the accompaniment is another extended formation, based on the complementary C-Phrygian-octatonic scale, C–[]–E♭–[]–F♯–G–(A♭)–[]. The repetition of the trichord, F–C–B, and its construction as a shifted-rhythm entity in the theme (mm. 1–6) confirms its presence as a cellular motif, namely, the gapped C Z-cell, C–F–[]–B. The complementary, gapped Z-cell in the accompaniment, C–[]–F♯–G, together with the repetition of F♯ in the ensuing bars (mm. 1–9), interacts with the thematic trichord to complete the Z-cell motif, C–F–F♯–B, as well as form a nine-tone polymodal pitch collection.

In measure 13, the viola solo plays an unaccompanied pentatonic configuration, B♭–A♭–G♭–E♭–D♭, where B♭ and D♭ complete the previously missing Phrygian degrees of the polymode. And the second degree, D♮, conspicuously absent to this point, makes its first appearance in the reprise of the theme (m. 15)—extending the polymodality to twelve tones. In retrospect, the interaction of octatonic, modal, and pentatonic configurations in the viola concerto is the last instance of a fundamental application in Bartók's unique tonal language.

During the first two weeks in September, Bartók, although depressed by his illness, was able to continue working at his desk. Then, when his condition suddenly worsened, the attending physician had him transported by ambulance to New York's West Side Hospital. Bartók's physical state was such that he was unable to work or even read, and he rarely spoke. Finally, on September 26, 1945, with his wife and younger son at his bedside, Bartók quietly passed away.[69]

Part Two

---- ❧ ----

CONCERTO FOR ORCHESTRA

Chapter 5

FIRST MOVEMENT
(*INTRODUZIONE*—ALLEGRO VIVACE)

The first link in the chain of events that ultimately led to the composition of Bartók's Concerto for Orchestra can be traced to 1941, the year
after he emigrated to the United States. As mentioned in the preceding
chapter, while Bartók was working on the transcription of Yugoslav folk
music he was particularly struck by a unique recording of Dalmatian two-
part melodies (see Example 4.23). As he later remarked, during his 1943
lectures at Harvard University, he was impressed by the "unity, higher development, and unusual effect on listeners" of the melodies.[1] The replica-
tion of this Dalmatian polyphonic style in the second movement of the
Concerto is a direct outcome of Bartók's scholarly research.

In April 1942, a letter from his publisher, Ralph Hawkes, proposed a
series of concertos for solo instrument or instruments and string orchestra.
"By this I mean piano and string orchestra, solo violin and string orchestra, flute and string orchestra, etc., or combinations of solo instruments
and string orchestra. I have in mind the Brandenburg Concertos by Bach,
and I believe you are well fitted to do something on these lines."[2] At that
time, however, Bartók was preparing his Yugoslav material, including a
highly technical introductory study and a detailed tabulation of material
for publication by Columbia University Press. Moreover, as he replied to
Hawkes August 3, "I am ill since the beginning of April. And the doctors
cannot find the cause, in spite of very thorough examinations. Fortunately,
I can continue my work at Columbia Univ. I only wonder how long this
can go on in this way. And whether it is a general breakdown? Heaven

123

knows. Just before my illness I began some composition work, and just the kind you suggested in your letter. But then, of course, I had to discontinue it because of lack of energy, tranquillity and mood—I don't know if I ever will be in a position to do some new works."[3] The overall structural concept and the title of the Concerto—particularly the plan of the second movement—indicate the extent to which Bartók was motivated by his publisher's ideas.

The Shostakovich Symphony no. 7 (*Leningrad*), broadcast by the NBC Symphony July 19, 1942, made a lasting, negative impression on Bartók. A parody of the third theme in the first movement appears as the third theme in the fourth movement (*Intermezzo Interrotto*) of the Concerto for Orchestra.[4] Concurrent with Bartók's work on Yugoslav folk music was the preparation of his monumental collection of Romanian folk music. In the first volume of instrumental melodies, which includes a chapter on folk dance and its choreography, he concludes that bagpipe dance tunes, seemingly of indeterminate structure, are actually composed of shorter or longer motifs strung together in a way recognizable by the dancers.[5] These bagpipe motifs and their imitations on violin and peasant flute were extracted, classified, and tabulated by Bartók as an appendix to his study. An outcome of this research was his idealization of bagpipe motifs as the thematic basis of the fifth movement of the Concerto.

Following the completion of the second volume of *Rumanian Folk Music* in December 1942, Bartók prepared a series of lectures to be given at Harvard University. In the second lecture, he refers to the influence of the "newly-discovered rural music" on his compositions:

> [W]e were rather surprised to find the common major and minor scales absent for the most part, especially in what seemed to us to be genuine folk melodies. Instead, we found the five most commonly used modes of the art music of the Middle Ages, and besides these, some others absolutely unknown from modal music [G–A–B♭–C–D♭–E♭–F, G–A♭–B♭–C♭–D♭–E♭] and furthermore, scales with seemingly oriental features (that is, having augmented second steps). . . . None [of them] can be expressed as octave segments of the diatonic scale; wherever they are begun on the keyboard, black keys will occur.[6]

The "unknown" modes are octave segments containing partial octatonic formations that Bartók discovered in the peasant music of eastern Europe and North African Arab oases. In the first movement of the Concerto, the *Allegro vivace* first theme begins with a five-note octatonic motif whose invention may have been prompted by similar motifs Bartók found in his Romanian and Yugoslav folk-song collections.[7] Mentioned above is Bartók's despair, following his third Harvard lecture in March 1943, when he suffered a sudden breakdown in his health: "They [the doctors] are groping about as in a darkness." On August 15 Bartók started work on the Concerto, beginning with the "lugubrious death-song" third movement and its prefatory transformation of the "Darkness" theme that opens and closes his opera *Duke Bluebeard's Castle.*[8]

When in May Bartók agreed to compose a symphonic work for the Boston Symphony Orchestra, the last and most important link in the chain of events was forged. With renewed energy he set to work and completed the Concerto October 15. The next year he wrote the following program note, "Explanation to Concerto for Orchestra," for the Boston premiere at Symphony Hall on December 1:

> The title of this symphony-like orchestral work is explained by its tendency to treat the single instruments or instrument groups in a *"concertant"* or soloistic manner. The "virtuoso" treatment appears, for instance, in the *fugato* sections of the development of the first movement (brass instruments) or in the *"perpetuum mobile"*-like passages of the principle theme in the last movement (strings), and, especially, in the second movement, in which pairs of instruments appear consecutively with brilliant passages.
>
> As for the structure of the work, the first and fifth movements are written in a more or less regular sonata form. The development of the first movement contains *fugato* sections for brass; the exposition in the finale is somewhat extended, and its development consists of a fugue built on the last theme of the exposition.
>
> Less traditional forms are found in the second and third movements. The main part of the second movement consists of a chain of independent short sections, by wind instruments consecutively introduced in five pairs (bassoons, oboes, clarinets, flutes and muted trumpets). Thematically, the five sections have nothing in common and could be symbolized by the letters *a, b, c, d, e*. A kind of "trio"—a short chorale for brass instruments and side-drum—follows, after which the five sections are recapitulated in a more elaborate instrumentation.
>
> The structure of the third movement is likewise chain-like; three themes appear successively. These constitute the core of the movement,

which is enframed by a misty texture of rudimentary motives. Most of the thematic materials derives from the "Introduction" to the first movement. The form of the fourth movement—"*Intermezzo interrotto*"—could be rendered by the letter symbols "ABA—interruption—BA."

The general mood of the work represents—apart from the jesting second movement—a gradual transition from the sternness of the first movement and the lugubrious death-song of the third movement, to the life-assertion of the last one.[9]

SYNOPSIS OF THE FIRST MOVEMENT

The two contrasting themes that form the slow Introduction have a four-section melodic structure characteristic of Hungarian folk song. The first theme, in the lower strings, is pentatonic in melodic structure and in the parlando (free) rhythm typical of old-style Hungarian melodies (Example 5.1)

While the last note is sustained, the upper strings play very soft tremolos. The repeated but slightly extended theme is again answered by similar tremolos. When the third, considerably extended repetition of the theme is answered, a short flute passage is heard that begins with the twin-bar motif of the second theme. The lower strings next play arpeggiated figurations that introduce and then accompany the theme in the trumpets. The rhythm schema of sixteenth-note values, as if the melody were fitted to eight-syllable text lines, is reminiscent of the oldest stratum of Hungarian folk song (Example 5.2).[10]

A variant of the second theme, in the high woodwinds and upper strings, is followed by an ominous pounding of the timpani during an ostinato-like repetition, *poco a poco accelerando e crescendo*, of a five-note

Example 5.1

Example 5.2

figure in the woodwinds and strings. This figure becomes Motif 1a of the main theme in the ensuing *Allegro vivace* exposition (Example 5.3).

A remarkable transition to the contrasting theme, assigned to the first trombone, is achieved through transformation of the main theme (Example 5.4), while the strings play tremolos and the woodwinds alternate renditions of Motif 1b.[11]

The lyrical contrasting theme, played by the first oboe, is for the most part an alternation of E and F♯, similar to the narrow-range, Arab folk-music style (Example 5.5).[12]

The pastoral mood is suddenly interrupted by the full orchestra, which introduces the development with a variation of the main theme consisting of alternation and juxtaposition of Motif 1a and 1b. Motif 2a and 2b then alternate, followed by Motif 2a as a four-part free canon in the strings and woodwinds. The second section features a transformation and development of the concatenated Motif 2a and 2b as a clarinet solo with string accompaniment and in the same pastoral mood as the contrasting theme (Example 5.6).

The third section is a reprise of the trombone transition theme (Example 5.4), which serves as the subject for a four-part fugato in the trombones and trumpets. A second fugato ensues when the horns enter with the inverted subject. In the last section the subject returns as a six-part canonic stretto, which is followed by a very loud, sustained unison on A♭

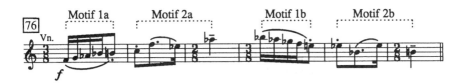

Example 5.3

Example 5.4

Example 5.5

Example 5.6

in the full orchestra. The development thereafter ends abruptly with the open fifth, A–E, as an eighth-note value.

The recapitulation begins with the contrasting theme as a clarinet solo, followed by woodwind variant. While the horns and lower strings take up the theme, Motif 1a is superposed in the violas and the violins—similar to change-song practice in the performance of Romanian carols and Christmas songs.[13] A reprise of the main theme is then heard in the strings, followed by passage work in the woodwinds when the strings switch to accompanying tremolos. A crescendo in the full orchestra leads to the eight-bar codetta, where the brass choir sounds the final reprise of the trombone transition theme. The movement ends with the superposition of Motif 1b by the woodwinds and strings in the last two bars.

Analytic Commentary

INTRODUZIONE (mm. 1–75)

1–6   The first theme (mm. 1–29), based on the symmetrical (Hungarian) form of the anhemitone-pentatonic scale, F♯–A–B–C♯–E, with B as the principal tone, has the quaternary heterometric structure typical of mixed-style Hungarian folk songs. The first melody section consists of antecedent and consequent phrases of markedly different character. The antecedent phrase shows the metric equivalent of seven-syllable structure, and the time signature, tempo, and metronome marks ostensibly indicate tempo giusto (i.e., strict) rhythm (Example 5.1). But the use of a hemiola (mm. 3–4) transforms the rhythm into a symmetrical parlando schema, 3/4 ♩. ♩. | 3/4 ♩ ♩ ♩ | 3/4 ♩. ♩. |. The alternation of perfect fourths and major seconds in the antecedent phrase, a prominent characteristic of Hungarian pentatonic structure, represents a melodic feature that takes on its own motivic life in the first movement and elsewhere in the Concerto. On the other hand, the analyst might point to those pentatonic turns as primarily programmatic in nature, such as the similar intervallic construction of the themes in Bartók's first Elegy (cf. Example 3.8) and second Dirge (Example 3.22), and of the "Darkness" motif in his opera, *Duke Bluebeard's Castle* (Examples 3.24 and 3.30).

6–11   The consequent phrase is constructed from nondiatonic pitch collections, with C as the principal tone, which are sounded above the sustained end note, C♯, in the lower strings. The tremolos in the upper strings, in two-part contrary motion, comprise complementary whole-tone scale segments: the pentachord, A♭–B♭–C–D–E (mm. 6–8), and the tetrachord, A–B–D♭–E♭ (m. 9). The flute parts, also in contrary motion, play an eleven-tone chromatic configuration (mm. 10–11), whose lowest half steps, C–C♯ and G–F♯, of the respective ascending and descending chromatic lines, imply the presence of a C Z-cell, C–C♯–F♯–G.

12–21   In the second melody section, the theme is extended to an eight-syllable structure. The added note, D, augments the pitch collection of the antecedent phrase (mm. 12–16) to a major hexachord with pentatonic turns (i.e., perfect fourths and major seconds), ending on the sustained end note, F♯. The structure of the whole-tone and chromatic scale segments in the consequent phrase, transposed to F, is identical to that of the first melody section. The flute parts, in contrary motion, are now literally symmetrical and bounded by an F Z-cell, E–F–B♭–B (m. 21).

22–25   Thematic extension to eleven-syllable structure in the third melody section includes three derivative fourth chords, C♯–F♯–B, E–A–D, A–E–B, and the added notes, C–G. This forms an eight-note segment of the cycle of fourths/fifths, C♯–F♯–B–E–A–D–G–C, bounded by a C Z-cell, C–C♯–F♯–G.

26–29   The metric number of the fourth melody section is the same as the first section, but the rhythm structure is the Hungarian dotted-rhythm type, ♩ ♩ ♩ ♩ | ♩ ♩ ♩. |. The added notes, G♯ and D♯, confirm the tonality of the first theme as pentatonic segments of the B-Mixolydian/Phrygian eleven-tone polymode, B–C♯–D♯–E–F♯–G♯–A/B–C–D–E–F♯–G–A.

30–38   This interlude serves as an introduction to the second theme. The first flute plays a variant of the first melody section, while the lower strings sustain the end note, D♯, followed by a twin-bar hemiola of fourth chords, 3/4 ♩. = 6/8 ♩. ♩..

39–50   The second theme has the quaternary isometric structure characteristic of old-style Hungarian folk songs, in which each melody section has eight syllables (see Example 5.2). The skeleton form (that is, main degrees) of the theme in the first trumpet is the E-Dorian mode, E–F♯–G–A–B–C♯–D. These notes and the parallel harmony in the second and third trumpets form nonfunctional minor, major, and diminished triads, while the upper and lower strings play accompanying figurations in two-part inversional counterpoint, which are based on diminution of the first theme.

51–57   A variant of the second theme, in the upper woodwinds and strings, is based on the G-Phrygian/Lydian twelve-tone polymode, G–A♭–B♭–C–D–E♭–F/G–A–B–C♯–D–E–F♯, and is accompanied by a different, additive-rhythm hemiola of 4 + 2 eighths in the lower strings.

58–75   Another interlude, in which the lower strings introduce an extended form of Motif 1a of the "Exposition" main theme, E♭–F–G–A♭–A♮–(F♯), while the upper strings play its inversion (Motif 1b) in augmented values, E♭–D♭–C–B♭–A (to m. 62). Motif 1a is then repeated as an ostinato, while the horns, trumpets, and timpani emphatically render its bounding tritone, E♭–A.

EXPOSITION (mm. 76–230)

76–78   The antecedent phrase of the main theme contains two motifs, 1a and 2a, which are repeated as nonliteral inversions (1b and 2b) in the consequent phrase (Example 5.3). Motif 1a, an octatonic pentachord bounded by the tritone, F–B, apparently stems from "a very peculiar scale formation . . . intermediate between the diatonic and the 'chromatic' scales" in Yugoslav folk songs and Romanian songs of mourning (Example 5.7).[14]

It is indeed interesting—if not prescient!—that Motif 1a and the first five notes of the Romanian melody sections (mm. 3 and 5) not only have the same interval sequence, but that the underlaid text lines of this funereal folk song read: "May the fire strike you, death, / Woeful is my heart inside me."[15] Motif 2a is a pentatonic tetrachord, F–A♭–C–E♭. The change of time from 3/8 to 2/8 reflects a 3 + 3 + 2 Bulgarian rhythm schema, ♫♩ ♫♩ ♩ |.

79–81   The inverted Motif 1b in the consequent phrase is an F-Phrygian tetrachord, F–G♭–A♭–B♭, bounded by the tritone B♭–E♮. Motif 2b adds B♭ to complete the F-pentatonic scale implied in Motif 2a. And the alteration of B♭ to B♮ (m. 81), together with the contrasting tritones of Motif 1a and 1b, clearly establish the tonic Z-cell framework of the main

Example 5.7. Bartók, Rumanian Folk Music, *vol. 2, no. 631, mm. 3–6.*

          theme, F–B–B♭–E. Furthermore, the antecedent and conse-
quent phrases of the main theme may be construed as forming the first in a series of melody sections that are based on
the variation principle.

82–85   The second section, transposed to B♭, is a truncated repetition of measures 79–81.

86–89   The antecedent phrase of the fourth section is based on the
E♭-pentatonic scale, E♭–G♭–A♭–B♭–D♭, and the concatenation
of Motif 2a and 2b.

90–94   The consequent phrase reverses the order of motifs in measures 76–78, where the woodwinds follow the transposed
Motif 1b with repetitions of Motif 1a and its emphasized tritone, F–B, as the lower strings descend with F–E♭–D♭. The
combined notes thus form B–D♭–E♭–F, the tritone transposition of the tonic F Y-cell (i.e., a whole-tone tetrachord), in
which B functions as a leading tone to the ensuing C-Aeolian
mode, C–D–E♭–F–G–A♭–B♭.

95–101   The antecedent phrase of the fifth section begins with Motif
2a in an altered rhythm schema, ♩♪♪|♩.|, melodically ex-
tended to include the flattened form of Hungarian dotted
rhythm, ♩ ♪|♪♩ |.

99–101   The consequent phrase features repetitions of Motif 1a, extended in range from the original octatonic form to diatonic
configuration.

102–109 The sixth section, transposed to B♭, is similar to the preceding one, with the exception that the consequent phrase consists of two literal repetitions of Motif 1b, transposed to F
(mm. 107–108), and a third, transformed repetition as a D♭-
major hexachord (m. 109).

110–121 The contrapuntal seventh section opens with the rhythmically altered Motif 2a in contrary motion that, together with
its melodic extension, serves as the subject of a two-part
stretto canon in the violins. Beginning at measure 117, the
consecutive entry of violins, violas, cellos, and basses thicken
the canonic texture to a four-part stretto. The violin notes on
the first beat of each bar, reinforced by the oboes and clarinets, form a pentachord of the B whole-tone scale,
B–C♯–E♭–F–G–A; those on the third beat form a complementary whole-tone pentachord, D–E–G♭–A♭–C.

122–133 The eighth section is an altered and extended return of the

Example 5.8

<table>
<tbody>
<tr><td></td><td>main theme, thus providing a rounded architecture to the variation form.</td></tr>
<tr><td>134–141</td><td>The transition to the contrasting theme is marked by a transformed concatenation of Motif 2a and 2b in the first trombone. The combined motifs in augmented values create a melodic entity that may be designated as a subordinate theme (Example 5.8)</td></tr>
<tr><td>142–154</td><td>A descending passage in the first flute, accompanied by semitone tremolos in the strings, leads to an interlude in which the first violins and cellos play a syncopated ostinato of open fifths, C–G.</td></tr>
<tr><td>154–159</td><td>The contrasting theme is a quaternary with five-bar melody sections of different content structure. The first section, played by the first oboe, consists of alternating E and F♯, and a rhythm schema derived from Motif 2a (Example 5.9).</td></tr>
</tbody>
</table>

The motivic structure stems from the narrow-range, *Qseida* type of North-African Arab folk song (a prayer chanted in honor of a personage)—collected by Bartók in 1913 and used in his Dance Suite for Orchestra (see the version for Piano in Example 3.43)—and particularly from his transcription of a related Yugoslav specimen (Example 5.10).[16] A similar adaptation of narrow-range motivic structure occurs in his Piano Concerto no. 1, first movement (R.N. 11).

Example 5.9

Example 5.10. Contrasting-theme related sources: (a) Bartók, "Die Volksmusik der Araber von Biskra und Umgebung," no. 16; (b) Dance Suite for Orchestra (1923), fifth movement, mm. 1–3; and (c) Yugoslav Folk Music, *vol. 1, no. 29.*

159–174	The second section is the retrograde form of the first section; the third is a chromatic, extended variant, of the first section; and the fourth is unrelated to the other sections.
174–191	A four-section variant of the contrasting theme is played by the clarinets. Constriction of the first two melody sections to four-bar lengths, together with the 3/8–4/8 change of time, approximates a $2 + 3 + 3 + 2$ Bulgarian rhythm schema.
192–209	This thematic reprise is harmonized for the most part with descending or ascending major triads in the upper woodwinds and strings, beginning with E♭ and ending on B.
210–230	The last variant of the contrasting theme is based on its first melody section and features a "dialogue in stretto," beginning and ending with the lower strings in alternation with the woodwinds, trombones, and first trumpet, respectively.

DEVELOPMENT (mm. 231–396)

231–237	The violins suddenly enter with the antecedent phrase of the main theme. Motif 1a is a D♭-major tetrachord, extended a

semitone to the tritone, G♮. Motif 2a, in the trumpets, also is extended to end with a tritone, G♯–C♯–B–F. "These sudden jolts," wrote one commentator, "correspond perfectly to the shocking modulations which Haydn and Beethoven liked to begin their development sections."[17] While the trumpets sustain their last note, Motif 1a is repeated in its original configuration as an octatonic pentachord, transposed upward a semitone, D–E–F–G–G♯, in successive layers by the strings and woodwinds. The unusual modulation by semitone is seamlessly accomplished by the traditional use of common tones, within the uniquely Bartókian context of Z-cell degrees, D♭–G–G♯–D, which interlock diatonic, pentatonic, and octatonic formations (Example 5.11).

238–241   The woodwinds respond with Motif 1b of the consequent phrase, transposed to E♭.

242–247   An ingenious stretto treatment of Motif 1a and 1b. The violins begin with Motif 1a on the first beat of each measure, ascending in a sequence of whole tones, E♭–F–G–A–B–C♯. The violas and cellos enter on the second beat, with the same sequence. The woodwinds follow on the third beat, with a descending sequence of Motif 1b pentachords.

248–257   Motif 2a and 2b are concatenated or otherwise extended to form a new phrase, which becomes the subject of a four-part stretto canon in the strings, oboes, and bassoons.

258–264   This four-part stretto canon, in the strings and based on Motif 2a only, begins with the G-octatonic scale as interlocked Z-cell partitions, G–C–D♭–G♭ and B♭–E♭–E–A, and

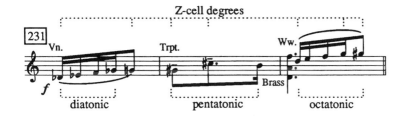

Example 5–11

Example 5.12

265–271   ends with the G-Phrygian/Lydian eleven-tone polymode, G–A♭–B♭–C–E♭–F/G–A–C♭–D♭–E–G♭.

The canon continues as twin-bar Z-cells that enter in whole-tone sequence—G–C–D♭–G♭, F–B♭–C♭–F♭, E♭–A♭–A–D—and ends, together with the woodwinds and horns, with emphatic rendition of the fourth-chord, C♯–F♯–B, to form the complementary hexachords of the chromatic scale.

272–287   Another transformation and extension of the concatenated Motif 2a and 2b results in a new, four-section theme in the first clarinet and with C as principal tone. The first half of the third melody section is bounded by a Z-cell, A♭–D♭–D–G, and the tempo and expression signs mark a return to the mood of the contrasting theme (Example 5.12).

While the phrase mark connecting the notes in the third melody section (mm. 278–283) indicates legato performance, they are obviously a transformed concatenation and extension of Motif 2a and 2b. Thus, the metric equivalent of the phrase is 7 + 7 syllables (that is, a double section), based on the heterometric syllabic structure, z z Z + Z z (i.e., 4, 4, 6 + 6, 4 syllables), of Slovak folk songs (Example 5.13).[18]

Tempo giusto, moderato

Example 5.13. Bartók, Slowakische Volkslieder, *vol. 1, no. 456a.*

288–312   The first reprise of the theme, in the English horn, is transposed to E. The second reprise, in the bass clarinet and transposed to C♯, has augmented values and twin-bar hemiolas (3/8 ♩. |♩. = 2/8 ♩ |♫♫|♩).

313–341   The return to Tempo 1 begins with repetitions of Motif 1a in the strings, then Motif 1b with the support of the woodwinds. When the latter motif is begun, however, the second trombone enters in Romanian change-song style with the subordinate theme (see Example 5.8) as the subject of a four-voice *fugato* in the B♭-Aeolian mode (m. 316). Continuing the change-song practice, the first trombone enters with the answer, in the B♭-Dorian mode, before the second trombone ends the subject and continues with the countersubject in the B♭-Lydian mode (mm. 322–324). Then the subject and answer return in the trumpets (mm. 328 and 334, respectively), while both trombones play individual lines in free, polymodal counterpoint until the bassoons and strings enter with Motif 1a and 1b as a twin-bar conclusion.

342–364   Another four-part *fugato*, with the inverted subject and answer in the C-Mixolydian mode, beginning with the horns and following in change-song style with the second trumpet, second trombone, and first trumpet, respectively. Here, too, the horn countersubject continues on, together with the other voices, as free contrapuntal lines.

363–379   The polyphonic treatment of the development continues with a six-part stretto canon in the trumpets and trombones, beginning with the third trumpet and in the B♭-Aeolian mode.

380–385   The horns join with the brasses in a contrapuntal mélange of arpeggiated fourth chords, B♭–E♭–A♭–D♭.

386–396   The woodwind-string superposition of Motif 1a as a pentachord bounded by the perfect fourth, F–B♭, during the continuation of the fourth-chord arpeggios, completes the B♭-pentatonic-scale configuration. But the following Motif 1b (mm. 387–88) shifts the tonality to the F-pentatonic scale, F–A♭–B♭–C–E♭. The ensuing tutti unison on A♭, the enharmonic equivalent of G♯, serves as the leading tone to the new tonal center, A, which marks the commencement of the "Recapitulation" (m. 396).

RECAPITULATION (mm. 396–521)

396–402   An interlude in the strings, based on the contrasting theme
             and consisting of parallel fifths, A–E, alternating with the
             neighboring semitones, Bb–F.

403–426   The four-section contrasting theme, played by the first clar-
             inet, opens the "Recapitulation" in the A-Phrygian/Lydian
             twelve-tone polymode, A–Bb–C–D–E–F–G/A–B–C♯–D♯–E–
             F♯–G♯.

426–456   Repetition of the theme by the flutes and oboes in the same
             polymode but transposed to G as principal tone and ending
             with an extended episode.

456–475   The same instruments present a three-section chromatic
             transformation of the theme in parallel triads, accompanied
             by string tremolos, followed by the first horn and lower
             strings performance of the first two melody sections in the E
             polymode.

476–487   The accelerando transition to the main theme juxtaposes
             fragments of the contrasting theme with repetitions of Motif
             1a as leading-tone Lydian tetrachords, E–F♯–G♯–A♯, in the
             violins and woodwinds.

488–514   The first two melody sections of the main theme, in F, are
             announced by the strings. The third and fourth melody-
             sections are freely developed episodes, for the most part
             based on Motif 2a, that are accompanied by scalar passages
             in the woodwinds.

514–521   The brasses enter with the first section of the subordinate
             theme, which ends with Motif 1b as a Phrygian cadence,
             C–Bb–Ab–G–Gb–F, superposed in the woodwinds and strings
             to close the movement.

Chapter 6

SECOND MOVEMENT
(*PRESENTANDO LE COPPIE*)

— ✌ —

hen Bartók completed the Concerto for Orchestra in 1943, the parenthetic subtitle of the second movement was *Giuoco delle coppie* (play or game of couples). Perhaps the ambiguous meaning of *giuoco* was the reason he changed the designation to *Presentando la* [*sic*] *coppie* (presenting the couples) in 1944.[1] The tempo mark, architectonic structure, and Bartók's own analysis indicate that the movement is a kind of orchestral scherzo, that is, a large ternary form with a contrasting central section—the trio—such as Beethoven defined in his symphonies.[2]

SYNOPSIS OF THE SECOND MOVEMENT

The movement opens with an introductory side-drum solo. The bassoons, at the interval of a major sixth, enter with a melody in imitation of Yugoslav *kolo* (i.e., round dance) style (Example 6.1).

The oboes continue with another melody in Yugoslav instrumental style, irregular in phrase structure and in minor thirds—the inverted form of the bassoon intervals (Example 6.2).

During Bartók's investigation of recorded Yugoslav folk music, he was struck by a type of folkloric duet performed on a pair of *sopile* (a kind of folk oboe) or sung by women or men (see Example 4.23). Bartók's paraphrase

Allegro scherzando

Example 6.1

Example 6.2

Example 6.3

Example 6.4

Example 6.5

of this genre is played by the clarinets in the next melody, with the unusual but characteristic intervals of a minor seventh (Example 6.3).

The fourth melody, a flute duet, emphasizes Yugoslav *kolo* rhythm patterns and the Slovak Lydian folk mode, and continues the polymodal chromaticism common to the preceding dance tunes. On the other hand, the use of parallel fifths suggests "foreign" (i.e., art music) influence (Example 6.4).

The last melody, in the muted trumpets, simulates the role of Dalmatian folk-singers whose striking duet in major seconds—the inverted form of minor sevenths—usually follows a *sopel* prelude (Example 6.2). Unlike folk-music performance, however, the trumpet duet is markedly different in rhythm and tonality (Example 6.5).

Part B, the "trio," verifies the apparent pastoral program of the movement. The preceding "Sunday order of dances"—a feature of village life that Bartók observed during his field trips to collect Romanian folk music—is interrupted by a chorale-tune imitation in the brass, as if the scene switches to the interior of a rural church (Example 6.6).

The closing da capo is a reprise of the dances in the same order of tone color and intervallic distance but with added instrumentation as well as contrapuntal passages in the strings. The movement ends with the last half of the side-drum solo that served as its introduction.

Example 6.6

Analytic Commentary

PART A (mm. 1–122)

MEASURES

1–8   The side-drum solo contains rhythm patterns characteristic of Romanian instrumental folk music: ♫♫, ♫♫, and ♫♫♫.[3]

9–24   Section a is a bassoon duet (Example 6.1), a quaternary melody partitioned into four-bar melody sections and based on D as the principal tone of a Phrygian/Lydian twelve-tone polymode, D–E♭–F–G–A–B♭–C/D–E–F♯–G♯–A–B–C♯. Certain structural features of the melody are related to Romanian and Serbian instrumental folk music (Example 6.7), such as nonarchitectonic (ABCD) form, heterometric or heterorhythmic melody sections, and Romanian rhythm patterns and shifted rhythm, where the motivic rhythm schema of four eighths (mm. 9, 19, and 17) is shifted from the beginning of the bar to its second half (m. 18).[4]

     The compositional techniques are inversion, such as the construction of the first motif (mm. 9–10), and sequential development. The harmonic treatment, including the string accompaniment, consists for the most part of syncopated triads and seventh chords, in which the lower strings play chains of open fifths.[5] The first half of the melody opens in D minor, and the second half begins with the tritone chord,

Example 6.7. (a) Bartók, "Musique paysanne serbe et bulgare du Banat," no. 4, and (b) Bartók, Rumanian Folk Music, *vol. 1, no. 152b.*

G♯ minor (m. 17), and ends in D major. A uniquely Bartókian feature, however, is the interaction between diatonic and
octatonic formations, which is highlighted by the shifted
rhythm in the third melody section (mm. 17–19).[6]

25–32   Section b is an oboe duet (Example 6.2), a three-section
melody in parallel thirds, based on Yugoslav *tambura* motifs
such as those Bartók recorded during a *Djurdjevka* (St.
George's-day dance) in 1912 (Example 6.8).[7]

The pitch content of the duet and the its string accompaniment is the D-Lydian/Mixolydian twelve-tone polymode,
resulting from the interaction of diatonic and octatonic scale
segments in the two-part melody.[8] The first melody section
opens with a D-major triad, the second section with an E
major seventh chord (m. 28). The close of the third melody
section, emphasized by the entry of the side drum, is on the
modal dominant (A-minor triad), in emulation of an imperfect "Yugoslav" cadence.[9]

33–41   An episode consisting of sequential sixteenth-note configurations, beginning with a ninth chord in F major, progressing
by way of a whole-tone scale in the strings, F–G–A–
B–C♯–D♯, to an octatonic tetrachord, D♯–E–F♯–G, and ending with a descending sequence of triads, B minor, A minor,
G major, and B major.

41–45   A transitional interlude in B major, in the lower strings, while
the first violin plays a tonic trill, B–C♯. The melody is based
on rhythm patterns that are characteristic of Romanian bagpipe motifs (Example 6.9).[10]

45–57   Section c, played by a pair of clarinets, emulates Dalmatian
sopel performance of a two-part folk-song melody (Example
6.3). The parts, mostly parallel minor sevenths in a narrow-
range chromatic style, are frequently added as interludes
in alternation with singers.[11] The melodic structure is a

Tempo giusto

Example 6.8. Bartók, "Musique paysanne serbe et bulgare du Banat," no. 9, mm. 5–8.

Example 6.9

quaternary with three-bar melody sections. The skeleton form (i.e., the principal notes) of the second section is an octatonic hexachord, D–C♯–B–A♯–G♯–G (mm. 48–50). The vertical sonorities formed by the combined duet and string accompaniment are fourth, seventh, and ninth chords. The fourth melody section concludes with a descending whole-tone scalar passage, D–C–B♭–A♭–G♯–E–D–C, in the *divisi* first violin (mm. 54–57).

58–60   A transitional interlude in the lower strings, ending on C♯ as the fifth degree of an F♯-major triad.

60–86   Section d is an ornamented melody in parallel fifths, in the first and second flutes (Example 6.4). The first melody section opens with an unusual rhythm schema, similar to one in a Serbian violin melody Bartók collected in 1912 (Example 6.10).[12]

The pitch content of the first melody section, including the string accompaniment, begins with the superposition of octatonic segments from all three octatonic collections, followed by complete octatonic scales in the flutes, E♯–F×–A–B–C♯–D–E and A♯–B♯–C♯–D♯–E–F♯–G–A.[13] The section is thereafter extended by a sequence of Lydian modal segments, end-

Example 6.10. (a) Bartók, "Musique paysanne serbe et bulgare du Banat," no. 1, staff 11, mm. 5–8.

ing on a pentatonic simultaneity, A♯–D♯–F♯–A♭–D♭ (m. 69). The second melody section begins with an F-major triad and ends on B♭ major (mm. 70–73). The third melody section, a variant of the second section, begins with an E♭-major triad and ends on G major (mm. 74–76). The last section consists of scalar passages in contrary motion, beginning with the G melodic-minor scale and ending on a sustained C♯-major chord (mm. 76–86).

83–90   This transitional interlude is a melodic variant of the first one (mm. 41–45; cf. Example 6.9), ending with viola configurations derived from the whole-tone scale, B♯–A♯–G♯–F♯–E–D–C (mm. 87–90).

90–101   Section e, the trumpet duet in major seconds, is stylistically related to Section c (the preceding clarinet duet in minor sevenths). In other words, the trumpets represent the part-singing of Dalmatian folksingers, and the clarinets are surrogate *sopile*, whose part-playing of the inverted intervals provides a dynamic contrast during the performance of a folk song (cf. Example 4.23 with Examples 6.3 and 6.5). The formal design is a quaternary melody and two variations, based on C as the principal tone, in which the skeletal rhythm schema, 2/4 ♩ ♩ | ♩ ♩ ♪ | ♩ ♩ | ♩ |, is a frequent occurrence in Slovak and Yugoslav seven-syllable folk-songs. The four-section melody, however, is Bartók's invention, whose structural features enable its superposition with the accompanying string tremolos to form alternating segments of the complementary whole-tone scales, C–D–E–F♯–A♭–B♭ and B–C♯–E♭–F–G–A.

102–108 In the second and third melody sections of the truncated first variant (from m. 104), the accompaniment changes to a melodic obbligato of whole-tone cluster chords.

109–116 The second variant also has three melody sections, in which the first two sections consist of a reprise and inversion, respectively, of the opening theme (mm. 90–92). The accompaniment, moreover, is for the most part based on the alternation of C and D as nonfunctional tertian sonorities—sevenths, ninths, or elevenths—ending in D major.

116–122 An interlude in D major, which ends with side-drum mimicry of the rhythm patterns from the preceding dialogue between the trumpet duet and its string accompaniment.

PART B (mm. 123–164)

123–146   The "trio," simulating the tone color of a church organ, be-
           gins with a five-part chorale-like theme in the trumpets,
           trombones, and tuba.[14] There are four isometric, isorhyth-
           mic melody sections, extended to accommodate side-drum
           solos whose rhythm schemata are derived from those in the
           preceding Section d (mm. 120–122).

           The polyphonic texture is remarkably similar to Bach's
           chorale settings, but there is a great difference in tonality:
           Bartók's chorale is based on an eleven-tone Phrygian/Ionian
           (major) polymode, with B as the principal tone, B–C–D–E–
           F♯–G–A/B–C♯–D♯–E–F♯–G♯–A♯. Another departure is the
           Bartókian Yugoslav (half-cadence) ending on the dominant,
           F♯.[15]

147–164   The trio is extended by a free variation of the first melody
           section, in the horns and tuba, which ends with a sustained
           B♭-major chord. The side-drum entry (beginning at m. 156)
           is followed by a dialogue between the oboe and flute (mm.
           158–164), which alternate playing the motivic upbeat tri-
           chord that initiates the first bassoon part in Section a.

PART A (mm. 165–263)

165–180   The da capo is essentially a literal reprise of Part A, with ad-
           ditional instrumentation and contrapuntal enhancements.
           Section a, the bassoon duet, shows an additional, contrapun-
           tal line in the form of scalar and arpeggiated configurations
           by the third bassoon.

181–197   Juxtaposed with the oboes in Section b are the clarinets that
           also play parallel thirds, but in contrary motion to form
           three- and four-part chords.

195–198   The three-bar interlude is constructed with different rhythm
           patterns than before.

199–211   Section c is a remarkable example of part writing, where the
           clarinet duet in minor sevenths is juxtaposed in parallel mo-
           tion with a pair of flutes at the same interval but with differ-

ent pitch content. The resultant tetrachords form whole-tone, pentatonic, fourth-chord, and other sonorities. The unisonal bassoons play an ascending sequence of motivic up-beat trichords (mm. 201–205), and the section ends with emphatic rendition of a D whole-tone chord, D–E–F♯–G♯–A♯.

212–218   The ingenious six-part polyphonic texture in Section d begins with the flute duet in fifths as before, the first and second oboes in parallel motion to form triads and four-part chords with the flutes, and the bassoons in contrary motion with various dyads.

219–227   The last melody section is for the most part the same as in Part A (cf. mm. 77–83), but the truncated transitional interlude that follows is based on different rhythm patterns.

228–263   Section d, the trumpet duet in major seconds, highlights the divisi strings: the violins with six-part whole-tone tremolos and violas with five-part whole-tone chords. Simultaneously, moreover, both harps play ascending and descending whole-tone glissandi as the unisonal clarinets and cellos play short, obbligato phrases (mm. 228–240). While the strings sustain a pianissimo D-major seventh chord, the side drum repeats rhythm patterns from its introductory section (cf. mm. 4–6) and ends the last three bars with the same solo, ♪♩ ♪|♩ ♩ |♩ ‖.

Chapter 7

THIRD MOVEMENT (*ELEGIA*)

———————————————— ✀ ————————————————

The *Elegia* represents Bartók's own "lugubrious death-song" and his first creative effort after he composed the String Quartet no. 6 (1939) in Budapest. The movement was the first one composed during the summer of 1943; it appears before the others in the field sketchbook he originally used for transcribing Turkish folk music in 1937.[1] Thus, so far as the compositional stages of the Concerto are concerned, his program note about the themes in this movement could read "appears in" instead of "derived from" (the introduction to the first movement). In a certain sense, Bartók has created a miniature symphonic poem in ternary (ABA) form and impressionist vein, whose "mysterious" background sonority implies an outdoor atmosphere to the extent that he has been designated "the worthy heir of Debussy."[2]

SYNOPSIS OF THE THIRD MOVEMENT

Part A begins with the foreboding "Darkness" motif in the basses, which is strikingly similar to the opening bars of Bartók's opera, *Duke Bluebeard's Castle* (Example 3.24) as well as the first movement *Introduzione* (Example 5.1) in terms of tone color and pentatonic orientation (Example 7.1).

Andante non troppo

Example 7.1

A stretto of "rudimentary" cellular motifs follows in the cellos, violas, and second violins, respectively, leading to a narrow-range chromatic melody in the first oboe and its accompanying variants of the "Lake of Tears" motif in the flutes, clarinets, and harp (Example 7.2).[3]

These undulating configurations begin Bartók's cherished "Night's music," as if in tearful remembrance of happier times he had during his many visits to collect folk music in the rural areas of Transylvania. The motivic stretto returns, slightly altered and with added instrumentation. The piccolo enters with a birdsong that provokes other nocturnal sounds of nature in the oboes, English horn, and French horns.

Part B is marked by a sudden change of mood: the melody sections of the Introduzione second theme (see Example 5.2) are partitioned into bar-length motifs in the clarinets and violins, where each motif is followed by swooping arpeggios, crashing chords, and fortissimo tremolos in the full orchestra. The tonal effect evokes the impression of a tormented soul in a hopeless struggle against a relentless fate. An attenuated reprise of the theme, in inverted form in the violins, is accompanied by a three-part stretto of descending configurations in the woodwinds and lower strings. A fortissimo chord in the horns signals the return of the "Night's music," here as a short interlude that ends with another birdsong in the piccolo.

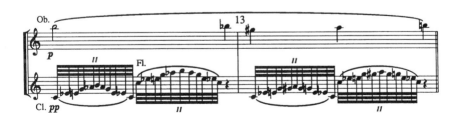

Example 7.2

Example 7.3

At the core of the movement and—from the formal point of view—the Concerto itself, is a new, lugubrious theme whose four melody sections are intoned by the violas (Example 7.3).

The chromaticism and other structural attributes of the new theme suggest that it stems from Romanian mourning-song melodies collected by Bartók in Transylvania, particularly the *zorilor* (at dawn) type.[4] When the theme is repeated in the woodwinds, the end tone of each melody section is punctuated by a loud chord and arpeggiation in the strings and harp—somewhat similar in effect to the preceding treatment of the *Introduzione* second theme. The fourth melody section is extended by chromatic passagework in the violins, in near relation to the melodic contour of the theme, that serves as a short interlude.

Part A returns with alternation of the "Lake of Tears" and the introductory "Darkness" motifs, followed by another birdsong in the piccolo. After the first violins take up the extended "Darkness" motif (*calmo*), the movement ends with nocturnal sounds in the muted horn and a twittering motif in the piccolo, which fades away into nothingness.

Analytic Commentary

PART A (mm. 1–33)

MEASURES

1–4   Although the melodic contour of the "Darkness" motif has
           so-called pentatonic turns, that is, an intervallic structure of

fourths, seconds, and thirds (Example 7.1), the leap of a fifth, G–D (m. 4) represents a plagal cadence and thus implies the continuity of the D-major tonality that ends the preceding movement.

5–10   Bartók's "rudimentary motifs" are not only tetrachordal partitions of octatonic scales—Z-cells and their inversion—organized as a stretto, but also include a tetrachordal partition of the D-chromatic scale—the motivic X-cell, D-E♭-E-F— which generates the Z-cells and, moreover, implies the presence of the D-Phrygian/Lydian polymode source, D–E♭–F– A–B♭–C/D–E–F♯–A♭–A–B (Example 7.4).[5]

An extraordinary nonfunctional chord progression (mm. 9–10) combines major sevenths, D♭–D and F♯–F, whose respective symmetrical resolutions to C–E♭ and G–E create the Bartókian neutral (i.e., major/minor) tonality, C–E♭–E–G.

10–22   The "Night's music" features repetitions of an X-cell motif in the first oboe, B–B♭–A–G♯, juxtaposed with alternation of the transformed "Lake of Tears" motif in the flute, clarinet, and harp, C–E♭–E–G–A♭–B (Example 7.2). It should be noted, however, that the transformation has an intervallic relationship to the preceding Z-cell motifs: perfect fourths are diatonically compressed to minor thirds, thus emphasizing the neutral C-major/minor tonality that serves as the chordal accompaniment in the strings. The section ends with a birdlike chirping in the piccolo.

22–33   The "Night's music" continues with a six-part canon in the flutes and clarinets, followed by an attentuated stretto in the strings, all based on the transformed "Lake of Tears" motif but in augmented values. The piccolo enters with a birdsong (m. 28) that is answered by diverse natural sounds in the oboe, English horn, and French horn, successively.

Example 7.4

PART B (mm. 34–100)

34–44   Part B is in itself a smaller ternary (aba) form, where the first
         subdivision is represented by the *Introduzione* second theme
         as a unisonal melody in the clarinets and violins (see Exam-
         ple 5.2), in place of the original, triadic form in the trumpets.
         The twin-bar motifs of the four melody sections, however,
         are treated as bar-length antecedent motifs concatenated with
         twin-bar X- and Z-cell consequent motifs in the first trumpet
         (Example 7.5).
             Concurrent with this unique motivic treatment are the
         descending modal passages in the flutes, oboes, and lower
         strings—whose initial and final notes form ascending octaves
         of the Phrygian mode—and the varied chordal punctuation
         in the tutti, where E functions as the harmonic ostinato.
         These diatonic and cellular interactions, based on E as the
         fundamental of a chromatic polymode, are in sharp contrast
         to the neutral tonality in Part A.

45–53   An inverted, transformed extension of the original twin-bar
         motif, with F as the principal tone, is played by the violins
         while the accompanying woodwinds and lower strings de-
         scend in a four-part polymodal stretto. An unexpected shift
         to the tritone, B♭ major, serves as the chordal background for
         a reprise of the X-cell consequent motif, G♯–A–A♯–B, by the
         first trumpet.

54–61   The transitional interlude begins with an X-cell trill figure,
         F✕–G♯–A–B♭, continues during the superposed X-cell-related
         birdsong in the piccolo, G♯–A–A♯–B–(C), and ends with a
         pizzicato C♯ in the cellos and basses.

Example 7.5

62–72   The core theme that initiates the second subdivision—a quaternary of twin-bar melody sections, each with an isorhythmic schema of eight eighth notes—is assigned to the violas. The first melody section is based on an X-cell motif, C♯–B♯–B–A♯ (see Example 7.3); the others consist of chromatic hexachords. A♯ suggested previously, the rhythm schema, chromaticism, melodic contour, and sustained section endnotes point to the octatonic, parlando mourning-song genre of the rural Transylvanian-Romanians as a possible source of inspiration (Example 7.6).

                The punctuation technique used in the first subsection is carried over during the sustained endnotes of each melody section, but as tremolo sonorities in the harp and major or minor chords in the violins. During the reprise of the theme in the woodwinds, however, the punctuation reverts to major or minor chords in the tutti.

73–83   This section, a reprise of the theme in the woodwinds, resumes the chordal punctuation of the first subsection. Here, however, the swooping is in the form of upward glissandos in the harp, and the simultaneities are played by the horns, trumpets, and pizzicato strings.

84–92   A twin-bar woodwind stretto in four parts, a transformation of the one previously met in Part A (cf. mm. 22–23), serves as an introduction to the reprise of the inverted *Introduzione* second theme (cf. mm. 45–53) in the violins and upper woodwinds. The homophonic treatment of the theme contrasts sharply with its previous monophonic texture. Additionally, the polymodal obbligato in the bassoons and lower strings is a stretto in free counterpoint, where the relationship of the two parts alternates between contrary and parallel motion.

93–100   This transitional interlude, played by the flutes and violins, is a twin-bar variant of the theme. The variant is repeated three

Example 7.6

times, each repetition an octave lower, whose principal degrees form an octatonic heptachord, E–D♯–C♯–C–B♭–
A–G. The descending octatonic treatment of the interlude,
which closes with a reprise of The "Lake of Tears" motif in
the flute and clarinet, is perhaps symbolic of a descent into
the "Darkness" motif that follows in the *Da capo*. The remarkable accompaniment in the tutti features the lower
strings in a progression of nonfunctional chords, from A
minor to G major, where the divisi violas, cellos, and basses
play three-part tremolos in close harmony.

DA CAPO (mm. 101–128)

101–105   Although the enharmonic reprise of the introductory "Darkness" motif in the lower strings maintains its pentatonic orientation, including the insertion of an additional fourth,
C–G (m. 104), the resulting hexachord forms an octatonic
segement, G♭–[]–E♭–D♭–C–B♭–[]–G. The motif again ends
with an ascending dyad, but altered to a tritone, B–F.

106–111   The "Night's music" returns with the "Lake of Tears" motif
in the flute and clarinet, which is extended in range to concatenated ascending/descending Z-cell arpeggios, B–E–F–
A♯–B and D–G–A♭–C♯, which together form the complete octatonic collection, D–E–F–G–A♭–A♯–B–C♯. Subsequent
stretto-like entries of these cellular formations in contrary
motion, accompanied by the tritone, B–F, as tremolos in the
strings, merge with an X-cell birdsong motif in the piccolo,
C–B–A♯–G×.

112–128   The final, extended reprise of the "Darkness" motif appears
for the first time as degrees of the symmetrical (i.e., Hungarian) form of the pentatonic scale, F♯–A–B–C♯–E, in the violins. This section, marked *calmo*, juxtaposes the descending
motif with a rising sequence of minor, major, and fourth
chords in the upper woodwinds. The sounds of nature are
heard in the muted first horn, followed by the last piccolo
birdsong that ends the movement.

Chapter 8

FOURTH MOVEMENT (*INTERMEZZO INTERROTTO*)

*I*n the first draft of his program notes, "Explanation to Concerto for Orchestra," Bartók struck out the opening words "The only programmatic" in the first sentence that introduces his discussion of the structural features of the *Intermezzo Interrotto*. Perhaps he felt that the quite obvious instrumental guffaws and snickering during the "interruption" section of the movement would be self-evident to the listener. While the programmatic content can be interpreted as a blend of Richard Strauss's objective treatment and Liszt's subjective approach in creating their symphonic poems, the structure is a Bartókian variation of the Beethovenian rondo form.

SYNOPSIS OF THE FOURTH MOVEMENT

A short, introductory phrase opens Part A, followed by the first theme in the oboe. This theme, invented by Bartók in the Lydian mode, emphasizes the modal augmented fourth degree, A♯, which is a characteristic feature of Slovak folk song. Thus, the melody represents an imitation of Slovak folk style—the penultimate level of Bartók's innovative approach for the transmutation of folk music into art music (Example 8.1).

The theme is repeated by the flute and clarinet, while the bassoon

Example 8.1

plays it as a mirror (i.e., literal) inversion. The first half of the inverted theme is then assigned to the flute, and the second half, in its original form, to the oboe. The oboe continues with the fourth rendition of the theme, while the flute plays a superposed obbligato.

Part B displays a most unusual change of mood, in which the lyrical second theme seemingly is a departure from Bartók's customary use of village folk-music sources (Example 8.2).

The second theme is Bartók's transformation of a song hit from *A hamburgi Menyasszonyi* (The Hamburg Bride), a Hungarian operetta composed by Zsigmond Vincze in 1926. The song, whose text reads "Szép vagy, gyönyöru . . . vagy, Magyarország" ("You are lovely, you are most beautiful, Hungary"), was used as the musical slogan of the Hungarian irredentist movement to rally support for the return of Transylvania to Hungary (Example 8.3).[1]

Through such transformation, Bartók emulates the metamorphosis process whereby certain urban folk songs (i.e., *magyar nótak* or popular art songs) are borrowed, transformed, and eventually assimilated by the Hungarian peasant class.[2] It seems likely, moreover, that Bartók was aware

Example 8.2

Lassan (Andante)

magyarosan (in Hungarian style)

Example 8.3

of a variant relationship between the operetta melody and his own transcription of a Hungarian folk song he collected in 1906 (Example 8.4).[3]

Returning to the second theme, its repetition is presented by the first violins and English horn in a canonic duet, while the violas take up an obbligato. The transitional interlude that follows is based on an extended form of the introductory phrase (mm. 1–3).

Part C, the "interruption" section, opens with the third theme in the first clarinet and its accompaniment in the strings (Example 8.5).

The original source of this theme is the vulgar *Chez Maxime* song hit from Franz Lehár's operetta, *The Merry Widow* (see Example 3.3). Bartók, however, arrived at his variant by way of the third theme in the first movement of the Shostakovich Symphony no. 7 in C Major (*Leningrad*), op. 60 (1941). According to the Russian composer's program note, this theme, which governs the middle passage of the movement, "presents the spirit and essence of those harsh events [when] our peaceful and pleasant life was disrupted by the ominous force of war" (Example 8.6).

Peter Bartók, the composer's younger son, recalls that in 1942

Parlando

Example 8.4. Bartók, The Hungarian Folk Song, *no. 304, mm. 1–4, 13–16.*[3]

Example 8.5

[t]he Shostakovich Symphony was broadcast with great fuss about the event; the score came from Russia by microfilm, it was an important work, etc. My parents and I listened to the broadcast. During the part of the work which I believe was supposed to signify the advance of the German armies, my father became aware of numerous repetitions of a theme which sounded like a Viennese cabaret song. . . . This part of the symphony was also referred to as the great crescendo. As the theme came again and again, we counted and the number of times it came was quite high, I believe several dozen. My father was quite surprised to hear such a theme used for such a purpose in such great abundance.

The years went by and it was after the war and after my father's death that I first had a chance to hear the Concerto. There I noticed this theme alternating with another very beautiful one. That the connecting bits represent laughter is only the product of my fantasy, as well as the assumption on my part that there should be any connection between our having heard the Shostakovich symphony during the war and the presence of the theme in the Concerto. Nevertheless, one thing is certain: my father was not quoting the symphony—he was quoting from a cabaret song.[4]

On the other hand, the recollection of the Hungarian-born conductor, Antal Dorati, who met with Bartók after the Concerto had been com-

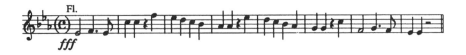

Example 8.6. Dmitri Shostakovich, Symphony no. 7 in C Major (Leningrad) *op. 60, first movement, third theme.*

posed, is that the third theme of the fourth movement was composed as a caricature of the tune in the Shostakovich work, and that in Bartók's view the public reception of the Seventh Symphony, then enjoying great popularity in America, was more than it merited.[5]

Returning to the discussion of Part C, the conclusion of the third theme is greeted with shrieking laughter by the orchestra, punctuated with trombone guffaws, and followed by a short, barrel organ-like episode of tonic–dominant chords in the woodwinds and brass. These trite harmonies serve as the accompaniment for the repetition of the third theme by the violins, which is again followed by an hysterical outburst in the orchestra. While the tuba attempts to restate the theme, the violins superpose its mirror inversion, but they are cut off when the orchestral forces suddenly erupt in a third demonstration of snickering that gradually subsides at the end of the section.

The reprise of Part A reverses the previous order of themes. The second theme, played by the first violins and violas, with an accompaniment by the other strings and the harp, is succeeded by the first theme in the English horn and the latter's inversion in the flute. A birdsong-like flute cadenza precedes the coda, where motifs from the inverted first theme are interchanged among the flute, oboe, and bassoon to end the movement.

Analytic Commentary

PART A (mm. 1–42)

MEASURES

1–3   The introductory tetrachord in the strings, B–A♯–E–F♯, indicates B major as the basic tonality of the movement. The cadential chord at measure 12 establishes the major mode.

4–12   However, the emphatic rendition of the fourth, fifth, and seventh degrees of the scale in the first three melody sections of the quaternary oboe theme (mm. 4–10) implies an underlying Y-cell (whole-tone tetrachord) motif, E–F♯–[]–A♯, in the E-Lydian mode, particularly because E, as the principal tone, is supported by its presence as sustained and pizzicato notes in the strings. Although the Lydian orientation of the theme is characteristic of Slovak folk song,[6] the alternation of

Example 8.7

G and G♯ in the accompanying second violins provides a Bartókian neutral (major/minor) atmosphere. More specifically, the three melody sections and their accompaniment form a hexachordal Lydian/Gypsy-minor polymode, E–F♯–G♯–A♯–B/E–F♯–G–A♯–B. The fourth melody section, on the other hand, ends, on the tonic B-major triad. So far as rhythm is concerned, the change of time in the first three melody sections—2/4 and 5/8—seems to serve as an optional replacement, for practical purposes, of their essentially Bulgarian rhythm schema, 2 + 2 + 2 + 3/8 (Example 8.7).

With regard to the Lydian orientation of the theme, the next illustration shows two of the numerous examples of the modal augmented fourth in Slovak folk song, which Bartók collected, beginning in 1906. He was the first to determine such intervals as a unique Slovak peculiarity (Example 8.8).[7]

It is striking that the inflected second degree, A♯, near the final cadence of no. 164 (m. 8) produces a transposition, G–A–B–C♯–D/G–A–A♯–C♯–D, of exactly the same Lydian/Gypsy-minor polymode, E–F♯–G♯–A♯–B/E–F♯–G–A♯–B, of

Example 8.8. Bartók, Slowakische Volkslieder, *(a) no. 164 and (b) no. 671f.*

the first three melody sections of the movement, referred to previously.

12–20 Repetition of the theme in the first flute and clarinet, varied in its last half, is again accompanied by the strings. The second violin adds the alternation of C♯ and D as well as the previous G♯ and G, and the first bassoon obbligato includes D, D♯, and A.[8] These degrees, together with repetition of the closing tonic B-major triad, confirm the tonality as a B-Major/Aeolian ten-tone polymode, B–C♯–D♯–E–F♯–G♯–A♯/ B–C♯–D– E–F♯–G–A. The obbligato itself begins with the retrograde form of the cellular motif, A♯–F♯–E, and continues as a more-or-less free inversion of the theme.

20–32 The second repetition begins with a free inversion of the first half of the theme by the flute in D harmonic minor, accompanied by harp arpeggios and sustained sonorities in the violins and violas. The third and fourth melody sections, on the other hand, return as variants of the original form, in the clarinet and first horn, respectively. The meandering polymodality, which begins with D as the principal tone, ends with a transitional C-Lydian chord, C–E–F♯–G, in the strings, harp, and horn, whose principal modal tones, C–F♯–G, imply the presence of a gapped C Z-cell.

32–42 Part A concludes with yet another reprise of the theme, here in its original form and played by the oboe. A flute obbligato consists of two octatonic pentachords, G♯–A♯–B–C♯–D (mm. 33–38), and, in the fourth melody section (mm. 38–40), C♯–[]–E–F♯–G–[]–A♯.[9] Even here, the modal folk source is evident, the first octatonic segment, G♯–A♯–B–C♯–D, together with the oboe theme, E–F♯–A♯, forming the larger nondiatonic folk mode, E–F♯–G♯–A♯–B–C♯–D.[10]

PART B (mm. 42–61)

42–50 The second theme, assigned to the violas, is a quaternary with C as the fundamental tone, in which the change of time (5/8, 3/4, 7/8, 2/4) evokes the impression of parlando-rubato rhythm. The first half of the theme is based on a rotation of the C melodic-minor scale, G–A–B–C–D–E♭ (Example 8.2).

The third melody section is essentially a rotation of the B♭ melodic-minor scale, F–G–A–B♭–C–D♭–E♭ (mm.46–47).[11] The harp accompaniment is constructed as a progression of functional chords.[12]

51–58   Repetition of the second theme is taken over by the violins and, in canonic stretto, by the English horn. The polyphonic texture is further enhanced by an obbligato in the violas, and the bass line in the harp accompaniment is doubled in the lower strings.

58–61   This short, two-part transition is played by the English horn and violas.

PART A (mm. 61–74)

61–69   The oboe reprise of the first theme, which includes a variation of its second half, is accompanied by obbligato figurations in the flute, clarinet, and second violins, while the other strings play sustained or pizzicato intervals.

69–74   A transition consisting of three sequences, G–D–A–B, E–B–F♯–G♯, and B–F♯–C♯–D♯—all variants of the contour of the introductory tetrachord in measures 1–3—played by the low strings while the oboes and first bassoon reiterate the last three notes of the theme.

PART C: INTERRUPTION (mm. 75–119)

75–91   The third theme begins with three bars of the accompaniment in 8/8 time, but the meter is in reality a Bulgarian rhythm of 3 + 2 + 3/8. This additive rhythm, featured in Bartók's *Fourth Dance in Bulgarian Rhythm* (*Mikrokosmos* no. 152), is described by the composer as "very much in the style of Gershwin."[13] Perhaps the syncopation is a musical memento of the time when "Toscanini and Koussevitzky publicly vied to perform [the Shostakovich Seventh Symphony] for the first time in America."[14] The parodic treatment of the Shostakovich theme, in the same key of E♭ major as the source melody, begins in the first clarinet (Example 8.5). When the melody ends on a B-major chord, it is greeted by two X-cell motifs in the form of two minor-second trills separated by a whole step in the muted trumpets, G♯–A, A♯–B, and minor-second tremolos separated by a whole step in the violins, B♭–A, A♭–G, whose combination approximates derisive cackling sounds (mm. 84–86). This in turn is followed by mockery in the clarinets, which descend in parallel seconds while the flutes and oboes repeatedly echo the trumpet trills (mm. 87–89), and finally by a snorting Z-cell motif (!) in the form of two tritone glissandi in the trombones, B–F–E–B♭ (mm. 90–91).

92–108   A four-bar street band accompaniment in the woodwinds and brass precedes the first reprise of the third theme by the violins. When the melody ends, this time on an E-major chord, it is again followed by repetition of the same trills in the muted trumpets and violins. These X-cell motifs, however are exchanged: the tremolos are given to the trumpets and the trills are played by the violins (mm. 103–104). The woodwind mockery, augmented by the addition of the oboes to the clarinets to form descending fourth-chords, includes those sonorities as descending glissandi in the violins and violas (mm. 105–108).

108–119   The tuba enters with the second repetition of the theme, together with a stretto entry of its inversion in the violins. And again the clamorous tremolos and trills are heard, now as major triads in the woodwinds and trumpets. The C major upward glissando in the violins and violas is followed by descending major chords in the oboes and clarinets to end Part C.

PART B (mm. 119–135)

119–127   The last reprise of the second theme is taken up by the muted first violins and violas, accompanied by chords in the harp, second violins, and cellos, and sustained notes in the basses.

127–135   These transitional bars begin with variations of the last four

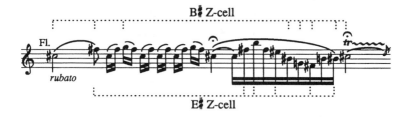

Example 8.9

notes of the theme in the oboe, within the context of an F Z-cell, F–F♯–B–C (mm. 127–130). Meanwhile, the flute obtrudes with a rhythm schema derived from the first theme, ♫ ♫♫ (mm. 128–129), continuing with the passage based exclusively on an octatonic collection, E–F–G–A♭–B♭–B–[]–D.

PART A (mm. 135–151)

135–139   A variation of the first two melody sections of the first theme in the oboe, by concatenation of a Y-cell and an octatonic tetrachord, E–F♯–G♯–A♮/A♯–B–C♯–D (again, the Romanian nondiatonic mode referred to above). These scalar degrees, together with the phrasal ending on a B-minor seventh chord in the string accompaniment, results in an E-Lydian/Phrygian tentone polymode, E–F♯–G♯–A♯–B–C♯–D♯/E–F–A–B–D .

139–142   The last two melody sections, played by the flute and accompanied by the strings, are variants of the inverted reprise (cf. mm. 20–24) but are constructed from an extended octatonic scale, [C♯–B♭]–A–A♭–G♭–F–E♭–D–C–B.[15]

143   This interlude is a flute solo, marked *quasi Cadenza,* which is partially accompanied by a sustained chord in the horns and strings. The scalar degrees of the accompaniment form the symmetrical (Hungarian) pentatonic scale, D♯–F♯–G♯–A♯–C♯, and those played by the flute are components of interlocking Z-cells (Example 8.9).

Example 8.10. Bartók, Rumanian Folk Music, *vol. 1, no. 743e., mm. 1–4.*

           The improvisational character of the flute solo suggests
that the source of creative inspiration may stem from more or
less similar *fluer* (peasant flute) melodies of the Transylvanian Romanians (Example 8.10).[16]

143–151   The movement ends in B major, with a Bulgarian rhythm
schema, 2 + 2 + 2 + 3/8, a piccolo variation of the second
melody section that is derived from the inverted reprise (mm.
22–24), and functional chord progressions in the strings.

Chapter 9

FIFTH MOVEMENT (FINALE)

───────────── ✂ ─────────────

$\mathcal{B}$artók's program notes state that the first and fifth movements of the Concerto "are written in a more or less regular sonata form." The Finale, however, is unquestionably much less regular—to the point where its structure is quite unique. The exposition, for instance, is a veritable apotheosis of Romanian instrumental folk music, based for the most part on a group of dance melodies of indeterminate structure. Such pieces, constructed of two- and four-bar motifs that are repeated without any plan or order, originally were played on the bagpipe and, when that instrument fell into disuse, on the violin and peasant flute (see Example 9.8).[1] The singular development, moreover, consists entirely of a fugal exposition whose unusual structure is far removed from the strict contrapuntal style of the German Baroque.

SYNOPSIS OF THE FIFTH MOVEMENT

A fanfarelike introductory phrase in the horns opens the exposition and is followed by pizzicato fourth chords in the lower strings (Example 9.1).

These chords serve as an ostinato accompaniment to the diverse motifs that constitute the first five sections of the exposition (mm. 8–43). The first motif is played by the second violins and consists of a four-bar structure

Example 9.1

with sixteenth-note configurations in "perpetual-motion" style (Example 9.2).

The second violins, divided into two parts, play the second section in parallel thirds. Finally, the first violins are added to form triadic sonorities in parallel and contrary motion in the third section, followed by their division into two parts to create diverse, four-voice chords in the fourth and fifth sections. The next section, a transitional one, is based on the characteristic Romanian rhythm schema, ♫♩♩ ♩, in the woodwinds and strings.

The seventh section, a stretto for strings, is scalar in construction; the eighth section, played by the woodwinds and the violins, returns to the type of whirling motifs characteristic of the first five sections. The ninth section is another transition, based on the rhythm schema of the sixth section but extensively permuted by the woodwinds and strings in polyphonic texture.

The tenth section has staccato chords on the first beat of each bar, played by the woodwinds, which are answered by scalar passagework in the strings. The woodwind configurations in the extended eleventh section have interesting rhythm schemata and are accompanied by syncopated chords in the strings. The antiphonal twelfth section features scalar tetrachords in the woodwinds and strings. Section thirteen continues the an-

Example 9.2

Example 9.3

tiphony in heptachords, followed by unisonal, narrow-range passagework
in section fourteen.

The remaining eleven sections of the exposition contain well-defined
themes and their variants, which can be identified as a subject or as a
compound theme constructed of melody sections. Section fifteen is a fugato for woodwinds, whose subject (Example 9.3) is a variant of the fanfarelike phrase that serves as an introduction to the movement (mm. 1–4).

Section sixteen is a short transition, consisting of string triads. The
next two sections contain a quaternary theme of Romanian provenance, in
the oboes and clarinets (Example 9.4), followed by its reprise in the violins and violas.

Section nineteen features the closing theme of the exposition (Example 9.5), a quaternary whose first melody section is a descending trichordal motif, played by the second trumpet while the violins and violas
repeat the preceding theme as an obbligato.

The obbligato continues in section twenty, but the first trumpet, supported by the first horn in the motivic first melody section, takes up the
theme in its inverted form. The ingenious counterpoint continues in section twenty-one, where the variegated obbligato is combined with the
theme in the horns and the inversion in the second trumpet as a stretto.

Example 9.4

Example 9.5

The full orchestra is heard in the next section, in which the trichordal motif is transformed in the woodwinds and second trumpet. The first trumpet then joins the woodwinds in a different obbligato; the strings return to the kind of whirling motifs heard earlier in the movement. In the last two sections, the configurations in the woodwinds and strings are organized as ostinatos, and the exposition ends when three staccato chords in the tutti are followed by a timpani roll and ascending glissando.

The development (m. 256) is introduced by the harps and divisi violins, in a short but striking passage. This introduction—perhaps a final homage to Debussy?—imitates the sound of an Indonesian gamelan orchestra. Bartók, like Debussy, was fascinated by this exotic music and its possibilities for composition, as evidenced by *From the Island of Bali* (*Mikrokosmos*, no. 109) and the second movement of *Contrasts*, for Violin, Clarinet and Piano (commissioned in 1938 by the renowned jazz clarinetist, Benny Goodman). Bartók's fascination apparently stems from the structural features of gamelan music, such as pentatonicism and melodic intervals of seconds and fourths, which are also characteristic of old-Hungarian folk music. The remainder of the development is an accompanied fugue in three sections—exposition, development, and recapitulation—whose subject is the quaternary closing theme of the exposition. The unmistakable musical atmosphere, however, is the art of the fugue merged with the spirit of the folk dance.

In the recapitulation (m. 384), the form returns to the sectional arrangement and motivic features of the exposition, until a new theme is played by the violins in slower tempo. This is followed by a very fast reprise of motifs, in triplet patterns, beginning with the lower strings.

While these passages are continued, the woodwinds play variations of the introductory fanfare motif and the brasses add chromatic obbligatos. When the brasses take up the harmonized closing theme in augmented values, the woodwinds join the strings in the performance of their triplet configurations. The latter instruments continue with transformed fanfare motifs and, in the piccolo and flutes, with variants of the head motif from the main theme of the first movement. The alternative ending, which is most frequently used, features a truncated reprise of the closing theme by the horns and trumpets, and a tutti cadence in F major.

Analytic Commentary

EXPOSITION (mm. 1–255)

MEASURES

1–4   These introductory, fanfare-like bars in the horns and trum-
            pets are based on F as the principal tone of an F-Mixolydian/
            Lydian nine-tone polymode, F–G–A–B♭–C–D–E♭/F–G–A–
            B–C–D–E. The timbre, rhythm patterns, and emphatic ren-
            dition of E♭, the characteristic lowered seventh degree of the
            Mixolyian mode, point to *bucium* (Romanian alphorn) motifs
            as the probable source of inspiration (Example 9.6).[2]

                A heptachordal variant from the same polymode, F–G–
            A–B–C–D–E♭, occurs in vocal melodies, particularly the *co-*

Example 9.6. Selected motifs from Bartók, Rumanian Folk Music, *vol. 1, Class E melodies.*

Tempo giusto

Example 9.7. Bartók, Rumanian Folk Music, *vol. 4, no. 73m, mm. 1–4.*

linde (carols and Christmas songs) of the Transylvanian Romanians (Example 9.7).[3]

5–11   The greater part of the exposition is organized as a series of sections that are transformed borrowings of Romanian instrumental melodies with motif structure (see Example 3.20). The viola-cello fourth chords that open the first section emulate the performance of a Romanian folk guitar that accompanies violin dance pieces (Example 9.8; cf. Example 3.38).[4]

Note the juxtaposition of fifths in the violin and guitar, which form dissonant sonorities, D–A–E–B (m. 28) and D–A–E (m. 31). The pitch collection in the complete melody is an A-Lydian/Mixolydian nine-tone polymode, A–B–C♯–D♯–E–

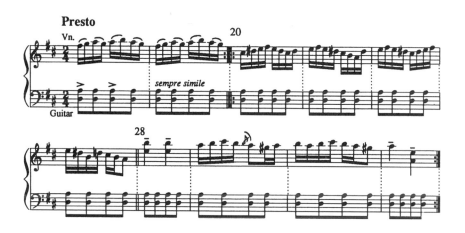

Example 9.8. Bartók, Rumanian Folk Music, *vol. 5, no. 161c, mm. 12–15, 20–23, 28–31.*

F♯–G♯/A–B–C♯–D–E–F♯–G. With regard to Example 9.2, the pitch collection in the first section of the exposition is a rotation of the same polymode, with E as the principal tone. The third horn plays A as a sustained tone.

12–15   The divisi second violins play a variant of the first section in parallel thirds. The second horn, entering with E, joins with the fourth horn in simulating Romanian *bucium* tonic and dominant drone pipes. The accompanying lower strings strum second-inversion A-major chords that resolve to the fourth chord, E–B–E–A.

16–20   While the second violins continue with another variant of the first section, the first violins enter a third above and thus form triads. The third horn adds A, an octave lower, to the sustained drone tones.

21–35   The extended fourth section features the divisi first violins that, with the second violins, form four-voice chords in contrary as well as parallel motion. While the other horns continue their notes, the first horn enters with E an octave higher, this forming pairs of fifths an octave apart. The timpani and divisi basses emphatically render A and E as syncopated rhythm schemata.

36–43   In the fifth section, the divisi violins play motifs that for the most part consist of two octatonic tetrachords, F♯–G–A–B♭ and E–F♯–G–A, in contrary motion. The bassoons join the lower strings in the A-major ostinato accompaniment, while the flutes play syncopated notes, B♭ and G♭, that reinforce the octatonic nature of the tetrachordal motifs.

44–51   This transitional interlude in the woodwinds and violins features the characteristic Romanian rhythm schema, ♫♩[5], whose degrees constitute a whole-tone pentachord, G–A–B–C♯–D♯. The ensuing enharmonic trill in the strings, D♭–E♭, together with the cadential articulation of the E♭-major triad in the flutes and trumpets (at m. 49), form a seventh chord that resolves to a C-major triad (mm. 47–50). The latter chord then serves as an introductory twin-bar ostinato accompaniment in the oboe, clarinet, and bassoon.

52–58   The ascending scalar motifs in the seventh section, in the C-Lydian/Mixolydian heptachordal polymode, C–D–E–F♯–G–A–B♭,[6] are organized as a four-part stretto in the strings.

59–73   A two-part stretto of whirling figurations in the woodwinds and violins is accompanied by chords in the horns and tremolos in the violas, while the cello and bass play a drone ostinato of fifths. The same polymode, transposed to F, has the Aeolian degree, E♭, as an added color note that extends the pitch collection to ten tones.

74–87   This extended transitional section, based on bagpipe rhythm schemata, ♪♪ ♩ and ♪♪ ♫, begins with the flutes and violins, punctuated by syncopated chords in the tutti. The pitch collection is the F- Lydian/Phrygian twelve-tone polymode, F–G–A–B–C–D–E/F–F♯–G♯–B♭–C–D–D♯ (mm. 74–78). A two-part inverted stretto, in the woodwinds and strings, includes a motif in the violins, whose accented notes outline a Z-cell, A–E♭–E–B♭ (mm. 78–80). The transition ends with the emphatic rendition of the tritone, B–F.

88–95   The return to scalar motifs in the tenth section consists of an octatonic heptachord in the violins and violas, D–E–F–G–A♭–B♭–C♭, which is accompanied by octave segments of the A♭-major scale, A♭–B♭–C–D♭–E♭–F–G, in the tutti (mm. 88–93). The principal notes of the combined scales outline the Z-cell, D–G–A♭–D♭. The same pitch collection, transposed to the enharmonic tritone, G♯, is harmonized to form diminished triads (m. 94). Harmonized D-Lydian modal formations are concatenated in the last bar of the section, while the bassoons and basses play an octatonic tetrachord, G–F–E♭–D, whose principal notes, G–D, and those of the Lydian mode, G♯–C♯, outline the enharmonic form of the preceding Z-cell.

96–111   The next section, in the flute and oboe, has a well-defined four-bar motif in the Dorian mode that is echoed as a variant, in the C-Aeolian mode, by the clarinets. The harp and violins play syncopated, more or less functional chords as the accompaniment (mm. 96–103). Other variations, initiated by the piccolo, follow in the same mode and end on the fifth degree, G.

112–118   Section twelve alternates F-Aeolian and F-major tetrachordal motifs between the antecedent violins and the consequent woodwinds, respectively. The last bar of the section ends on an octatonic configuration, D♯–E–F♯–G–A, in the woodwinds and violins, while the accompanying horns and lower strings play an A-major triad.

119–126   The antiphonal, extended passagework continues in reverse order of entry, beginning with the woodwinds and followed by the violins. The pitch collections, however, are Lydian/Mixolydian octachordal polymodes: A-Lydian/Mixolydian, A–B–C♯–D♯/D♮–E–F♯–G and its transposition to F, F–G–A–B/B♭–C–D–E♭, respectively (mm. 119–121). In the remaining bars the alternating pitch collections are between the D-Lydian/Mixolydian polymode, D–E–F♯–G♯/G–A–B–C, and the preceding transposition to F.

126–147   Section fourteen consists for the most part of repetitions of the X-cell motif, E–F–G♭–G, in the strings and high woodwinds, while the brass play an ostinato of syncopated fourth-chords, A–D–G.

148–175   A five-part fugato in the woodwinds, where the four-bar subject is derived from the introductory phrase (mm. 1–4; see Examples 9.1 and 9.3). The second bassoon enters on A♭ with the subject; the first bassoon follows with the answer a fifth higher, on E♭; the clarinets play the reprise of the subject a fifth higher, on B♭, instead of the traditional return to the original pitch (A♭); and the second and first oboes continue the interval cycle with their entries of the subject on F and C, respectively. Put in another way, the fugato entries are based on a pentatonic pitch collection, within the context of twelve-tone polymodal chromaticism.

            The transition from subject to answer, and so on, is by Z-cell transformation of the second half of the theme (Example 9.9): A♭–A–D–E♭ (mm. 150–151), E♭–E–A–B♭ (mm. 153–155), B♭–B–E–F (mm. 157–158), and C–G–G♭–D♭ (mm. 159–161). While the continuation of the second bassoon could be construed as a countersubject, the other parts carry out Bartók's propensity for free counterpoint in fugal writing.

            The flute entry with the inverted and modified subject on G♭, in slower tempo (m. 161), is answered likewise by the first bassoon, transposed to A♭ (mm. 171–175).

175–187   A three-section, homophonically textured melody in the E-Lydian/Phrygian twelve-tone polymode, played by divisi violins and violas and ending on a fifth-chord, E–A–D–G–C.

188–195   An unprepared change of tonality to D♭ major marks the presentation of a new theme in the clarinet (see Example 9.4). The apparent progenitor of this imitation of Romanian

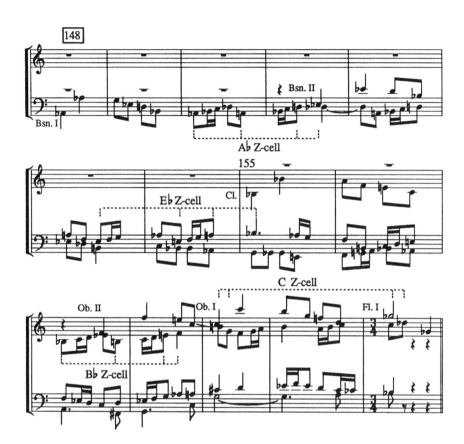

Example 9.9

melodic style is the instrumental music of northern Transylvania, particularly with regard to the rhythm schemata (Example 9.10).

It is obvious that this section imitates bagpipe timbre: the
first oboe reinforces the clarinet "chanter pipe" motifs, and
the second oboe, second bassoon, and cello sustain the tonic
and dominant "drone pipe" notes, D♭–A♭ (mm. 188–191).
Repetition of the theme includes pizzicato chords in the violins as additional accompaniment.

196–200   Section eighteen is a variation of the preceding one, in the violins and viola, while the woodwinds, cello, and bass take up
the tonic/dominant accompaniment.

Example 9.10. Bartók, Rumanian Folk Music, *vol. 5, no. 155a, mm. 18–23.*

201–211   The variations continue while the second trumpet introduces the closing theme (see Example 9.5). The theme consists of four melody sections: a trichordal fanfare motif (cf. Example 9.6) as the first melody section; a repeated-note motif and its variation as the second and third melody sections;[7] and concluding with another fanfarelike motif whose principal notes are related to the descending melodic contour of the first melody section. Expressed in Bartókian alphabetic terminology, the theme can be construed as having an architectonic (rounded) ABBA melodic structure.[8]

211–221   The reprise of the theme is an inversion, in which the first motif, A♭–D♭–A♭, is played by the first trumpet and supported by the first horn that sustains the uppermost note for five bars (mm. 213–217). While the source of the fanfare motif as well as its inversion may stem from Romanian alphorn music, there is a distinct possibility that their provenance may lie elsewhere, namely, the opening motif in the Strauss symphonic poem, *Also sprach Zarathustra,* op. 30, and the related one in the third movement (Scherzo) of Bartók's Suite no. 1 op. 3, for Large Orchestra (Example 9.11).

In his autobiography, Bartók credits the 1902 performance of the Strauss symphonic poem as a "lightning stroke" that led him to a new way of composing.[9] Another unforgettable experience occurred on December 29, 1935, when he read that the Budapest Kisfaludy Society had awarded him the Greguss Prize for his 1905 Suite no. 1 op. 3, for Large Orchestra. Incensed by this apparent disregard of his later works, he informed the society that "I do not wish to accept the Greguss Medal, neither now, nor in the future, nor during my life-time, nor after my death."[10] With regard to the origin of the repeated-note motif in the second and

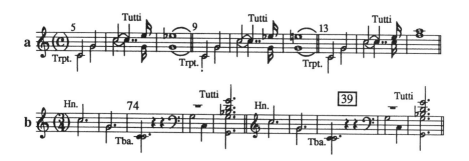

Example 9.11. (a) Strauss, Also sprach Zarathustra *op. 30, and (b) Bartók,* Suite no. 1 *op. 3, for Large Orchestra (1905), third movement.*

third melody sections, the first two bars of the clarinet duet in the second movement show a variant relationship (cf. Example 6.3). Another, closer connection is with the "Seventh Door" motif that marks the last scene in *Duke Bluebeard's Castle* (cf. Examples 3.27 and 3.29).

221–231   Section twenty-one is a two-part stretto, in which the closing theme begins in the horns, in the E-Mixolydian mode, and is followed in the next bar by the inverted theme in the second trumpet. The fanfare motif by the latter instrument is altered to a fourth chord, E–A–D, thus highlighting the characteristic lowered-seventh degree of the mode. The accompaniment continues as before, excepting the reduced instrumentation in the woodwinds.

231–238   The stretto continues when the clarinets and second trumpet take up the reprise of the fanfare motif, in D♭, followed by motivic diminution to quarter-note values in the woodwinds and second horn (mm. 233–234). In place of the other three melody sections, the woodwinds and the first trumpet play a Hungarian pentatonic strain whose rhythm schema is derived from Slovak folk song (Example 9.12).[11]

    Meanwhile, the string accompaniment consists of ostinato trichords in sixteenth notes, and the lower brass and basses sustain the fifths, D♭–A♭.

239–244   During the continuation of the string accompaniment, the woodwinds and first trumpet play shifted-rhythm patterns, resulting in an unusual cross rhythm between the two groups.

Bartók, *Slowikische Volkslieder* I, No. 409.

Example 9.12

244–256   The last section of the exposition is a transitional interlude,
           which ends forcefully with neutral (C-major/minor) seventh
           chords, C–Eb–E–G–Bb, and an ascending timpani glissando
           from G to B.

DEVELOPMENT (mm. 256–383)

256–265   These introductory bars feature a melody in the first harp
           and its chordal accompaniment in the second harp, where
           the pitch collection is the Chinese (i.e., major) form of the
           pentatonic scale, B–C#–D#–F#–G#.
266–277   The development is based on the exposition's closing theme
           as the subject of a monumental fugue. The fugal exposition
           section, in B major, commences with the subject and its
           pizzicato accompaniment in the divisi second violins (cf. Ex-
           ample 9.5). The repeated-note second and third melody-
           sections are ornamented with acciaccaturas (very short ap-
           poggiaturas), in the style of bagpipe melodies collected in
           1910 by Bartók, in the Hungarian-inhabited southern part of
           Czechoslovakia (Example 9.13).[12]
               These acciaccaturas, notated as grace notes in Bartók's bag-
           pipe transcriptions, produce "typical squeaky effects" that he

Example 9.13

emulates as minor seconds, F♯–G, in his piano piece, *Bag-pipe*, from *Mikrokosmos* (Example 9.14).[13]

    An interesting addition to the accompaniment is the alternation of decorative X-cells in the woodwinds, which supplement the squeaky bagpipe effects in the subject.

277–288   The tonal answer begins on the fifth degree, F♯, and is played by the divisi first violins (m. 277). The second violins continue with the countersubject, in eighth-note triplets, while the woodwind configurations are expanded to octatonic, major, and minor tetrachords. The countersubject pitch collection, however, is the B-Lydian/Phrygian twelve-tone polymode, B–C♯–D♯–E♯–F♯–G♯–A♯/B–B♯–D–E–F♯–G–A.

288–291   In this episode, the violas join with the divisi second violins to form descending pizzicato triads as the accompaniment. The divisi first violins play a passage in free counterpoint, in B major, rather than a repetition of the second-violin countersubject. The latter instruments, on the other hand, also

Example 9.14. Bartók, Mikrokosmos *for Piano, no. 138, mm. 32–35.*

continue with passagework in free counterpoint, but in the preceding chromatic polymode.

292–301   In accordance with more or less traditional practice, the subject returns in the tonic, in the divisi cellos, an octave lower and with the second and third melody sections truncated to one-bar length. The violins carry on with their counterpoint as juxtaposed B-major and B-Lydian/Phrygian lines, while the flutes and clarinets alternate X-cell tetrachords in octaves.

300–316   The last statement of the answer is made by the violas, in which the trichordal fanfare motif is compressed to a fourth-chord, E–B–F♯, and the second and third melody sections are truncated as before.

The alternation of cellular tetrachords in the woodwinds is continued, and the pizzicato chords in the string accompaniment, augmented to four parts, are syncopated. The intricacy of the polyphonic texture is extended by the introduction of contrary-motion strettos in the divisi strings and woodwinds (m. 309ff.). The cello plays a sequence of ascending motifs in B major, whose rhythm schema consists of an eighth-note triplet, a pair of eighths, and a quarter note. Imitative sequential patterns are followed on the first beat of the next bar in the viola (m. 310). On the second beat of that same bar the first violin initiates the motif in descending sequences, which are imitated by the second violin on the first beat of the next bar (m. 311). The flutes and clarinets enter with scalar trills in contrary motion, together with the contrary-motion pizzicato triads in the other divisi strings, which ends the exposition section.

317–321   The fugal development section begins with the fanfare motif as a four-part ascending stretto in the strings, with the successive entry of the parts as ascending, interlocked X-cell motifs, E♭–E–F–F♯ and B♭–B–C–C♯, and with a progressive diminution of values (Example 9.15).

Meanwhile, the oboes and clarinets play a counterpoint in which scalar configurations of triplet eighth notes, in parallel thirds, are in contrary motion between the two instrumental groups. The configurations are based on the E♭-Mixolydian mode, E♭–F–G–A♭–B♭–C–D♭ (mm. 317–318), followed by the same mode transposed a semitone higher.

321–324   The oboes and clarinets continued with the truncated sec-

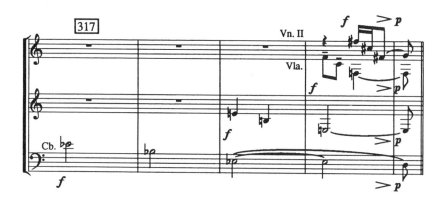

Example 9.15

ond and third melody sections, where the first section has harmonic minor seconds, F–E (cf. Example 9.13). The second section has the same type of intervals, which form ascending, parallel Y-cell motifs, F–G–A–B and E–F♯–G♯–A♯. And these combined cellular constructions, moreover, may also be construed as an E Z-cell, E–F–A♯–B, and its component X-cell degrees, F♯–G–G♯–A. The string accompaniment consists of syncopated sonorities, including the characteristic Slovak rhythm schema, ♪♩ ♪|♩ ♩|. The subject is further abbreviated by the elimination of the fourth melody section.

325–329 The diminution-stretto in the strings is repeated as a real (exact intervallic order) inversion of the fanfare motif, transposed to G. The entries thus form descending, interlocked X-cell motifs, G–F♯–F–E and C–B–B♭–A (Example 9.16).

The contrapuntal scalar configurations of triplet eighth notes, in parallel thirds and in contrary motion between the flutes and the clarinets, form the eleven-tone D-Phrygian/Mixolydian polymode, D–E♭–F–G–A–B♭–C/D–E–F♯–G–A–B–C♯.

329–332 The woodwind inversion of the truncated second and third melody sections, an octave lower, has F♯ and E♯ as the harmonic intervals, and descending parallel Y-cell motifs, F♯–E–D–C and E♯–D♯–C♯–B. The combined cellular constructions may also be construed as a B Z-cell, B–C–E♯–F♯,

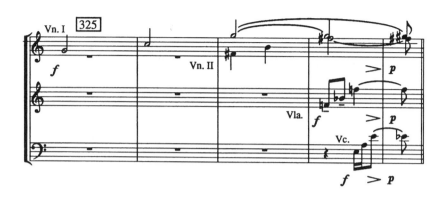

Example 9.16

and its component X-cell degrees, C#–D–D#–E. The string accompaniment continues in the same rhythmic style as before.

333–337   In this transitional episode, the complexity of the polyphonic texture is an outcome of dual, four-part strettos, whose interwoven degrees constitute twelve-tone polymodal chromaticism. The thematic stretto is based on an ingenious, abridged transformation of the second and third melody sections. In each twin-bar section, where the first and second flutes are in contrary motion, the previously antecedent repeated-note bar is shifted to consequent position (mm. 333–336). The clarinets echo a somewhat similar procedure (mm. 334–337). In the second half of measure 333 the oboes, also in contrary motion, play harmonic intervals that are X-cell degrees, E–E♭–D–D♭ and B–B♭–A–A♭ (mm. 334 and 336). They, in turn, are followed by the bassoons whose contrary-motion intervals form the fourth, noncellular entry.

The first violins, violas, and cellos are organized as a two-part stretto, for the most part consisting of the above-mentioned characteristic Slovak rhythm schema. The violins double the oboe harmonic X-cells (mm. 333ff.), and the viola-cello rhythm schemata form contrary-motion linear X-cells, G–F#–F–E and B–A#–A–G# (mm. 334ff.). Another two-part stretto in the second violin contains half-step trills a tritone apart, G#–A and D–D# (mm. 333–336).

337–344   The transition continues, for the most part with the rhythm schema in the clarinets and violins, where the descending E-chromatic scale is partitioned into three X-cells.

345–352   The fugal recapitulation is a remarkable illustration of the art of counterpoint. The subject returns—again without the fourth melody section—as a six-part woodwind stretto (Example 9.17).

The first harp enters with a two-part stretto (at mm. 345–346) that culminates in parallel thirds (mm. 347–356). The second harp begins and ends likewise (mm. 347–348), and continues with parallel thirds in contrary motion to the first harp. The tonality of the woodwind and harp combined strettos is for the most part octatonic in the combined layers.

Example 9.17

353–356   A transitional episode in which the high woodwinds and vio-
           lins play a chain of descending nonfunctional minor-seventh
           chords, C♯–A♯–F♯–D♯–B–G♯, which ends on a G-major triad.
357–364   The four-part stretto in the clarinets and bassoons, based on
           an inversion of the first two melody sections of the subject, is
           accompanied by string trills. A Z-cell, B♭–E♭–E–A, in the
           first and second clarinets follows their entry as the fourth part
           (at m. 361). This cellular construction marks an abrupt
           changeover from the subject to a chain of minor-seventh
           chords that are the vertical projection of sequential fourths in
           the individual parts.
365–383   This extended retransition section features an unusual clus-
           ter chord in the strings—the outcome of a five-note octatonic
           simultaneity, D–[]–E♯–[]–G♯–[]–B–C♯—during a three-part
           stretto in the woodwinds (to m. 369). The latter instruments
           then return to descending chord sequences, which are orga-
           nized as 3/8 hemiolas (to m. 369), followed by paired
           eighths, in 2/4 time. The strings emphatically render the
           cluster chords as sixteenth-note patterns, which are inter-
           spersed with harmonic X-cell motifs, such as the juxtaposed
           major seconds, C♯–D♯/D–E (to m. 378). The retransition
           section ends with the addition of G as the cluster-chord fun-
           damental, thus forming repeated-note octatonic hexachords,
           while the brass sustains or otherwise amplifies the same
           sonority.

                    RECAPITULATION (mm. 384–625)

384–386   The exposition sectional arrangement returns, that is, in imi-
           tation of Romanian instrumental melodies with motif struc-
           ture (see Example 3.20). The violas and cellos present a
           three-bar motif in the F♯-Lydian/Mixolydian heptachordal
           polymode, F♯–G♯–A♯–B♯–C♯–D♯–E, while the rhythm pattern
           in the basses restates the fundamental.
387–389   Another three-bar section in which the first violins take up a
           motif in the A-Lydian/Mixolydian polymode, A–B–C♯–D♯–
           E–F♯–G, while the violas and cellos play eighth-note dyads,
           D♯–E, and the basses sustain C♯.

390–393   A motif in the third section, extended to four-bar length, is
           played by the second violins in the D-Lydian/Mixolydian
           polymode, D–E–F♯–G♯–A–B–C. The viola-cello dyads are
           C♯–D, and the first violins join the basses in sustained thirds,
           F♯–A.
394–403   The fourth, ten-bar section continues the buildup of orches-
           tral forces, where the first violins resume their motivic leading
           role, in the F-Lydian/Mixolydian polymode, F–G–A–B–C–
           D–E♭. The horns provide a syncopated accompaniment of
           ostinato thirds, F–A, and the second violins play a sustained
           trill on C, thus forming the F-major triad as an accompani-
           ment. The dyads in the cellos and basses, B–C and A–B,
           change to trichordal hemiolas (i.e., 3/8 patterns), B–C–D
           and A–B–C (mm. 401–402 and 404–405, respectively).
           When the second violins double the the motif an octave
           lower (m. 399ff.), the clarinets and flutes alternate doubling
           the horn accompaniment an octave higher (mm. 400ff.).
404–407   The fifth section returns to four-bar format, and the instru-
           mentation continues as before. The polymode, however,
           changes to an F-Lydian/Dorian neutral octachord, that is,
           with the juxtaposition of major and minor thirds, F–G–A–
           B–C–D/F–G–A♭–C–D–E♭.
408–417   A sectional interlude, where F♯-minor chords introduce a
           four-part stretto in the bassoons and strings. The tritone en-
           tries form a Z-cell, G♯–D–A–E♭, and the ensuing scale pat-
           terns, including the introductory F♯, begin with an octatonic
           formation, F♯–G♯–A–B–C–D–E♭–F. The last note, moreover,
           serves as the fundamental of the concatenated Lydian/
           Mixolydian polymode, F–G–A–B–C–D–E♭ (mm. 409–411).
           In the next bar, C♯-major chords introduce two Y-cells,
           G♯–A♯–B♯–C× and A–B–C♯–D♯, which are punctuated by a
           B-major and A-major chord, respectively. A third Y-cell fol-
           lows, B♭–C–D–E, whose rendition is emphasized by repeti-
           tion (mm. 425–417).
418–425   The seventh section divides the full orchestra into three in-
           strumental groups—trumpets and horns, upper woodwinds
           and strings, and lower woodwinds, brasses, and strings—that
           play four-bar motifs in triple counterpoint and in the F-Aeo-
           lian/Lydian nine-tone polymode, F–G–A♭–B♭–C–D–E♭/F–
           G–A–B–C–D (Example 9.18).

Example 9.18

426–432   While the trombones and basses sustain G as the pedal
          point, the contrapuntal mélange continues among the
          strings, woodwinds, and combined bassoons and horns. Al-
          though the polymodality incorporates the twelve degrees of
          the chromatic scale, there is accentuation of sequential
          fourths, in contrary motion, whose degrees comprise the C-
          Aeolian mode, C–D–E♭–F–G–A♭–B♭. The section ends with
          the repetition of staccato dyads in the woodwinds and violins,
          G–A♭ followed by G♭–A♭, that recall the second melody sec-
          tion of the exposition closing theme (mm. 429–432).

433–448   The skeletal form of the rhythm in the ninth section is
          a Ukrainian *kolomyjka* (round-dance) schema, 2/4 ♪♪♪♪|
          ♪♪♪♪|♪♪♪♪|♩ ♩ |. The polymodal motif, played by the vio-
          lins and violas, consists of an octatonic tetrachord, G♭–F–
          E♭–D, concatenated with an F-Dorian hexachord, F–A♭–B♭–
          C–D–E♭ (to m. 436). Simultaneously, the woodwinds con-
          tinue playing staccato dyads whose varied intervallic size adds
          to the chromaticism. The motif is then transposed down
          a fourth, which changes the fundamental to C (mm.
          437–440). The next transposition of the motif, to D (begin-
          ning at m. 441), is truncated to three bars and is followed by
          sustained major seconds in the woodwinds and disjunct
          dyads in the strings: all in the D-Phrygian/Lydian ten-tone
          polymode, D–E♭–F–A♭–B♭–C/D–E–G♭–A♭–B–C♯.

Example 9.19

449–468   An abrupt change in tempo marks the appearance of a new, four-section theme in the first violins, accompanied for the most part by sustained notes in the woodwinds, horns, and basses, and tremolos in the other strings. The theme is in the D-Lydian/Phrygian twelve-tone polymode, D–E–F♯–G♯–A–B–C♯/D–D♯–F–G–A–B♭–C, and the second melody section is a transposition of the first section (Example 9.19).

469–481   This transitional section features three chains of augmented triads in contrary motion. The first chain, in the woodwinds and horns (Example 9.20), is accompanied by an F♯ pedal point in the basses and the same note as tremolos in the other strings.

    In the second chain, the flutes and second oboe sustain the augmented triad, B♭–D–F♯. The third chain, in half-note values, omits the oboes.

482–497   The twelfth section not only marks the change to a much faster tempo (*Più presto*) but introduces eighth-note triplets

Example 9.20

as the motivic rhythm schema, in place of the preceding, characteristically Romanian patterns.[14] The extraordinary organic growth of the motif is achieved by means of stretto in four parts, extension in range and phrase length, and harmonic densification from dyads to whole-tone sonorities. The section begins with a bass-drum roll and a twin-bar motif, shared between the cellos and violas, in the A♭-Lydian/Mixolydian octachordal polymode, A♭–B♭–C–D♭–D–E♭–F–G. This pitch collection is a transposition of the same polymode with which the introductory fanfare motif opens the movement (cf. Example 9.1). The same note is sustained as tremolos in the cellos and a drone in the basses. In the next two bars, the cellos and violas repeat the motif as tritone dyads, A♭–D, B♭–E, and so on, while the timpani replaces the bass-drum roll in the accompaniment. In addition the parallel tritones supply the four degrees—E, F♯, A, and B—that convert the preceding octachord into a twelve-tone polymode.

Another three-part "obbligato" stretto, based on a transformation of the fanfare motif, is initiated by the second bassoon (mm. 484ff.). Meanwhile, the entry of the second violins with the original motif on A♭, the repetition of the preceding viola part on the tritone, D, and the cello part transposed a minor third upward to D, result in parallel diminished triads, A♭–C♭–D, B♭–D♭–E, and so on. Moreover, the motif is extended to a tenth in range and three bars in length (mm. 486-489).

When the first violins enter with the fourth part, the motif is extended to a twin-bar concatenation of ascending D-Lydian and C-octatonic hexachords, D–E–F♯–G♯–A–B and C–D–E♭–F–G♭–A♭, respectively. The other three parts have the same hexachords transposed to form tritone pairs in parallel motion (Example 9.21).

The resultant sonorities are also tetrachordal degrees of the two whole-tone scales that partition the chromatic scale. When the second bassoon concludes the transformed fanfare motif (m. 489), the endnote, A♭, is sustained as an additional drone, and the first bassoon enters with that motif transposed a tritone upward.

Example 9–21

       The next two bars are for the most part descending octa-
tonic formations that maintain the dual tritones as whole-
tone sonorities (mm. 491–492). The third entry, a variant of
the transformed fanfare motif, is played by the bass clarinet
during the repetition of the previous Lydian-octatonic configuration in the strings. The component degrees of the configuration, however, are restructured as minor sixths, A♭–C
and D–G♭, in the violins and combined violas and cellos, respectively. The resultant chords are nevertheless the same
whole-tone sonorities as before but in open position (mm.
493–494). Although the last three bars of the section continue the restructured whole-tone formations, the descending
contour of the four parts is adjusted to begin with chromatic
configurations and end with octatonic degrees, thus enabling
the transition from A♭ to F♯ as the fundamental in the ensuing
motif.[15]

498–514   These bars initiate the series of overlapping sections in which
continuously transformed fanfare motifs are treated as three-
part, foreground strettos in the woodwinds; chromatic motifs
appear as two-part, middle-ground strettos or contrapuntal
obbligatos in the brasses; and four-part configurations as
background sonorities in the violins, violas, and cellos, while
the basses continue playing sustained notes as a drone.

       The woodwind strettos begin in the clarinets, with repeti-
tions of the characteristic octave leap that opens the fanfare
motif, although in contrary motion. A transformation of the

complete motif, also in contrary motion, follows in the English horn. The first bassoon then plays its transformation of the motif in its original contour (mm. 504–507). The stretto continues with repetitions of the motif, in contrary motion, by the first oboe. The second entry of the motif, returning to its original contour in the bass clarinet, includes a diatonic (Phrygian) hexachord, E♭–D♭–C–B♭–A♭–G. The third entry of the motif, in likewise intervallic contour, is played by the English horn (mm. 508–514).

As regards the brasses, a three-part stretto of chromatic motifs begins with contrary-motion fragments in the first trombone and tuba (mm. 498–501). The first trombone continues with an extended passage, followed by the second trombone with an X-cell motif, F♯–E♯–E–D♯ in contrary motion (mm. 502–505). The tuba reenters with another X-cell motif, in augmented values, A–G♯–G–F♯. The second horn and the trumpets then proceed with the stretto to the end of the section (mm. 512–516).

The four-part arpeggiated configurations in the strings are divided between the violins and the combined violas and cellos. The former play parallel minor thirds in one direction and the latter play similar dyads in the other direction. The individual configurations, however, are the same for each instrument: interlocked augmented triads resulting from the alternation of minor thirds and minor seconds.[16] Similar intervallic progressions occur in the third movement, as variants of the "Lake of Tears" motif from *Duke Bluebeard's Castle* (see Example 7.2). Although dissonant sonorities are formed by the coincidence of four parts, such as minor-seventh chords, diminished triads, and whole-tone clusters, opposing streams of consonant dyads in fast tempo and as sixteenth-note sextuplets create a linearity that precludes any sonic impression of functional or nonfunctional harmonic progression.

515–525 In this section, the trumpets play a reprise of the second melody section of the exposition's closing theme, in augmented values (Example 9.5). Meanwhile, the characteristic octave leaps of the fanfare motif are repeated in the woodwinds, in opposite directions (mm. 515–519). A two-part stretto ensues, between the first flute and clarinet in octaves and the first bassoon in contrary motion, all based on a truncated version of the fanfare motif. The horns and trumpets close the brass portion of the section with a chromatic chain of major-seventh chords, B♭–D–F–A, B–D♯–F♯–A♯, and so on, that are structured as parallel pairs of major thirds (mm. 522–525).

The strings, reorganized in terms of intervals and direction, reverse the preceding configurations by alternating minor seconds and minor thirds, in parallel motion of the four parts. However, the vertical distance between the violins is a major seventh; between the violas and cellos, a major sixth; and the resultant intervallic juxtaposition is a sequence of major-seventh chords. The drone in the basses is discontinued.

525–531   The fifteenth section shows chromatic compression of the inverted fanfare octave to a minor sixth, F♯–A, in the woodwinds, while the trombones play an obbligato in octaves (mm. 525–529). To a certain extent the strings continue their configurations of interlocked augmented triads. When the four parts change to minor-second tremolos, thus forming an alternation of major-seventh and whole-tone chords, G♯–D♯–C–G and A–E–B–F♯, the horns enter with a sustained C-minor seventh chord, C–E♭–G–B♭ (mm. 529–532).

532–542   An extended transformation of the fanfare motif, in the woodwinds, is accompanied by cellular motifs in the horns, glissandos in the divisi basses, and four-part modal as well as whole-tone configurations in the other strings. The horn Z-cell motifs, B–C–F–F♯ and C–C♯–F♯–G, are preceded by juxtaposed X- and Z-cells in the strings. The motifs end with a unique progression: a whole-tone tetrachord, B–C♯–F–G, to a major-seventh chord, A–C♯–E–G♯ (Example 9.22).

The trumpets enter with a two-part stretto, based on the first melody section of the exposition's closing theme (mm. 535ff.). The four-part string configurations in this section, which are organized as tritones in parallel motion, partition the chromatic scale into ascending and descending whole-tone hexachords. The resultant sonorities, moreover, form a chain of Y-cells.[17]

543–555   In section seventeen, the addition of the trombones extends the trumpet stretto to five parts, while the woodwinds play the motivic interval sequence of minor seconds and thirds

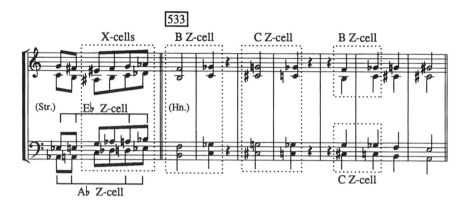

Example 9.22

that form interlocked augmented triads. The basses take up
the tritone, E♭–A, as a sequence of tremolos, and the other
strings resume alternation of both whole-tone scales that are
extended in range to two octaves. These configurations are
later restructured as descending octatonic scales or segments
(mm. 553–555), and the section ends with a sharply dissonant simultaneity, E♭–G♭–A♭–A♮–C♯, in which the tritone,
A–E♭, is emphasized.

556–572 A final return of the closing theme by the brass, in augmented values and harmonized to begin with a G-minor
triad and end abruptly with an F-minor seventh chord.
While the basses play alternately ascending and descending
glissandi, the other strings and the woodwinds begin their
twin-bar, unisonal configurations with a reprise of the motivic interlocked augmented triads, followed by a succession
of scalar constructions that end with the A♭-Lydian mode,
A♭–B♭–C–D–E♭–F–G (mm. 570–572).

573–586 This codalike section begins with transformations of the fanfare motif (cf. Example 9.3), during repetitions of an ascending chain of mixed triads in the F-Aeolian mode, that end in A
major (mm. 573–578). Note, too, the transformed (retrograde) reprise of Motif 1a from the first movement main theme
(cf. Example 5.3) in the piccolo and flutes (Example 9.23).
        Successive motivic transpositions are accompanied by

Example 9.23

another set of chained triads in the C-Phrygian/Dorian octa-chordal polymode, C–D♭–D–E♭–F–G–A–B♭. The polymode is extended by means of a sequence of fourths, F–B–E–A, in the motif (m. 584). These notes, together with connecting ones in the preceding and following bars, form overlapping Z-cells, B♭–F–B–E/E–A–B♭–E♭.[18] The last transposition of the motif and its accompaniment is in the G-Lydian/Dorian nine-tone polymode, G–A–B–C♯–D–E/G–A–B♭–C–D–E–F, while the piccolo and flutes play a transformation of Motif 1b from the first movement's main theme.

587–593   The piccolo and flute take up repeated transformations of Motif 1a, while a two-part stretto between the strings and woodwinds alternates ascending transpositions of Y-cell motifs and the horns enter with a twin-bar scalar passage.

594–602   While the woodwinds, horns and trumpets sustain E♭, then E♭ and B, the strings play a rotation of the C-melodic minor scale, with G as the principal tone, in a three-octave configuration. The fundamental is then sustained while the piccolo plays anonuplet of the same scale, within the boundary of an F♯ octave, as a leading-note passage to the ensuing bars.

603–606   The original ending of the Concerto, based on the F-Mixolydian mode, F–G–A–B♭–C–D–E♭, consists of descending arpeggiated triads in the upper woodwinds, brasses, and strings, and ascending harmonic triads in the other instruments, v–vi–VII–I (i.e., C minor, D minor, E♭ major, and F major). This concludes the work with a modal (i.e., Dorian) cadence in which the final chord is perfect—that is, the fundamental, F, is in the upper parts (Example 9.24).

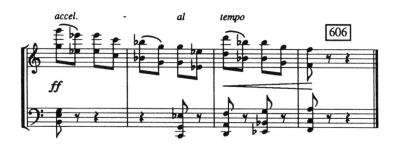

Example 9.24

603–621   The Concerto pocket score (B. & H. 9009) is published
           with an additional, alternative ending that is invariably cho-
           sen by conductors for concert and recording purposes.

One commentator questioned the need for an optional choice:

> To publish these alternative endings is surely strange. . . . If the original
> ending is a bit too abrupt or the revised ending a shade too bombastic for
> my taste, why should the composer direct me to choose between them? I
> should like to have only the one *he* preferred, or else, perhaps to have lib-
> erty to compromise between the two.[19]

The answer to this question perhaps resides in a letter to Bartók from
his publisher, after the first performance of the Concerto in Boston and
the later one in New York.

> As I was told that I should not call on you before next Monday I thought
> I should let you know that I had a most pleasant meeting with [Serge]
> Koussevitzky this morning. He asked me to tell you how happy he is
> about the new ending and that he will play the Concerto "many times"
> next season. He will repeat it again in New York among others.[20]

Comparison of the two endings in terms of unusual structural characteristics and instrumental peculiarities suggests that Bartók intended the
alternative ending as a "Koussevitzky Coda" to satisfy the conductor's wish

Example 9.25

for a longer, more stirring ending. This is accomplished by extending each arpeggiated triad into a twin-bar motif (mm. 604–614) and adding a transformation of the closing theme by way of its second melody section in augmented values (mm. 616ff.). The similarity of the transformation to the ending of the last piece in Bartók's *Mikrokosmos* is striking (Example 9.25).

And, from the psychological viewpoint, the transformation closely resembles the last, "Seventh Door" motif in *Duke Bluebeard's Castle* (cf. Example 3.27).[21] Other probable manifestations of Bartók's apparently negative reaction to the Koussevitzky request are the swooping Lydian mode (mm. 621ff.) and, in the penultimate bar, the unique polyrhythm formed by the juxtaposition of triplets, quintuplets, sextuplets, septuplets, and glissandos in the horns and trombones (cf. the trombone guffaws in the fourth movement, mm. 90–91). In addition (!), note the imperfect F-major chord that ends the Concerto with emphatic rendition of the third and fifth degrees in the upper parts, in place of the tonic in the original ending (Example 9.26).[22]

It has been suggested that the second melody section of the closing theme (Example 9.5) may have had an additional, more recent melodic source underlying the composition of the theme.[23] During 1943, the Latin-American song hit, *El Cumbanchero*, pervaded the music radio channels. Composed by Rafael Hernandez and published by Peer International, lead sheets of the piece were provided to prominent musicians,

Example 9.26

such as Xavier Cugat, the renowned Latin-American bandleader, for orchestration purposes, well in advance of the August 1943 copyright date
(Example 9.27).[24]

A comparison of Bartók's sketches of the Concerto suggest that the
closing theme and other elements of the fifth movement were added after
the basic construction of the five movements had been completed.[25] In
that event, and assuming that the remarkable similarity between the two

Example 9.27

melodies is not pure happenstance, perhaps Bartók considered the Latin-American popular song as worthy of the same level of adaptation as he accorded the Hungarian operetta melody underlying the fourth movement's second theme (Example 8.2). Whatever the case, the closing theme uniquely represents the concept of life assertion that Bartók attributes to the character of the fifth movement.

Part Three

BARTÓK'S LEGACY

Chapter 10

THE INFLUENCE OF BARTÓK'S MUSIC
ON LATTER-DAY COMPOSITION

The Concerto for Orchestra was given its premiere performance by the Boston Symphony Orchestra, Serge Koussevitzky conducting, in Boston's Symphony Hall on the afternoon of December 1, 1944. Cyrus Durgin's review includes these waffling remarks:

> The conventional view of the music of Béla Bartók probably can be expressed thus: "It's awfully modern, don't you think? Full of discords and crazy rhythms and—well, you know—awfully modern. I may not know music, but I know what I—well, it's awfully modern."
>
> The Friday audience seemed to like the Concerto and it applauded the short, white-haired composer when he appeared on stage and bowed with grave shyness. So much new music is heard once or twice and then forgotten that I hope Mr. Bartók's Concerto will be a fortunate exception to the role. Let's hear it again this season.[1]

The review by Rudolph Elie Jr., on the other hand, is remarkably prescient:

> It is hardly necessary at this point to remark on the strength of the musical personality disclosed by Bartók's music. His Orchestral Concerto, given yesterday for the first time, is a work which must rank as the composer's masterpiece, which is to say it must also rank among the musical masterpieces of recent years.

201

. . . It may be reading things into the work which are not there, but the feeling of increasing optimism, of increasing strength and vigor is strongly conveyed in this work, and I have more than a suspicion that it is a highly personal, even autobiographical music.

. . . The composer came to the stage to acknowledge the applause, of which there was a heartening volume. Yes, if a composition of transcendent musical art may be defined as one which, in its own way, is a summation of all that has gone before, then the Concerto for Orchestra is a work of art . . . and a great one.[2]

When the work was performed by the Boston Symphony Orchestra in Carnegie Hall, New York, on January 10, 1945, the audience applauded while Koussevitzky repeatedly led Bartók from the wings and finally left him alone on the stage to savor—at long last!—this unprecedented acclamation of his genius. Oscar Thomson's review, however, was far less enthusiastic:

In the writing for the instruments all is clear and vital. But there is much that eludes, perplexes and mystifies the listener. He is confronted with a clutter of ideas that do not seem significant. The themes, in their multiplicity, tend to pass him by. Yet the spirit of Bartók is in this music. The listener feels it, and it leaves him troubled.

. . . What will be the future of this concerto? It is a brash soul that attempts to say. What, indeed, is the future of any of Bartók's major works?[3]

The response to Thomson's pessimistic queries was given four years later, in Howard Taubman's review of the first recording of the Concerto for Orchestra, by the Pittsburgh Symphony Orchestra under the leadership of Fritz Reiner:

Since the première by the Boston Symphony under Serge Koussevitzky in December 1944, it has won increasingly wide acceptance. And one can unhesitatingly predict that before long it will become one of the staples of the contemporary repertory.

. . . It deserves no less. It is one of Bartók's most powerful, moving and accessible scores. It combines rugged strength and affecting sentiment in a wholly indigenous mixture. The rhythms, harmonies and instrumental effects are the composer's own, but everything is unified knowingly for expressive purpose. This is the work of a master whose form and style are indivisible, and who has something meaningful to say.[4]

In 1981, the centenary of Béla Bartók's birth was commemorated by the international music world. Leading the way were performances of his Concerto for Orchestra—the most frequently performed orchestral composition of this century—and the six string quartets that are acknowledged as the greatest chamber works since Beethoven's last quartets. Also featured were such major works as the three concertos for piano and two for violin, the opera, *Duke Bluebeard's Castle*, *The Miraculous Mandarin* ballet, *Cantata Profana*, and Music for Strings, Percussion, and Celesta. Scholarly symposia were convened for the presentation of papers on analytical, theoretical, and ethnomusicological aspects of Bartók's compositions, and these were followed by a substantial number of publications in various languages. One of the outstanding contributions is the essay by György Kroó, Hungary's distinguished musicologist, in which certain works composed by eleven of his Hungarian contemporaries are described in terms of Bartókian influence. He adds:

> From the ethical point of view—and this is very important to a generation turning away from its hypocritical predecessors—Bartók became a symbol of uncompromising purity, the ideal of the lonely revolutionary in sharp contrast to the state-subsidized poet of the people. . . . Bartók held up a mirror to the Hungarian composers, so that they could learn there is more to art than service and fun; art also has to tackle, interpret, and give utterance to the great issues of the age and life itself. It is in this respect that Bartók contributed to molding the character of Hungarian music in the 1960s. If he had not existed, the feeble sprout of new Hungarian composition would have been withered by winds from Darmstadt, Warsaw, or even from Rome or Paris.[5]

Today the "massive and complex" literature about Bartók's life and music is another affirmation of his stature in music history, yet the question of his influence on other composers is inadequately addressed.[6] In a number of cases, the literature refers to Bartók in a general way, without substantive evidence. The purpose of this closing chapter, therefore, is to explore the impact of Bartók's musical language on specific works by those latter-day composers who have achieved widespread international recognition: Alberto Ginastera (Argentina), Benjamin Britten (United Kingdom), György Ligeti (Hungary), George Crumb (United States), Witold Lutosławski (Poland), and Olivier Messiaen (France).

Alberto Ginastera (1916–1983)

At age fifteen, during his years as a piano student at the Buenos Aires Conservatory, Ginastera attended a piano recital by Artur Rubinstein. When Bartók's *Allegro Barbaro* was played, Ginastera recalls that he felt the impact of a discovery and the bewilderment of a revelation: the music provided him with a new approach to forging a national music based on South American musical folklore. He was struck by the rhythmic strength of the piece, the cellular melodic construction, and the new, percussive piano technique. In 1937, under Bartók's influence, he composed his Argentine Dances for Piano, a work that initiates Ginastera's period of objective nationalism: "My folklore imaginaire begins there, with its polytonal harmonizations, its strong, marked rhythms—the Bartókian feverish excitement—all within a total pianism where the spirit of a national music is recreated." Later on, when he was able to acquire and analyze Bartók scores, he found the answer to another long-held concern: the problem of form and style.[7]

The outcome of his Bartók research was a change in style from objective to subjective nationalism or, in Bartókian terms, to compositions that reflect the spirit or atmosphere of folk music. The new style marks Ginastera's second period, whose first significant work is the Sonata no. 1 for Piano (1952), "written with polytonal and twelve-tone procedures. The composer does not employ any folkloric material, but instead introduces in the thematic texture rhythmic and melodic motives whose expressive tension has a pronounced Argentine accent."[8] The first movement, in sonata form and with A as the fundamental tone, has its first theme based on the five degrees of the symmetrical (Hungarian!) form of the pentatonic scale, A–C–D–E–G. The harmony is derived from a hexachord of the A-octatonic scale, A–C–C♯–E♭–E–F♯, which interacts with the pentatonic melody to form an octachordal polymode. And the rhythm emulates Bartókian "Bulgarian rhythm" (m. 8: 8/8 = 2 + 3 + 3) and multiple time signatures (Example 10.1).

Example 10.1. Ginastera, Sonata no. 1 for Piano, first movement, mm. 1–7.

The pentatonic structure of the lyrical second theme is likewise symmetrical, transposed to B as the fundamental, B–D–E–F♯–A. The contrapuntal bass part consists of the octatonic hexachord, B–C–F–F♯–G♯–A, with an added degree, E, as a diatonic intrusion. Example 10.2 shows a Z-cell (a tetrachord consisting of two tritones), B–C–F–F♯, that appears

Example 10.2. Ginastera, Sonata, first movement, mm. 52–55.

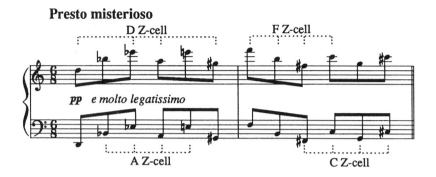

Example 10.3. Ginastera, Sonata, second movement, mm. 1–2.

prominently as a local adjacency.[9] The interaction of pentatonic, octa-tonic, and cellular components thus yields another octachordal polymode.

The second movement opens with twin-bar unisonal arpeggios that are configured as interlocked Z-cells: D–E♭–G♯–A and A–B♭–E♭–E in measure 1, F–F♯–B–C and C–C♯–F♯–G in measure 2 (Example 10.3). The ingenious cellular organization, moreover, is derived from the partition of the twelve-tone chromatic scale into two octatonic substructures, each with D as the principal tone, D–E♭–F–F♯–G♯–A–B–C and D–E–F–G–G♯–B♭–B–C♯.

The first theme in the third movement represents an apotheosis of the normal chord (E–A–D–G–B–E) of the six-string guitar, which is "the

Example 10.4. Ginastera, Sonata, third movement, mm. 1–7.

characteristic instrument of the gauchos and of the folk music of the pampas. From [Ginastera's] earliest works to the most recent, this chord appears as a sort of 'signature.'"[10] An early example is the first bar of Ginastera's *Malambo* for piano (1940), in which the natural hexachord appears as an unmeasured arpeggio. In the Sonata the signature chord is transformed into a D-octatonic hexachord, B–F♯–C–E♭–A–D, which appears as a prelude, interlude, and postlude in the movement (Example 10.4).

The fourth movement is a rhythmic tour de force based on the Aeolian mode that combines the hemiolic meter of the *gato*—the most important dance of the Argentine countryside—with such *malambo* rhythm schemata as (6/16) ♫♫ ♫, ♫ ♫♫, and ♫ ♫.[11] Example 10.5 shows the twin-bar hemiola that pervades the movement (mm. 1–2) and the C♯, D, and A (tonic) Z-cells (mm.168, 171, and 183, respectively). The work ends with emphatic rendition of tetrachords representing the lower strings of the Argentine guitar.

Example 10.5. Ginastera, Sonata, fourth movement, mm. 1–2, 168–171, and 182–184.

Benjamin Britten (1913–1976)

Britten's early studies with the English composer, Frank Bridge, included an intensive examination of works by Bartók, Schoenberg, and other contemporaries. His admiration for the great Hungarian composer is evident in a musical tribute to Bartók's memory, which appears in *A Young Person's Guide to the Orchestra*. This work—composed in 1946, the year after Bartók's death—is a set of variations based on a theme from Henry Purcell's incidental music (ca. 1697) to the tragedy, *Abdelazer or the Moor's Revenge*. The D-minor triad that opens Purcell's theme (Example 10.6a) is transformed into a major-seventh chord, G–B–D–F♯, in Britten's Variation B (Example 10.6b). A subsequent transposition of the seventh chord, D–F♯–A–C♯, appears in Variation F (Example 10.6c).

Variation F, moreover, is in the same key and in close motivic and rhythmic connection to the first theme in Bartók's *Two Portraits*, op. 5, for Orchestra (Example 10.7).[12]

In Britten's choral masterpiece, *War Requiem* (1961), "traditional forms and procedures (fugue, chaconne, ritornello, etc.) serve as the framework for nontraditional pitch-set relations, which include the modal, octatonic, and whole tone interactions characteristic of the Bartók and

Example 10.6. Britten, A Young Person's Guide to the Orchestra, *(a) Theme A, (b) Variation B, and (c) Variation F.*

Andante

Example 10.7. Bartók, Two Portraits *(1907–1908), first movement, mm. 1–4.*

Stravinsky idioms."[13] In the "Confutatis" for men's voices, orchestral accompaniment consists of triads based on the Aeolian mode, A–B–C–D–E–F–G (mm. 1–2), followed by the ascending form of the A-melodic-minor scale, A–B–C–D–E–F♯–G♯ (mm. 3–4) and the emphatic timpani rendition of broken-chord inversions of the tonic triad, A–C–E, during the baritone setting of "Be slowly lifted up"(Example 10.7).[14]

The tritone setting, A–E♭, of the text "black arm" (a metaphor for a cannon), and the minor-second degree in the chordal accompaniment (m. 5: B♭), transform the bimodal pitch collection on A into an eleven-tone, Phrygian-colored polymode, A–B♭–C–D–E♭–F–G/A–B–C–D–E–G♭ (= F♯)–G♯. Moreover, the cadential melodic tritone, A–E♭, is vertically projected into the final chord, where it is combined harmonically with a whole-tone segment, G♭–B♭–C–D. This produces a symmetrical formation, G♭–A–B♭–C–D–E♭–[G♭], that implies the presence of two gapped Z-cells, A–B♭–E♭–[] and A–D–E♭–[], both framed by the polymode's tonic

Example 10.8. Britten, War Requiem *("Confutatis"), "Be slowly lifted up,"mm. 1–5.*

tritone. Thus, traditional modal constructions are absorbed into a nontraditional harmonic context.

In the opening of the *War Requiem*, we already find the twelve-tone chromatic scale partitioned into contrasting pitch collections: the antiphonal declamation of the tritone degrees, F♯ and C, by the chorus and tolling bells; the theme in D–harmonic minor, D–E–F–G–A–B♭–C♯, by the upper winds and strings; the E-octatonic scale, E–F–G–G♯–A♯–B–C♯–D, in the lower winds; and the pedal on A, by the tuba, timpani, and piano. "At the second (ritornello) orchestral statement (m. 6 to no. 1), the original E-octatonic scale is replaced in the lower winds by ascending parallel five-note segments of two whole-tone scales, a minor third apart, B–C♯–D♯–F–G and D–E–F♯–A♭–B♭."[15]

Another reminiscence of Bartókian procedure occurs in Britten's opera, *Death in Venice* (1973). In Act I, Scene 4, the novelist Gustav von Aschenbach arrives at his hotel and is welcomed by the Manager, then shown to his room "with a specially fine view. The wide sweep of this panorama recalls the moment in Bartók's *Duke Bluebeard's Castle* when Judith flings open the fifth door to reveal a vast, magnificent landscape. But here it is a lagoonscape instead of a landscape that meets Achenbach's gaze."[16]

György Ligeti (1923–)

The Ligeti family had been Hungarian citizens, domiciled in Transylvania until the Treaty of Trianon (1920) ceded the territory to Romania. György Ligeti's musical education began in 1941, at the Conservatory of Music in the Transylvanian provincial center of Kolozsvár (now Cluj-Napoca, Romania). In September, 1945, after the end of World War II, he resumed his composition studies at the Budapest Academy of Music, did field research in Romanian folk music, and was appointed to the faculty of the Budapest Academy in 1950, where he taught harmony and counterpoint. During the next six years, following in the footsteps of his Hungarian contemporaries, he was greatly influenced by Bartók's works.

> You know, he was the great Hungarian composer, and I knew very little other modern music: a little bit of Stravinsky—*Petrushka* but not yet *Le Sacre*—no Schoenberg. Bartók was the big genius: I still think he is, for

me. I have several of those early pieces. The style isn't totally Bartók: you know, when you are young you oscillate a bit, so there are some little Stravinsky influences. Even my first quartet, from 1953–4, is still Bartók. . . . In those last two years in Budapest, 1955 and 1956, very gradually I came to know all of Bartók. . . .[17]

Ligeti fled to Austria after the Hungarian uprising of 1956, and in 1957 wrote the analytic notes that preface the reprinted pocket score of Bartók's String Quartet no. 5 (Universal Edition, W. Ph. V. 167). Following a brief exploration of electronic music composition in 1961, he "developed his technique of chromatic complexes, taking it almost to its ultimate consequence: the removal of melody, harmony, and rhythm as distinct features."[18] This technique stems from his work in the electronic music studio.

For instance, I had to read up psychoacoustics at that time, and I learned that if you have a sequence of sounds where the difference in time is less than fifty milliseconds then you don't hear them any more as individual sounds. This gave me the idea of creating a very close succession in instrumental music. . . . [T]his kind of cluster thinking I think probably came from the area of Bartók, much more than from the Viennese.[19]

In May 1978, Ligeti composed *Hungarian Rock (Chaconne)*, for Harpsichord, which in certain respects owes much to Bartók as the source of inspiration. The piece is based on the seventeenth- and eighteenth-century keyboard *chaconne*, a set of variations in triple meter, where the theme is a harmonized basso ostinato (a constantly repeated set of bass notes) and the melodic material (the variations) is often connected to the theme by certain motives. Ligeti's "theme" is really a one-bar motif, G–F–C–D–A, repeated to form a quaternary ostinato in which the harmony includes the twelve degrees of the chromatic scale (Example 10.9).

The polymetric time signatures indicate additive rhythm in the bass staff, structured in Bartók's so-called Bulgarian rhythm, and divisive rhythm (compound 9/8 time) in the treble staff. The harmonization of the fixed theme changes from bar to bar—similar to the innovative procedure in Bartók's opera, *Duke Bluebeard's Castle* (the "fifth door" scene: Bluebeard's domain)—where the chord progressions are triads in root position, G–F–C–D–A (m. 1), second inversion, C–B♭–F–G–D♯ dim. (m. 2),

Vivacissimo molto ritmico

Example 10.9. Ligeti, Hungarian Rock (Chaconne), *mm. 1–4.*

and first inversion, E♭–D♭–A♭–B♭–F (m. 3), and also appear as implied third-inversion seventh chords, A–G–D–E–B (m. 4).

The variations begin in the first section, based on the G-Dorian mode, G–A–B♭–C–D–E–F, where each melodic degree is juxtaposed as a concordant member of the respective underlying chord (mm. 5–16). Dissonant polytonality and interesting cross rhythms occur when a motif is rhythmically displaced (Example 10.10). Bartók called such displacement "shifted rhythm,"which he found in certain Romanian instrumental folk melodies.[20] The use of shifted rhythm results in the creation of a phrase-length entity based on a single motif, and Ligeti uses the device for that purpose throughout the work.

In a more recent interview (1990), Ligeti was reminded that in earlier ones he indicated that Bartók had been crucial at the beginning of his career. In response to a question about his present relationship to Bartók's music, he stated that "as far as tonality is concerned, I have returned to Bartók, while at the same time I have done with atonality altogether. . . . Now I have the courage to be 'old-fashioned.' I don't want to return to the nineteenth century, but I am no longer interested in such categories as avantegarde, modernism or atonality."[21]

Example 10.10. Ligeti, Hungarian Rock (Chaconne), *mm. 78–81.*

George Crumb (1929–)

The influence of Bartók's "Night's music" is apparent in Crumb's early works: *Night Music I*, for Soprano, Piano, Celesta, and Two Percussion (1963), and Four Nocturnes *(Night Music II)*, for Violin and Piano (1964).[22] He turned again to Bartók in 1972, dedicating the first volume of *Makrokosmos* for amplified piano to "B.B. IN MEMORIAM,"and in 1973, the second. The third volume (1974), for two amplified pianos and percussion, "symbolic of Bartók's Sonata for Two Pianos and Percussion, makes use of three fundamental pitch-collections which summarize the composer's vocabulary."[23] It features three fundamental pitch collections: a chromatic trichord, consisting of a whole tone and an intermediary semitone that is usually displaced by an octave (i.e., G–A♭–F♯); a whole-tone trichord, such as a major second or major third combined with a tri-tone (G–A–C♯ or G–B–C♯); and a third type, a tritone combined with a major seventh (G–C♯–F♯). These pitch collections apparently are attenu-ated derivatives of Bartók's tetrachordal pitch-collections: the X-cell (F–F♯–G–A♭); Y-cell (G–A–B–C♯); and Z-cell (G–C–C♯–F♯).

Bartók's *Mikrokosmos* (1926–1939) is a multipurpose work consisting of 153 pieces for teaching piano technique and musicianship, many of which are suitable for concert purposes, and which incorporate the various folk- and art-music aspects of his "little world" of composition.[24] On the other hand, each of the first two volumes of Crumb's *Makrokosmos* is for a piano with a conventional microphone suspended over the bass strings, requiring additional techniques for activating the piano strings with the finger or metal objects and consisting of "Twelve Fantasy-Pieces after the Zodiac."

> The zodiac, like the metaphor implied in the idea of a macrocosmos, is a spatial concept, with a special implication of the night—the only time when the cosmos as astronomical/astrological phenomenon can be ob-served. The complex associations of the zodiac provided the composer with an ideal motivation: verbal, suggestive, expandable but not so spe-cific as to delimit form or to require a voice or a text.[25]

There are no time signatures or bar lines; brackets with numerals specify the time in seconds to be allocated to specific notational configura-tions. The autographic, oversize score apparently was required to enter the

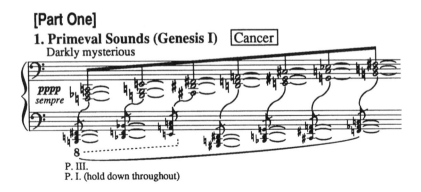

Example 10.11. Crumb, Makrokosmos I, *no. 1, first system.*

substantial number of conventional and invented signs and symbols, explanatory text blocks, and special music notations. The first piece in Volume I opens with a series of nonfunctional minor triads in their root position, first inversion and second inversion in both staves, where the grace-note chords in the lower staff are positioned a tritone below the principal-note chords in the upper staff. The twelve-tone chromatic scale is partitioned into an array of discrete six-note octatonic segments. These unfold as hexachords formed by the paired, tritone-related (grace-note/principal-note) triads (Example 10.11).

Witold Lutoslawski (1913–1994)

When a state publishing house was founded in postwar Poland in 1945, to promote national music culture, Lutosławski received a commission to write piano music based on Polish folk melodies. Unlike Bartók, whose work he had studied with great admiration, he had no background in ethnomusicology as collector or researcher. He therefore selected twelve previously published folk tunes, representing several different parts of Poland, and transcribed them as Folk Melodies for Piano (1945). Because he had neither the time nor the inclination to devise an original tonal language based on Polish folk music, he applied certain ingredients of Bartók's tonal language for the accompaniment and melodic variation (Example 10.12).

Example 10.12. Lutosławski, Folk Melodies, no. 3, mm. 5–12.

Inasmuch as the modality of the D-minor melody is ambiguous—the modal sixth degree (Dorian B or Aeolian B♭) is missing—the composer provides both degrees (in mm. 7–8) in the octatonic tetrachord, F–A♭–B♭–B, which accompanies the caesura (that is, end tone) of the first melody section. This tetrachord is an octatonic expansion of the preceding Z-cell, D–G–A♭–D♭, both chords together forming the heptachordal octatonic segment, D–[]–F–G–A♭–B♭–B–D♭. The modal-diatonic tetrachord, D–E–F–G (R.H.), which also belongs to this octatonic collection, completes the latter by providing the missing degree second degree (E). The upper (gapped) modal tetrachord, A–[]–C–D (mm. 9–12, R.H.), is also reinterpreted by its accompaniment as part of a more complex polymodal symmetry, A–C–D–E♭–E–F♯–[]. The latter implies the presence of two interlocking, inversionally related octatonic segments, A–C–D–E♭–F♯ and A–F♯–E–E♭–C, which represent the two remaining octatonic collections, respectively. Thus, the diatonic-octatonic interactions between antecedent and consequent phrases of the melody and accompaniment, and their fusion, produce all twelve tones of the D-chromatic scale.

Two years later Lutosławski completed his First Symphony (1941–1947). The second movement, *Poco adagio*, opens with a "long and fully developed melody [whose] brooding accompaniment recalls the first movement of Bartók's Music for Strings, Percussion, and Celesta."[26] The second theme begins with an octatonic pitch collection (Example 10.13).

Bucolics, a five-movement suite for piano (1952), is based on a collection of folk tunes from the Kurpie region of Poland. The first piece is a fast round-dance melody in G major, whose rhythm stems from the Ruthenian (Ukrainian) kolomyjka (Example 10.14).[27]

Example 10.13. Lutosławski, First Symphony, mm. 39–40.

In the middle section of the ternary form the folk tune appears in the lower staff, transposed to E♭ as principal tone (Example 10.15). The accompaniment, on the other hand, emphasizes a seemingly unrelated trichord, A–C♯–D. The juxtaposition of theme and accompaniment, however, produces a nine-tone Lydian/Mixolydian polymode, E♭–F–G–A–B♭–C–D/E♭–F–G–A♭–B♭–C♯ (mm. 39–44). And in place of the expected folk-tune ending, B♭–B♭–C–D–E♭–E♭, the last two bars are configured as passagework in the minor form of the C-octatonic scale, C–D–E♭–F–G–G♯–A♯–B. This concatenation of modal and octatonic entities for the transmutation of folk music into art music is one of the fundamental procedures in Bartók's system of composition.

Lutosławski's Concerto for Orchestra (1950–1954) is a monumental work in three movements, based on folk-music sources from Masovia (the region around Warsaw). In it, writes Steven Stucky, "folk songs and dances are mere raw material from which he fashions not only themes but also the tiny motivic fragments of which to build up an elaborate contrapuntal edifice. Folk tunes are never simply quoted: they are radically transformed, manipulated, made to serve the composer's vision."[28] Other than the use of folk-music sources, Lutosławski's composition has little in common with Bartók's Concerto for Orchestra, according to Stucky.

Example 10.14. Lutosławski, Bucolics 1: source melody from the Kurpie region.

(poco sostenuto)

Example 10.15. Lutosławski, Bucolics 1, *mm. 39–46.*

It is easy to suppose that Lutosławski's Concerto for Orchestra must have been deeply influenced by the well-known Bartók work of the same name. Lutosławski had indeed come under Bartók's influence in the late forties, and it is difficult to believe that his love for that composer's music did not filter into his own concerto. But aside from the obvious coincidence that both composers' works contain a chorale, one can search in vain for clear traces of Bartók in the actual musical text of the Lutosławski concerto.[29]

The *Funeral Music,* for String Orchestra (1954–1958), intended to commemorate the tenth anniversary of Bartók's death (1955), has as its distinctive feature "the application of limited serial techniques in quite novel ways . . . is an experiment he has never really repeated . . . a 'diversion' from the main stream of the composer's stylistic evolution."[30] The work opens with a twelve-tone row, beginning with F and ending with C, which consists of alternating tritones and semitones. The series may also be construed as interlocking Z-cell partitions of the chromatic scale, which cycle at the interval of a perfect fifth (Example 10.16).

Example 10.16. Lutosławski, Funeral Music, *mm. 1–4.*

According to Joe Brumbeloe, "While Lutosławski did not attempt to imitate Bartók's style in this work for string orchestra, he did admit that his lifelong study of Bartók's music could lead to some unintentional resemblances. Perhaps one of the most interesting manifestations of Bartók's influence can be seen in the extent to which Lutosławski makes use of symmetrical relationships to organize various structural levels of *Trauermusik*."[31]

Olivier Messiaen (1903–1992)

In 1918, at the precocious age of ten, Messiaen's harmony teacher gave him the score of Debussy's opera, *Pelléas et Mélisande*, to study. He later recalled this event as "a real bombshell . . . probably the most decisive influence of my life."[32] He entered the Paris Conservatoire in 1926, where he studied composition with Paul Dukas and became "very well acquainted with the music of Bartók and Stravinsky."[33] During his last year at the Conservatoire, Messiaen composed his Eight Preludes for Piano (1929), which to a certain extent commingles the tonal languages of Debussy and Bartók with derivative or innovative pitch collections from Messiaen's so-called Modes of Limited Transposition.[34] Thus, for example, the whole-tone scale is designated as Mode 1, the octatonic scale is Mode 2, and Messiaen's nine-tone pitch collection is Mode 3 (Example 10.17).

The fourth piece, *Instants défunts*, is in a rondo form that contains two alternating themes, an "Interlude" and a "Coda," with D as the principal tone. The first theme opens with a tonic Z-cell motif in the lower staff, D–G–A♭–C♯ (Example 10.18).

The rhythm schema of the Z-cell motif represents the first application of Messiaen's invention, "non-retrogradable rhythm":

> It consists of two groups of time-values, the one is the retrograde of the other, and they enclose a free value in the middle which is common to both groups. Whether we read the rhythm from left to right or from right

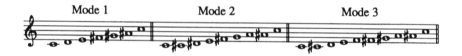

Example 10.17. (Messiaen Modes)

Example 10.18. Messiaen, Prelude no. 1, for Piano, mm. 1–4.

to left, the arrangement of the time values remains the same. It is an absolutely self-contained rhythm.[35]

The Interlude features a sequence of Z-cells, C–F♯–B–E×, B♭–E–A–D♯, and A–D♯–A♭–D (mm. 27–30), and the Coda ends ambiguously with a melodic configuration of tritones from the D whole-tone scale, D–G♯–E–A♯–F♯–B♯, in the upper staff (mm. 45–46).

Messiaen's preoccupation with rhythm schemata led him to investigate Greek versification, the provincial "decî-Tâlas" of ancient India, and Bulgarian rhythm in Bartók works. His interest in Bulgarian rhythm apparently stems from such "non-retrogradable" rhythms as 3 + 2 + 2 + 3/8 and 2 + 3 + 3 + 2/8 in the Scherzo movement of Bartók's String Quartet no. 5, and 3 + 2 + 3/8 in *Bulgarian Dance 4* (*Mikrokosmos* no. 151). In any event, Bulgarian rhythm appears as 2 + 3/16 in Messiaen's *Regard de l'Esprit de Joie* (*Vingt Regards sur l'Enfant-Jésus*, for Piano [1944], no. 8).[36] It is also noteworthy that Bartók's "Night's music" and birdsong motifs were other sources which became features of Messiaen's musical language. In *Regards des hauteurs* (*Vingt Regards*, no. 5), the lark's song begins with a high-pitched motif, B♭–A–E♭–E.[37]

BÉLA BARTÓK'S STYLISTIC
DEVELOPMENT: AN OVERVIEW

Excepting aspects of the lifework of Alberto Ginastera, Bartók's musical growth differs markedly from that of the composers listed. His compositions can be divided into three distinct stages, each one preceded

by a two-year period of creative "stagnation." The first stage, which
Bartók modestly referred to as his student years, was the recapitulation of
nineteenth-century Hungarian musical dialect. This dialect is based on
the national melodies composed by dilettantes from the upper classes,
which were widely disseminated by Gypsy bands and the romanticized
keyboard and orchestral transcriptions of Liszt, Brahms, Sarasate, and
other contemporaries.[38] Bartók used these melodies or their imitations in
his early works, such as the *Kossuth* symphonic poem and Rhapsody
op. 1, for Piano and Orchestra, together with harmonic procedures derived from the works of Richard Strauss and the technique of thematic
transformation, including the use of whole-tone and octatonic pitch collections, from Liszt.

The second stage began when Bartók and his close friend Zoltán Kodály
embarked on field trips to collect musical folklore—the true folk music of
Hungary—in peasant villages. Since the rural areas were also inhabited by
minority peoples of what was then Greater Hungary, who were for the most
part Slovaks and Romanians, Bartók collected and transcribed multiple
thousands of their melodies and, in addition to remarkable modal, rhythmic, and performance peculiarities, discovered reciprocal relationships in
the material of those peasants living in close proximity to the Hungarians.
His scholarly studies of the collected material eventually led to monumental
publications and international recognition as an outstanding ethnomusicologist. Concomitantly, Bartók's absorption and fusion of the peculiarities of
peasant music, including those later discovered among Yugoslav minorities
and North African Arabs, provided him with a unique musical mother
tongue, enabling him to devise different levels in the transmutation of folk
music into art music.[39]

He began with the traditional folk-song setting, but his accompaniments
to such exclusively monodic melodies were based on their structural attributes rather than on the commonplace tonic-dominant progressions then in
vogue. A second type of transcription emphasizes the accompaniment, so
that the peasant tune serves only as a musical motto. A third type is the invention of a theme that imitates a folk melody, and the highest level is
reached when the composition reflects the atmosphere or spirit of folk
music. Thus, for example, an abstract work might have Hungarian dotted
rhythm and pentatonic turns, Slovak emphatic rendition of the Lydian tritone, or Romanian bagpipe motif structure and nondiatonic folk modes.
With regard to Western art-music sources, Bartók turned to Debussy's in-

novations in harmonic construction and progression, and to Beethoven's further development of such architectonic forms as the sonata and the rondo. But the major stylistic development was in tonal language, namely, the concept of polymodal chromaticism. Following Bach's juxtaposition of ascending and descending forms of the melodic minor scale in contrapuntal passages, Bartók observed that juxtaposition of Lydian and Phrygian folk modes, based on the same fundamental note, provides the twelve tones of the chromatic scale. Furthermore, the characteristic "color" degrees of these modes—the lowered Phrygian second and the raised Lydian fourth—when combined with their common tones, the first and fifth modal degrees (posthumously designated the "Z-cell"), provides tonal centricity. Thus Bartók found the means to create a unique species of twelve-tone polymodality, which antedates and is unrelated to the composition of atonal or serial music.

The third stage of his compositional development reflects another, previously held Bartók concept: to synthesize Bach's transcendent counterpoint, Debussy's harmonic innovations, and Beethoven's progressive form, assuring the validity of the twentieth-century product by incorporating the newly won fusion of folk-music sources. Bartók, a virtuoso pianist and editor of teaching editions of Bach keyboard works, nevertheless concluded that the latter's strict contrapuntal style would be incompatible with his Hungarian temperament, which included an obvious bent toward transformation and variation of his musical subject matter, and he looked elsewhere for adding the polyphonic dimension to his works. Fortuitously, during a concert tour in Italy, he acquired and performed the keyboard works of Italian Baroque composers—Frescobaldi, della Ciaia, Rossi, Marcello, and Zipoli—and subsquently edited them for publication as piano transcriptions. Style analysis of this music disclosed modal juxtaposition, free counterpoint, chromatic motifs, and other attributes, which Bartók applied for the first time in his Concerto no. 1, for Piano and Orchestra (1926).

Bartók continued his folk-music research, extending it to Bulgarian and Turkish ethnic areas, and added a number of their characteristic peculiarities to his musical language. His increasing use of the Phrygian form of the octatonic scale (the alternation of minor and major seconds)—whose mirror inversion produces the minor form of the octatonic scale (alternating major and minor seconds), where the common fundamental note serves as the dual axis of symmetry of the combined scales—provides another means of partitioning the twelve-tone chromatic scale and enables the seamless interaction of diatonic and nondiatonic pitch collections. Finally, Bartók's treatment of the piano as a percussion instrument, somewhat similar to the hammered cimbalom (Hungarian-Gypsy dulcimer); invention of special methods of tone production on stringed and other instruments; and creation of works that highlight the standard percussion instruments of the orchestra are other features of his unique style of composition.

On January 10, 1931, Bartók wrote a lengthy letter to a Romanian ethnomusicologist in connection with the latter's forthcoming radio talk about the composer. In the letter, Bartók unequivocally objects to being labeled as a Romanian composer:

> My views are as follows: I consider myself as a Hungarian composer. The fact that the melodies in some of my own original compositions were inspired by or based on Rumanian folk-songs is no justification for classing me as a *compositorul român*. . . . If your view were correct, I could just as easily be called a "Slovak composer;" and then I should be a composer of three nationalities! As I am being so frank, I should like to give you some idea of what I think about all this.
>
> My creative work, just because it arises from 3 sources (Hungarian, Rumanian, Slovakian), might be regarded as the embodiment of the very concept of integration so much emphasized in Hungary today. . . . My own idea, however—of which I have been fully conscious since I found myself as a composer—is the brotherhood of all peoples, brotherhood in spite of all wars and conflicts. I try—to the best of my ability—to serve this idea in my music; therefore I don't reject any influence, be it Slovakian, Rumanian, Arabic or from any other source. The source must only be clean, fresh and healthy![40]

Bartók's idea is nowhere more transparent than in his Concerto for Orchestra, a monument of Western music that also represents an embodiment of his compositional processes. Indeed, this representation has been compared to the role of *The Art of the Fugue* in Bach's oeuvre. So far as Bartók's place in twentieth-century music is concerned, the pithy conclusion of Mosco Carner is offered as an equally fitting close to this book:

[O]f the three musicians who dominated the musical scene during the first half of the twentieth century—Stravinsky, Schoenberg, and Bartók—it is the Hungarian master who, despite his immense intellectual control, remained nearest to the instinctual, the irrational in music and thus to the Dionysian spirit in art. He is the supreme example of the artist who, in the dialectic between emotional "primitivism" and intellectual sophistication, never allowed the second ascendancy over the first.[41]

NOTES

PART ONE

Bartók's Musical Language

Chapter 1:   *Childhood and Youth: 1881–1899*

1. *Béla Bartók Essays,* ed. Benjamin Suchoff (Lincoln, Nebr., and London, 1992), 408.The town is now Sînnicolau Mare, Romania.

2. Béla Bartók, Jr. "Béla Bartók's Diseases,"*Studia Musicologica* 23 (1981): 427.

3. *Bartók Béla levelei* (Béla Bartók Letters), ed. János Demény (Budapest, 1951), 203–217. Readers interested in other details concerning Bartók's childhood and adolescence, in English and including extracts from his mother's memoirs, should refer to Halsey Stevens, *The Life and Music of Béla Bartók*, rev. Malcolm Gillies (London, 1992), 3–11; Jószef Ujfalussy, *Béla Bartók* (Budapest and Boston, 1971), 15–35; Lajos Lesznai, *Bartók* (London, 1973), 1–35; and Tibor Tallián, *Béla Bartók* (Budapest, 1981), 25.

4. The first page, consisting of thirty-two bars, appears in facsimile in Ferenc Bónis, *Bartók Béla élete képekben és dokumentumokban* (Béla Bartók's Life in Pictures and Documents, Budapest, 1980), 36. According to Denijs Dille, the complete piece contains ninety-two bars and its duration is approximately two minutes. See his *Thematische Verzeichnis der Jugendwerke Béla Bartóks 1890–1904* (Budapest, 1974), 53.

5. The *ländler* is an Austrian folk dance in slow 3/4 time; it was the precursor of the waltz.

6. According to the Hungarian-born musicologist Otto Gombosi (1902–1955), Bartók played "the opening movement of Beethoven's C Major Sonata op. 2,

no. 3, not of the 'Waldstein' Sonata. (This was confirmed to me in a conversation by
Bartók, in 1943)." See Gombosi's unfinished biography of Bartók in the private collection of Peter Bartók.

7. The composition is preserved in a student's six-stave manuscript book; it
consists of thirty-two pages in Paula Bartók's autograph. See Dille, *Thematische Verzeichnis*, 63–69.

8. The *csárdás* is a Hungarian dance in duple time, with alternating slow and
fast sections.

9. *Kolomyjka* rhythm is a characteristic feature of a Ruthenian (that is, Ukrainian) round dance type that appears in Bartók's mature works (see Example 3.43) as
well as in the vocal and instrumental music of Hungarian, Romanian, Slovak, and
other rural villages of eastern Europe.

10. *Béla Bartók Essays*, 408. Ferenc Erkel was the most popular and important
Hungarian nationalist composer in the nineteenth century. His position in the history
of Hungarian music might be compared to that of Bedrich Smetana (1824–1884) in
Czechoslovakia. Although Erkel's style is less thoroughly and authentically national,
and his talent considerably less, his work was important at that time and found a
strong response in the Hungarian public. His *Festival* Overture and operas on national subjects, *Bánk Bán* and *Hunyadi László* are still performed in Hungary today,
and are available on Hungaraton (Budapest) records.

11. *Béla Bartók Essays*, 408.

12. Ibid., 489–490.

Chapter 2:   Summary of Hungarian Musical Dialect: 1900–1905

1. Béla Bartók, *The Hungarian Folk Song*, ed. Benjamin Suchoff (Albany,
1981), 99.

2. *The Selected Writings of Zoltán Kodály*, ed. Ferenc Bónis (London, 1974),
103.

3. *Béla Bartók Essays*, ed. Benjamin Suchoff (Lincoln, Nebr., and London,
1992), 453.

4. Ibid., 409.

5. The third theme is borrowed from the Scherzo (third movement) of Bartók's
Symphony in E-flat (1902). Publication details are given in Elliott Antokoletz, *Béla
Bartók: A Guide to Research* (New York, 1988), 30.

6. The outcome of the transformation is a melodic construction remarkably
similar to the first theme of the *Kossuth* symphonic poem.

7. The open fifth as a neutral closing chord is an attribute of Bartók's later polymodal chromaticism.

8. *Manchester Guardian,* February 19, 1904. See also Malcolm Gillies, *Bartók in Britain* (New York, 1989), 5–8.

9. *Béla Bartók Essays,* 409.

10. In 1909, Zoltán Kodály collected the peasant version in a village in northern Hungary (now Slovakia).

11. The Székely (or Seklers) are a Transylvanian-Hungarian people. Because of their remote geographical position, they "were naturally better enabled to preserve the old style of highly ornamented singing." See Bartók, *The Hungarian Folk Song,* 16, 38.

12. Letter dated August 15, 1905. See *Béla Bartók Letters,* ed. János Demény (London, 1971), 50.

13. Zoltán Kodály, "Matyusföldi gyűtés," *Ethnographia* 16 (1906): 300–305. In his essay "Bartók the Folklorist," Kodály recalls that Bartók made a thorough study of this collection. See *The Selected Writings of Zoltán Kodály* (London, 1974), 105.

14. *Béla Bartók Essays,* 409.

15. The Hungarian melody is reprinted in György Kerényi, *Népies dalok* (Popular Songs) (Budapest, 1961), 141, with the remark that it was first published in 1883.

16. Bartók, *The Hungarian Folk Song,* 77.

17. *Béla Bartók Essays,* 452.

18. Halsey Stevens, *The Life and Music of Béla Bartók,* rev. Malcolm Gillies (London, 1992), 260.

Chapter 3:   Fusion of National Musical Styles: 1906–1925

1. Foreword to Béla Bartók and Zoltán Kodály, *Magyar népdalok* (Hungarian Folk Songs), prepared by Kodály for joint signature and published under the imprimatur of Rozsnyai Károly, Budapest, in December 1906.

2. Zoltan Kodály, *Folk Music of Hungary* (New York and Washington, D.C., 1971), 97–98.

3. The first edition, beginning in the fall of 1907, was J. S. Bach, *The Well-Tempered Clavier,* published in four volumes according to degree of difficulty. In addition, Bartók's annotations describe for the first time his concept of piano technique regarding touch-forms, including their related signs. See *Béla Bartók Essays,* ed. Benjamin Suchoff (Lincoln, Nebr., and London, 1992), 447–448.

4. Inasmuch as time signatures are not applicable in the notation of *parlando*

228 NOTES TO CHAPTER 3

rhythm, the bars mark only structural articulation and are irregularly unequal.See Bartók, *Rumanian Folk Music*, ed. Benjamin Suchoff, (The Hague, 1967–1975), vol. 2: 7, 43.

5. The transcription for piano, *Három Csíkmegyei népdal* (Three Hungarian Folk Songs from the Csík District), was published by Rozsnyai Károly in 1907.The other transcriptions were published in 1908, as "Székely balladák" in the January and March issues of *Ethnographia* (Budapest).

6. *Béla Bartók Essays*, 410.

7. An earlier notation of the leitmotiv, C♯–E–G♯–B♯ appears in Bartók's undated (probably mid-September) "Wednesday" letter to Stefi. Of greater significance, however, is his incredulous remark, "Do you mean to say that you wouldn't have the courage to read Nietzsche's *Zarathustra*, even though you would be intrigued by Strauss's?!" See *Béla Bartók Letters*, ed. János Demény (New York, 1971), 86–87.

8. Bartók not only included an instrumental variant as No. 3 in *Három csíkmegyei népdal* (1907; see note 5 above) but transcribed the folk song as No. 5 in Eight Hungarian Folksongs for Voice and Piano (1917). A vocal variant is published as No. 60 in Béla Bartók, *The Hungarian Folk Song*, ed. Benjamin Suchoff (Albany, 1981), 234.

9. The French poet A. M. Louis de Mamartine (1790–1869) was also a novelist and statesman. It is noteworthy that Bartók studied *Les Préludes* during his second year as a student at the Budapest Academy of Music. See *Thematische Verzeichnis der Jugendwerke Béla Bartóks 1890–1904*, ed. Denijs Dille (Budapest, 1974), 233.

10. *Béla Bartók Essays*, 518. On January 9, Bartók made his first purchase of Debussy piano music, *L'Isle Joyeux* (1904), a work in the romantic style of virtuoso piano technique, but whose new tonal language is for the most part whole-tone scales and their related Lydian octave-segments.

11. Béla Bartók, Jr., *Apám életének krónikája* (Chronicles of My Father's Life) (Budapest, 1981), 97.

12. Elliott Antokoletz, "The Musical Language of Bartók's 14 Bagatelles for Piano," *Tempo* (June 1981), 8.

13. Letter dated October 7, 1908. See *Béla Bartók Letters*, 92. The melodies are published in Bartók, *Rumanian Folk Music*, vol. 2, nos. 56e, 120, 628l; vol. 4, no. 42b.

14. Letter dated August 31, 1909. See *Béla Bartók Letters*, 95.

15. *Béla Bartók Essays*, 119–120.

16. The illustrated melodies were revised by Bartók in the 1930s for inclusion in Bartók, *Rumanian Folk Music*, vols. 1 and 2.

17. Cf. Liszt, Piano Sonata in B Minor (mm. 13–17, 309–313) and Bartók, Sonata for Violin and Piano (Example 2.12).

18. Bartók, *Rumanian Folk Music*, vol. 1, 13.

19. That is, the characteristic Hungarian-Gypsy scales—minor and Phrygian forms—which are a feature of urban-Gypsy bands. See Bartók, *The Hungarian Folk Song*, 55.

20. *Béla Bartók Essays*, 367–371.

21. Victor Bator, foreword to Bartók, *Rumanian Folk Music*, vol. 1, ix.

22. Letter to Frederick Delius, June 7, 1910, in *Béla Bartók Letters*, 104. In her book *Bartók Béla a népdalkutató* (Béla Bartók, the Folk Music Researcher), 92, Julia Szegő notes that "Well known is the embarrassing scandal at the first Bartók-Kodály evening [concert], which went so far as the throwing of rotten eggs by cliques from the upper class. It was at time that the vulgar mock-poem appeared in a daily newspaper circulated throughout Hungary: 'Kot-kot-kot- Kodály, little Zoltán do not compose!' Similar verses about Bartók were on everybody's lips, too."

23. Jószef Ujfalussy, *Béla Bartók* (Budapest, 1971), 107.

24. Béla Bartók, "Debussyről," in *Bartók Béla Válogatott Írásai* (Béla Bartók Selected Writings), ed. András Szőllősy (Budapest, 1956), 342–343.

25. Donald Grout, *A Short History of Opera* (New York, 1947), 421.

26. Sándor Veress, *"Bluebeard's Castle"* in *Béla Bartók: A Memorial Review*, 45.

27. See Elliott Antokoletz, "Bartók's *Bluebeard*: The Sources of its Modernism," *College Music Symposium* 30, no. 1 (Spring 1990): 79–80. See also Antokoletz, *The Music of Béla Bartók* (Berkeley and Los Angeles, 1984), 91, for an illustrated discussion of the first appearance of this tetrachord in the opera, at no. 4, mm. 5–6.

28. The Ruthenians, a Ukrainian people, inhabited the easternmost province of then Hungarian Slovakia (now part of Ukrainia).

29. Benjamin Suchoff, "Ethnomusicological Roots of Béla Bartók's Musical Language," *World of Music* 29, no. 1 (1987): 56–57.

30. *Béla Bartók Essays*, 157.

31. The Bulgarian Christmas song, transcribed by Bartók in 1935 and published by him in a pamphlet of Serbian and Bulgarian folk melodies, is reprinted in *Documenta Bartókiana* 4, ed. Denijs Dille (Budapest, 1970), 244.

32. Sabin Drăgoi and Tiberiu Alexandru, foreword to Béla Bartók, *Rumanian Folk Music,* vol.5, x.

33. *Béla Bartók Essays,* 11.

34. The Arab melodies are published in Béla Bartók, "Die Volksmusik der Araber von Biskra und Umgebung" (The Folk Music of the Arabs of Biskra and Environs), *Zeitschrift für Musikwissenschaft* 9, no. 2 (June 1920), 510.

35. Such as those found in nos. 10 (*With Alternate Hands*) and 25 (*Imitation and Inversion*) in Bartók's *Mikrokosmos.*

36. *Béla Bartók Essays,* 411.

37. Ibid., 375.

38. See the complete analysis of the work in Antokoletz, *The Music of Béla Bartók,* 55–62, 103–109, 154–157, and 213–219.

39. János Kárpáti, *Bartók's String Quartets* (Budapest, 1975), 25.

40. Bartók, *Rumanian Folk Music,* vol. 1, 55.

41. The relationship is illustrated in Rudolph Reti, *The Thematic Process in Music* (New York, 1951), 94.

42. Bartók, *Rumanian Folk Music,* vol. 1, 45–46.

43. See also Benjamin Suchoff, "Notes on the Music" in *Béla Bartók: A Celebration* (Camp Hill, Penn., 1981), 9–11.

44. *Béla Bartók Essays,* 379–380.

45. See Bartók, *Hungarian Folk Song,* 73–75, and melody no. 303a.

46. *Béla Bartók Essays,* 165.

47. Benjamin Suchoff, "The Impact of Italian Baroque Music on Bartók's Music," in *Bartók and Kodály Revisited,* ed. György Ránki (Budapest, 1987), 189.

Chapter 4: Synthesis of East and West: 1926–1945

1. Serge Moreux, *Béla Bartók* (London, 1953), 92.

2. Three pieces, eventually numbered as *Mikrokosmos* 81, 137, and 146, were drafted during the composition of Nine Little Piano Pieces.

3. József Ujfalussy, *Béla Bartók* (Budapest, 1971), 221.

4. Elliott Antokoletz, *Twentieth-Century Music* (Englewood Cliffs, N.J., 1992), 268–272.

5. Edwin von der Nüll, *Béla Bartók. Ein Beitrag zur Morphologie der neuen Musik* (Halle, 1930), 108–109.

6. Béla Bartók, Jr., "Remembering my father, Béla Bartók," *New Hungarian Quarterly* 7, no. 22 (Summer 1966): 203.

7. See melodies nos. 404 and 385 in Bartók, *Rumanian Folk Music*, ed. Benjamin Suchoff (The Hague, 1967–1975), vol. 1 (Instrumental Melodies) and vol. 2 (Vocal Melodies) respectively.

8. A discussion of the Shaker tune appears in Antokoletz, *Twentieth-Century Music*, 207. See also the illustrated analysis of the complete work in Suchoff, "Notes on the Music" in *Béla Bartók: A Celebration* (Camp Hill, Penn., 1981), 13–15.

9. *Béla Bartók Essays*, ed. Benjamin Suchoff (Lincoln, Nebr., and London, 1992), 412.

10. See pp. 70–71 and 78–79 above. See also Example 3.34 for the similarly-styled Arab peasant melody collected by Bartók in 1913.

11. J. H. Douglas Webster, "Golden-Mean Form in Music," *Music and Letters* 31 (1950): 242–245. Ernő Lendvai, the first Bartók theorist to undertake and promulgate similar structural analysis, published his findings in Hungarian (Akadémiai kiadó, 1955) and English (*Béla Bartók. An Analysis of His Music* [London, 1971]).

12. See the analyses and Bartók's related sketches in Antokoletz, *The Music of Béla Bartók* (Berkeley and Los Angeles, 1984), 88–89, 122–123, 235–236, 274–279, and the illustrations numbered 10 and 11.

13. Bartók had collaborated with a younger colleague, Sándor Reschofsky (who prepared the technical exercises), in the preparation of several volumes for teaching the piano from the beginning to the highest degree.

14. John Vinton, "Toward a Chronology of the *Mikrokosmos*" (*Studia Muscologica*, 1966) 41–42.

15. Benjamin Suchoff, "Synthesis of East and West: *Mikrokosmos*," in *A Bartók Companion*, ed. Malcolm Gillies (Portland, Or., and London, 1993), 191.

16. Cf. melody no. 81 in Bartók, *The Hungarian Folk Song*, ed. Benjamin Suchoff (Albany, 1981), 241.

17. Béla Bartók, *XVII and XVIII Century Italian Cembalo and Organ Music* (New York, 1990), 59.

18. Cf. *Béla Bartók Essays*, 367, example 3.

19. Ibid., 379, example 15.

20. Ibid., 334–335.

21. Benjamin Suchoff, *Guide to Bartók's Mikrokosmos* (New York, 1983), 75.

22. Ibid., 86.

23. *Béla Bartók Letters*, ed. János Demény (New York, 1971), 233. The facsimile reprint of Bartók's pamphlet, titled "Musique paysanne serbe (No. 1–21) et bulgare (No. 22–28) du Banat," is published in Dille, ed. *Documenta Bartókiana* 4 (Budapest, 1970) 221–244.

24. The publications are listed in Jaap Kunst, *Ethnomusicology* (The Hague, 1958), 197.

25. *Béla Bartók Essays*, 44.

26. Suchoff, *Guide to Bartók's Mikrokosmos*, 100.

27. Bartók's interest in Wassil Stoin's Bulgarian folk-music collections (see note 24, above) was preceded by his study of the latter's 1927 treatise, *Bulgarska narodna muzika: metrika i ritmika* (Bulgarian folk music: meter and rhythm; see note 24, above) which contains an explanation of Bulgarian rhythm and 187 folk songs as examples.

28. Béla Bartók, *Yugoslav Folk Music*, ed. Benjamin Suchoff (Albany, 1978), vol. 1, 17.

29. *Béla Bartók Essays*, 381.

30. It is interesting that the eighty-nine bars comprising the first movement are in relation to golden section proportions (see Lendvai, *Bartók. An Analysis of his Music*, 41–42).

31. Ujfalussy, *Béla Bartók*, 320. The "fixed idea" is the recurrent "Dearly Beloved" theme which appears in all five movements of the Berlioz *Symphonie fantastique*.

32. *Béla Bartók Essays*, 381.

33. Ibid., 416.

34. Kodály recorded the example and Bartók later transcribed it as no. 879 in Bartók, *Slowakische Volkslieder*, ed. Alica Elscheková and Oská Elschek (Bratislava, 1970), vol. 2, 534. The 1907 specimen appears in the first volume as no. 53e.

35. See Suchoff, "Synthesis," 196–197.

36. Antokoletz, *The Music of Béla Bartók*, 135.

37. *Béla Bartók Essays*, 139–141.

38. Ibid., 141.

39. Béla Bartók, *Turkish Folk Music from Asia Minor*, ed. Benjamin Suchoff (Princeton, 1976), 190.

40. See p. 20 above.

41. Yehudi Menuhin, *Unfinished Journey* (London, 1977), 165.

42. *Béla Bartók Essays*, 338–339, 345.

43. Suchoff, "Notes on the Music," in *Béla Bartók. A Celebration* (Camp Hill, Penn., 1981), 12.

44. Facsimiles of the sketch appear in Benjamin Suchoff, "Structure and Concept in Bartók's Sixth Quartet" (London, 1968), 8–10. See also Kárpáti, *Bartók's String Quartets* (Budapest, 1975), 244–266, for his analysis of the manuscript.

45. Bartók, *The Hungarian Folk Song*, 241. See also Kodály, *Folk Music of Hungary*, rev. ed. Lajos Vargyas (New York, 1971), 62–71.

46. *Béla Bartók Essays*, 389.

47. The added note, B♭, also extends this octatonic hexachord into a nondiatonic folk mode that, transposed to D, opens Bartók's *Cantata Profana*. See Antokoletz, *The Music of Béla Bartók*, 242–249.

48. Bartók, *Rumanian Folk Music*, vol. 1, 16. Cf. melodies nos. 425 and 426; see also the compendium of bagpipe motifs in appendix 1.

49. A fascinating account of the underlying events and dramaturgy in the quartet is given in György Kroó, *A Guide to Bartók* (Budapest, 1971), 215–221.

50. *Béla Bartók Letters*, 279.

51. Benjamin Suchoff, "Bartók and Serbo-Croatian Folk Music," *Musical Quarterly* 58, no. 1 (October 1972), 560.

52. Bartók, *Yugoslav Folk Music*, 1:xxi.

53. *Béla Bartók Letters*, 306.

54. Suchoff, "Bartók and Serbo-Croatian Folk Music," 569–571. The book, titled *Serbo-Croatian Folk Songs* and published posthumously in 1951, was reprinted as the first volume in Bartók's *Yugoslav Folk Music*.

55. See p. 143.

56. Bartók, *Yugoslav Folk Music*, vol. 1, 59–62.

57. Ibid., 72–73.

58. Bartók, *Turkish Folk Music*, 12–14. See also Suchoff, "Bartók in America," *Musical Times* 117, no. 1596 (February 1976), 123–124.

59. *Béla Bartók Letters*, 324.

60. See *Béla Bartók Essays*, vii–viii, 354–392.

61. As quoted in Halsey Stevens, *The Life and Music of Béla Bartók*, rev. Malcolm Gillies (London, 1992), 98.

62. *Béla Bartók Letters*, 326.

63. Suchoff, "Notes on the Music," 6.

64. *Béla Bartók Letters*, 342.

65. Ibid., 344.

66. János Kovács, Notes to *Béla Bartók Complete Edition* (Budapest, n.d., SLPX 11421), 9.

67. Robert Haven Schauffler, *Beethoven: The Man Who Freed Music* (New York, 1946), 438. Schauffler also notes that Beethoven's use of the Lydian mode "fore-shadowed that freer use of the old church modes which has more recently been stimulated by the influence of Moussorgsky."

68. Tibor Serly completed the fair copy.He also reconstructed the Viola Concerto sketches in accordance with Bartók's expressed plan that "the orchestration will be transparent." See Tibor Serly, "Béla Bartók's Last Works," *The Long Player* 2, no. 10 (October 1953), 26–27; and his "Story of a Concerto: Bartók's Last Work," *New York Times*, December 11, 1949.

69. Ditta Bartók, "26. September 1945. Zum 20. Todestag von Béla Bartók," *Österreichische Musikzeitschrift* 20, no. 9 (September 1965), 448.

PART TWO

Concerto For Orchestra

Chapter 5:   First Movement (Introduzione—Allegro vivace)

1. *Béla Bartók Essays*, ed. Benjamin Suchoff (Lincoln, Nebr., and London, 1992), 377.

2. Benjamin Suchoff, "Notes on the Music," in *Béla Bartók. A Celebration* (Camp Hill, Penn., 1981), 6.

3. Ibid.

4. Cf. Examples 8.5 and 8.6.

5. Béla Bartók, *Rumanian Folk Music*, ed. Benjamin Suchoff (The Hague, 1967–1975), vol. 1, 659–669.

6. *Béla Bartók Essays*, 363.

7. The related Romanian source melody is given in Example 5.7. See also note 14 below.

8. Suchoff, "Notes on the Music," 6.

9. *Béla Bartók Essays*, 431.

10. Bartók, *The Hungarian Folk Song*, ed. Benjamin Suchoff (Albany, 1981), 37.

11. The original form of Motif 1b is shown in Example 5.3, m. 79.

12. Cf. Example 3.36.

13. This peculiarity occurs during the exchange of stanzas between two groups of singers. Just before the first group ends its stanza, the second group enters with the next stanza (there is no pause during the interchange). See Bartók, *Rumanian Folk Music*, vol. 4, 24–25.

14. Béla Bartók, *Yugoslav Folk Music*, ed. Benjamin Suchoff (Albany, 1978), vol. 1, 61. The idiosyncratic pitch collection Bartók refers to as "a very peculiar scale" is designated "octatonic" by Arthur Berger in his essay, "Problems of Pitch Organization in Stravinsky," *Perspectives of New Music* 2 (1963), 27. A number of octatonic Yugoslav folk songs are published in *Yugoslav Folk Music*, vol. 1, no. 36 and vol. 4, nos. 311a–c, 485b, 486, and 802d.

15. The folk song is a *bocet* (a proper song of mourning, with improvised text) whose text and translation appear in Bartók, *Rumanian Folk Music* vol. 3, 559–561. Bartók prepared his Romanian and Yugoslav materials for publication in the two-year period prior to the composition of the concerto.

16. The Arab melody has a religious text, the A♭ is sung a quarter tone higher, and the rhythm schema resembles the *kolomyjka* dance rhythm. "Die Volksmusik der Araber von Biskra und Umgebung" (The folk music of the Arabs in Biskra and environs), *Zeitschrift für Musikwissenschaft* 9 (1920): 492, 507.

17. William Austin, "Bartók's Concerto for Orchestra," *The Music Review* 18, no. 1 (February 1957): 26–27.

18. Although double sections are commonplace in the folk songs of eastern Europe, the z z Z + Z z formula is a characteristic Slovak syllabic structure (cf. Béla Bartók, *Slowakische Volkslieder*, ed. Alica Elscheková, Oskár Elschek, and Jozef Kresánek (Bratislava, 1959), vol. 1, 29 and vol. 2, xiii–xv). It should be noted that Bartók invented the use of the letter Z in different type sizes to represent the proportion of syllabic numbers in heterometric folk songs. The use of the same letter to designate Z-cell structure in Bartók's works came into being many years after his death.

Chapter 6: Second Movement (Presentando le Coppie)

1. Bartók enclosed a list of "Changes for the 'Concerto for Orchestra'" with his January 27 letter to Hans Heinsheimer, editor of Boosey & Hawkes, Inc., New York

(collection of Peter Bartók). See also Benjamin Suchoff, "Notes on the Music," in *Béla Bartók. A Celebration* (Camp Hill, Penn., 1981), 7.

2. See p. 125.

3. Bartók found that the rhythm of the greater portion of Romanian folk music can be reduced to a skeleton pattern of 2/4 = ♪♩♪, and that a pair of sixteenths is substituted for most of the single eighths. See Bartók, *Rumanian Folk Music,"* ed. Benjamin Suchoff (The Hague, 1967–1975), vol. 1, 42.

4. Cf. Example 3.42. The Serbian melody, a *Veliko kolo* (round-dance for adults), is reprinted in Bartók, *Yugoslav Folk Music,* ed. Benjamin Suchoff (Albany, 1978), vol. 1, 457.

5. William Austin, "Bartók's Concerto for Orchestra," *The Music Review* 18, no. 1 (February 1957), 29–30.

6. Elliott Antokoletz, *The Music of Béla Bartók* (Berkeley and Los Angeles, 1984), 256–257.

7. Bartók, *Yogoslav Folk Music*, vol. 1, 460. "The *tambura* is a stringed instrument with frets, about the size of a viola, played with a plectrum" (ibid., 239).

8. Anokoletz, *The Music of Béla Bartók*, 258.

9. See Bartók, *Yugoslav Folk Music*, vol. 1, 60–61.

10. Cf. Bartók, *Rumanian Folk Music*, vol. 1, no. 596b.

11. Bartók, ibid., 62–64, 72–73. See also Wolfgang Laade, "The Diaphonic Music of the Island of Krk, Yugoslavia," liner notes to Folkways Record Album No. FE 4060, 1975. Laade indicates that the basic narrow-range "Istrian" scale used in this music consists of alternating half steps and whole steps, that is, an octatonic hexachord bounded by a perfect fifth.

12. The Serbian melody, a *Malo kolo* (round-dance for youths), is reprinted in Bartók, *Yugoslav Folk Music*, vol. 1, 453–454. The repetition of such dotted rhythm trochees as ♪.♪ ♪♪ in peasant music may indicated art-music influence: see Bartók, *The Hungarian Folk Song*, ed. Benjamin Suchoff (Albany, 1981), 29.

13. Antokoletz, *The Music of Béla Bartók*, 258.

14. The assertion by Yves Lenoir, that Bartók's theme is a free paraphrase of the chorale *Nun komm, der Heiden Heiland* is erroneous. See his book, *Béla Bartók, folkore et transcendence dans l'œuvre américaine de Béla Bartók [1940–1945]* (Louvain-la-Neuve, 1986), 356–359. There is neither a lexicographical (same or similar melodic contours) nor a grammatical (same section end notes) connection between the two melodies. According to the Bartók system of classifying folk-music materials,

a variant relationship cannot be established between melodies solely on the basis of identical metrical structure (e.g., seven-syllable underlying text lines).

15. See the figured, harmonic progressions in Austin, "Bartók's Concerto for Orchestra," 31.

Chapter 7:   Third Movement (Elegia)

1. Bartók Archive MS 80 FSS1, p. 10, in the collection of Peter Bartók. See p. 125.

2. William Austin, "Bartók's Concerto for Orchestra," *The Music Review*, 18, no. 1 (February 1957), 33.

3. See Bartók, *Duke Bluebeard's Castle*, R.N. 91ff, and Example 3.26 above.

4. *Zorilor* lamentations are sung by relatives in the house of mourning at dawn, prior to the burial of the deceased. See Bartók, *Rumanian Folk Music*, ed. Benjamin Suchoff (The Hague, 1969–1975), vol. 2, 27 and vol. 3, 567–573.

5. For a detailed analysis of the cellular construction, including a graphically enhanced view of the full score, see Elliott Antokoletz, *The Music of Béla Bartók* (Berkeley and Los Angeles, 1984), 298–300. The first prominent instance of a cellular stretto occurs in Bartók's String Quartet no. 4 (movement 1, mm. 5–6), where the X-cell answer C–C#–D–D# expands to a Y-cell (whole-tone tetrachord), Bb–C–D–E (ibid., 110).

Chapter 8:   Fourth Movement (Intermezzo Interrotto)

1. In June 1920, after the end of World War I, defeated Hungary was required to sign the Treaty of Trianon, which ceded Transylvania to Romania. Later on, the political situtation in Hungary compelled the government to prohibit performance of the song in public.

2. Béla Bartók, *The Hungarian Folk Song*, ed. Benjamin Suchoff (Albany, 1981), 1–3.

3. Bartók's note to this melody indicates a probable art song source (ibid., 217).

4. Roberta London, program notes to Bartók, Concerto for Orchestra (Columbia MS 6140).

5. Antal Dorati, "Bartókiana," *Tempo* 136 (1981): 12.

6. It should be noted, however, that among the Transylvanian-Romanian instrumental melodies Bartók collected, beginning in 1909, are a number of violin

pieces in the Lydian folk mode. Cf. Béla Bartók, *Rumanian Folk Music*, ed. Benjamin Suchoff (The Hague, 1967–1975), vol. 1, 87.

7. In 1924. See *Béla Bartók Essays*, ed. Benjamin Suchoff (Lincoln, Nebr., and London, 1992), 128.

8. In m. 19, the first bassoon part of the print score erroneously shows the sharp sign preceding the penultimate A instead of the end note. See Bartók Archive MSS 80FSFC1–3 in the collection of Peter Bartók.

9. See the related music notation and its detailed analysis in Elliott Antokoletz, *The Music of Béla Bartók* (Berkeley and Los Angeles, 1984), 259–260.

10. See table 2, pattern 15 in Bartók, *Rumanian Folk Music*, vol. 4, 20 and melody no. 73m.

11. Antokoletz, *The Music of Béla Bartók*, 260–261.

12. The notated theme and its suggested figured bass is given in William Austin, "Bartók's Concerto for Orchestra," *The Music Review* 18, no. 1 (February 1957): 36.

13. Benjamin Suchoff, *Guide to Bartók's* Mikrokosmos (New York, 1982), 138.

14. Austin, "Bartók's Concerto for Orchestra," 37. Austin further comments that "the theme Bartók refers to is in itself a blatant exaggeration of a stiff symmetry, and in the first movement of his Symphony Shostakovich repeats it twelve times, with only the most rudimentary variation, as if he were determined, like other Soviet orators, to wear out everybody's patience."

15. See the related music notation and detailed analysis of mm. 135–142 in Antokoletz, *The Music of Béla Bartók*, 63.

16. See also Bartók's transcriptions for piano, Three Hungarian Folk Songs from the Csík District (1907).

Chapter 9: Fifth Movement (Finale)

1. See also Béla Bartók, *Rumanian Folk Music*, ed. Benjamin Suchoff (The Hague, 1967–1975), vol. 1, 50–53.

2. Beginning in 1910 Bartók collected more than forty Transylvanian-Romanian alphorn melodies. The instrument, constructed from the trunk of a fir tree and about eight feet in length and five inches in diameter, was played by professional shepherds. The useful harmonics consist of a Mixolydian hexachord, and certain motifs may be traced to trumpet calls of the Austro-Hungarian army. For further details and the complete notation, see Bartók, *Rumanian Folk Music*, 23–25 and 635–658, respectively.

3. This polymode, also referred to as a "nondiatonic folk mode," occurs in

many transformations in Bartók's *Cantata Profana* and, in a number of instances, in the fourth movement of his String Quartet no. 4. See the illustrated analyses in Elliott Antokoletz, *The Music of Béla Bartók* (Berkeley and Los Angeles, 1984), 241–249.

4. The ordinary guitar, strung with only two strings that are tuned in fifths, is played in a 2/4 ostinato rhythm of accented and unaccented eighth-notes. See Bartók, *Rumanian Folk Music,* vol. 5, 29–30.

5. Ibid., melodies nos. 173h and 173j.

6. This pitch collection has been referred to as the "acoustic scale" by Hungarian theorists. See Ernő Lendvai, *Béla Bartók. An Analysis of his Music* (London, 1971), 67.

7. According to William Austin, the "rapid, emphatic repeated notes recall several other memorable themes of Bartók, such as that of the second Quartet, second movement, the sixth Quartet, third movement, and *Contrasts*, last movement. "See his article, "Bartók's Concerto for Orchestra," *The Music Review 18,* no. 1 (February 1957), 43. See also the comments and music notations in John W. Downey, *La musique populaire dans l'œuvre de Béla Bartók* (Paris, 1966), 365–366, and Example 9.13.

8. This structural schema is the most frequent form in new style (Class B) Hungarian folk songs. See Béla Bartók, *The Hungarian Folk Song,* ed. Benjamin Suchoff (Albany, 1981), 39.

9. See Example 2.2 and its related commentary. Bartók's autobiography (1921) appears in *Béla Bartók Essays,* ed. Benjamin Suchoff (Lincoln, Nebr., and London, 1992), 408–411.

10. *Béla Bartók Letters* (New York, 1971), 245, 419–420.

11. Two Hungarian Class C melodies with a related rhythm-schema appear in Bartók, *The Hungarian Folk Song,* nos. 284 and 285.

12. The complete melody appears in *Béla Bartók Essays,* 260. The region is now part of Slovakia.

13. Benjamin Suchoff, *Guide to Bartók's Mikrokosmos* (New York, 1982), 120.

14. Cf. the appendix 1 motifs in Bartók, *Rumanian Folk Music,* vol. 1, 659–669.

15. See also the related music notation and analysis in Antokoletz, *The Music of Béla Bartók,* 263–264.

16. Ibid., 265, 300–302.

17. Ibid., 301.

18. Ibid., 303.

19. Austin, "Bartók's Concerto for Orchestra," 47.

20. The letter, dated March 15, 1945, was written by H. W. Heinsheimer, then editor of Boosey & Hawkes, New York.

21. In his essay, "Quotations in Bartók's Music," Ferenc Bónis illustrates similar "keystone" motifs of Bartók's *Allegro barbaro* and the second movement in the Sonata for Two Pianos and Percussion. See *Studia Musicologica* 5 (1963), 380.

22. The polyrhythmic treatment is the first instance of such complex juxtapositions in Bartók's works. It is also interesting that Bartók dated his final draft "1943. okt. 8." in the Bartók Archive MS. 80FSFC2 (collection of Peter Bartók), but omitted another entry for the added pages of the alternative ending.

23. According to a conversation in 1982 with my informant, George Jellinek, music director of WQXR Radio, New York, and confirmed in a telephone communication in 1993.

24. I am also indebted to Todd Vunderink, music editor of Peer International, Inc., for information related to copyright procedures and performance practice of the 1940s. A reprint of the sheet music appears in *The New York Times Great Latin Songs* (New York, 1947), 82–85.

25. Cf. Bartók Archive MSS 80FSS1 and 80FSSS2,3 in the collection of Peter Bartók.

PART THREE

Bartók's Heritage

Chapter 10: The Influence of Bartók's Music on Latter-Day Composition

1. *Boston Daily Globe,* December 2, 1944.

2. *Boston Herald,* December 2, 1944.

3. *New York Sun,* January 11, 1945.

4. *New York Times,* December 12, 1948. The long-playing record was produced by Columbia Records as ML 4102.

5. György Kroó, "Bartók and Hungarian Music (1945–1981)" in *Bartók and Kodály Revisited,* ed. György Ránki (Budapest, 1987), 142–143.

6. See Elliott Antokoletz, *Béla Bartók. A Guide to Research* (New York, 1988), 251–252.

7. Alberto Ginastera, "Homage to Béla Bartók," *Tempo* 136 (March 1981), 3–4.

8. Gilbert Chase, "Alberto Ginastera: Argentine Composer," *The Musical Quarterly* 43 (1957), 451.

9. This cell appears as early as 1903, as a motif in Bartók's *Kossuth* symphonic poem (cf. Example 2.6).

10. Chase, "Ginastera," 449.

11. The *gato* is described in Gustavo Duran, *Recordings of Latin American Songs and Dances* (Washington, D.C., 1942), 4–5. The hemiola results from alternating subdivisions of six units (e.g., 6/16 followed by 3 x 2/16. Chase ("Ginastera,"454–455) lists other *malambo* schemata and notes that the genre is a regional, archetypal gaucho dance that has become an Argentine national symbol.

12. The first movement, "Ideal," was composed in 1905 as the first movement in Bartók's Concerto no. 1 for Violin and Piano (published posthumously in 1959. See Example 3.5).

13. Elliott Antokoletz, *Twentieth-Century Music* (Englewood Cliffs, N.J., 1992), 509.

14. An illustrated discussion of the "Confutatis" section is given in Peter Evans, "Britten's 'War Requiem,'" *Tempo* 61–62 (1962): 29–31.

15. Antokoletz, *Twentieth-Century Music*, 511. An extended essay on Bartók's influence, including a comparative analysis of the *War Requiem* and Bartók's *Cantata Profana*, appears in E. J. Lundergan, "Benjamin Britten's *War Requiem*: Stylistic and Technical Sources" (D.M.A. treatise, University of Texas at Austin, 1991), 46–63.

16. Eric Walter White, *Benjamin Britten: His Life and Operas* (Berkeley and Los Angeles, 1983), 273. See the related analysis of Bartók's opera on pp. 64–65 below.

17. From a 1982 interview published in Paul Griffiths, *Györgi Ligeti* (London, 1983), 18, 22.

18. Ove Nordwall, "Ligeti, György (Sándor)" in *The New Grove Dictionary of Music and Musicians*, (London, 1980). The author points to Ligeti's String Quartet no. 2 as "one of his most profound works, somewhat resembling the combined variation and arch form of Bartók."

19. Griffiths, *György Ligeti*, 26.

20. See Example 3.42.

21. Tönde Szitha, "A Conversation with György Ligeti," *Hungarian Musical Quarterly* 3 (1992), 14.

22. Antokoletz, *Twentieth-Century Music*, 522.

23. Robert Moevs, "George Crumb: *Music for a Summer Evening (Makrokosmosmos III)*," *The Musical Quarterly* 62 (1976), 295–296.

24. See p. 92 below.

25. Edith Boroff, *Three American Composers* (Lanham, Md., 1986), 210.

26. Steven Stucky, *Lutosławski and His Music* (Cambridge, 1981), 28.

27. The melody was drawn from a collection by Father Wladyslaw Skierkowski (cf. Example 3.31).

28. Stucky, *Lutosławski*, 49. Eight of the tunes are printed on p. 50 of Stucky's work.

29. Ibid., 49. There is also a more obvious conicidence that has led to the misconception: the pairing of the Bartók and Lutosławski concertos on recordings (Seiji Ozawa and the Chicago Symphony Orchestra, EMI Records, Ltd., 1984; and C. von Dohnanyi and the Cleveland Orchestra, London 49772CD).

30. Ibid., 70.

31. That is, *Funeral Music*. Joseph Brumbeloe, "Symmetry in Lutosławski's *Trauermusik*," *Indiana Theory Review* 6, no. 3 (Spring 1983), 4.

32. Roger Nichols, *Messiaen* (London, 1975), 7.

33. Claude Samuel, *Olivier Messiaen. Musique et couleur. Nouveaux Entretiens avec Claude Samuel* (Paris, 1986), 120 (interview first published in 1967, in Samuel, *Entretiens avec Olivier Messiaen*).

34. See Olivier Messiaen, *Technique de mon langage musicale* (Paris, 1956), chap. 14.

35. Almut Rößler, *Contributions to the Spiritual World of Olivier Messiaen. With Original Texts by the Composer* (Duisberg, 1986), 42. See also Michèle Reverdy, *L'œuvre pour piano d'Olivier Messiaen* (Paris, 1978), 10, 17.

36. Madeleine Hsu, "Olivier Messiaen, the Musical Mediator and His Major Influences, Liszt, Debussy, and Bartók" (Ph.D. diss., New York University, 1984), 129.

37. Paul Griffiths, *Olivier Messiaen and the Music of Time* (Ithaca, N.Y., 1985), 120. This symmetrical tetrachord is, of course, a Z-cell construction.

38. These Hungarian melodies (*magyar nótak*) were later designated by Bartók as popular art music or urban folk music.

39. See figure 1 in Benjamin Suchoff, "Folk Music Sources in Bartók's Works," in *Gedenkschrift Kurt Reinhard* (Laaber, 1984), 200.

40. *Béla Bartók Letters*, 201.

41. Mosco Carner, "Béla Bartók," in *The Modern Age 1890–1960*, ed. Martin Cooper (London, 1974), 299.

CHRONOLOGICAL LIST OF CITED BARTÓK COMPOSITIONS

1890	Waltz for Piano
1890–1904	*The Course of the Danube*
1894	Sonata no. 1 in G Minor
1898	Intermezzo in C Minor
1902	Four Songs for Voice and Piano
1903	*Kossuth* symphonic poem
	Sonata for Violin and Piano
1903–1904	Piano Quintet
1904	Rhapsody op. 1, for Piano and Orchestra
	Székely Folk Song for Voice and Piano
1905	Suite no. 1, op. 3, for Large Orchestra
1906	Twenty Hungarian Folk Songs (with Zoltán Kodály; nos. 1–10 by Bartók) for Voice and Piano
1907	Three Hungarian Folk Songs from the Csík District for Voice and Piano
1907–1908	Concerto no. 1, for Violin and Orchestra (op. posth.)
1907–1908/1911	*Two Portraits*, op. 5, for Orchestra
1908	Fourteen Bagatelles op. 6, for Piano
	Ten Easy Pieces for Piano
1908/1909	Two Elegies op. 8b, for Piano
	For Children, for Piano
1908–1917	Eight Hungarian Folk Songs for Voice and Piano
1909/1910	Two Romanian Dances op. 8a, for Piano
	Four Dirges op. 9a, for Piano
1911–1918	*Duke Bluebeard's Castle* op. 11, opera in one act
1913/1929	Piano School (*Zongora Iskola*, with Sándor Reschofsky); *The First Term at the Piano.*
1914–1917	*The Wooden Prince*, ballet in one act
1916	Suite op. 14, for Piano

1920	Improvisations on Hungarian Peasant Songs op. 20, for Piano
1921	Sonata no. 1, for Violin and Piano
1922	Sonata no. 2, for Violin and Piano
1923/1925	Dance Suite for Orchestra; for Piano
1924	*Five Village Scenes*, for Voice and Piano
1926	Sonata for Piano
	Out of Doors, for Piano
	Nine Little Piano Pieces
	Concerto no. 1, for Piano and Orchestra
1926–1939	*Mikrokosmos*, for Piano
1928	Rhapsody no. 1, for Violin and Piano
	String Quartet no. 4
1930	*Cantata Profana: The Nine Enchanted Stags*, for Double Mixed Chorus, Tenor and Baritone Soloists, and Orchestra
1936	String Quartet no. 5
1937	Music for String Instruments, Percussion, and Celesta
1938/1940	Sonata for Two Pianos and Percussion; Concerto for Two Pianos and Orchestra
1938	*Contrasts*, for Violin, Clarinet, and Piano
	Concerto no. 2, for Violin and Orchestra
1939	Divertimento for String Orchestra
	String Quartet no. 6
1943	Concerto for Orchestra
1944	Sonata for Solo Violin
1945	Concerto no. 3, for Piano and Orchestra (unfinished; last seventeen bars completed by Tibor Serly)
	Concerto for Viola and Orchestra (unfinished; reconstructed and orchestrated by Tibor Serly)

EXPLANATION OF TERMS

ADDITIVE RHYTHM.   The regular recurrence of groupings composed of longer and shorter units $(3 + 2, 2 + 3, 2 + 2 + 3, \text{etc.})$.

ARCHITECTONIC FORM.   A rounded structure in which the last part or melody section is similar in content to the first one (ABA, ABBA, ABCA, etc.).

BAGPIPE MOTIF.   Two- or four-bar fragmentary melodic structures, generally consisting of a pentachord.

BULGARIAN RHYTHM.   Additive rhythms in fast tempo, resulting in a very peculiar and exciting "limping" effect.

CHANGE-SONG.   A type of Romanian Christmas song, sung by two alternating choruses of youngsters, where the first note of the new entry or stanza falls on the last note of the preceding stanza.

CHROMATIC COMPRESSION.   Melodic transformation by changing diatonic degrees into chromatic ones.

CLUSTER-CHORD.   A chromatic chording, generally in close position (i.e., within the span of an octave), where the individual degrees usually form octatonic or whole-tone pentachords or hexachords. (A Bartókian innovation, unrelated to the tone-cluster sonorities invented by Henry Cowell.)

DIATONIC EXTENSION.   Melodic transformation in which the succession of chromatic degrees is extended into diatonic ones. Such extension in range may change the character of the original structure to the extent that it sounds like an entirely new melody.

DIVISIVE RHYTHM.   A series of beats at equal distances, organized in patterns through equally recurring accents (2/4, 3/4, 6/8, etc.).

DOTTED RHYTHM.   A peculiarity of new-style Hungarian folk songs, in which a dotted value is preceded or followed by its complementary short value (eighth–dotted quarter or dotted quarter–eighth), and most frequently in combinatorial patterns that form distinctive syncopated rhythms.

245

FOLK MODE.   Any of the five most commonly used modes—Dorian, Phrygian, Lydian, Mixolydian, or Aeolian—of the art music of the Middle Ages.

GOLDEN MEAN (or SECTION).   A geometric proportion, applied to musical form, that uses bar or note values according to the number series 1, 2, 3, 5, 8, 13, 21, and so on (each number being the sum of the previous two). This "Fibonacci series" is named after Italian mathematician Leonardo Fibonacci (b. c.1170).

GYPSY SCALES.   Nondiatonic configurations with two augmented seconds. The Hungarian-Gypsy (minor) form has flat third and sixth, augmented fourth, and major seventh degrees. The *kalindra* (Gypsy-Phrygian) form has flat second and sixth, major third, and major seventh degrees.

HEMIOLA.   The alternative subdivision of metrical units, e.g. 6/8 ♫♩ ♫♩| ♩♩♩|, or 2/4 ♩♩|♩ ♫♩ ♫♩|.

HETEROMETRIC STRUCTURE.   Melodies with sections of unequal length or meter (i.e.,with a different number of feet or syllables).

HETERORHYTHMIC STRUCTURE.   Melodies with sections of unequal rhythm.

INDETERMINATE STRUCTURE.   Melodies coinsisting of shorter or longer motifs that are repeated without any plan or order.

ISOMETRIC STRUCTURE.   Melodies with the same number of feet or syllables in each section.

ISORHYTHMIC STRUCTURE.   Melodies with the same rhythm in each section.

MELODY SECTION.   The portion of a vocal melody corresponding to one line of text. Instrumental melody sections are generally determined by musical articulation, that is, by recurring end tones (i.e., the caesuras, which mark the point between melody sections).

MOTIF.   A fragmentary, recurrent figure of characteristic melodic and/or rhythmic structure, usually a unifying element derived from a theme or subject.

NEUTRAL TONALITY.   A polymodal configuration with a doubled third: one minor, the other major.

NONDIATONIC SCALE.   A scale formed by the chromatic alteration of one or more degrees of the diatonic scale.

OCTATONIC SCALE.   An eight-note symmetrical scale with alternating half- and whole-steps or whole- and half-steps. In the case of polymodal chromaticism (based on a single fundamental tone), there are two complementary octatonic scales. The one beginning with a half-step is referred to as the "Phrygian" form, and the other is the "minor" form.

OCTAVE SEGMENT.   Any tetrachord or pentachord that is identifiable as an explicit partition of a scale or folk mode.

OSTINATO.   The persistent repetition of an unchanging motif or chord.

PARLANDO RHYTHM.   *Parlando* (or *parlando-rubato*) means free, declamatory rhythm which does not involve the recurrence of equal values and is nearly equivalent to recitative style in western European art music.

PENTACHORD.   A five-tone segment of a scale or mode.

PENTATONIC SCALE.   A five-tone scale without semitones. The fifth, symmetrical mode of the scale (e.g., A–C–D–E–G) is the only one used in ancient Hungarian melodies.

POLYMODAL CHROMATICISM.   The superposition of two modes with a single fundamental tone, where the chromaticized degrees have only a diatonic-melodic function. In other words, the altered degrees of a polymode are not constituents of a certain chord that lead to degrees in a following chord, but ingredients of the specific modes to which they belong.

PRINCIPAL TONE.   The fundamental tone or first degree of a scale or folk mode. The same term is used in the plural form to identify the main degrees of an embellished melody.

QUATERNARY.   A vocal melody with four text lines, or an instrumental tune with four melody-sections.

SHIFTED RHYTHM.   A peculiarity of instrumental dance melodies in which a phrase is repeated so that the accentuated parts lose their accent during the repetition while the nonaccentuated parts gain one.

SKELETON FORM.   The reduction of an embellished melody to its principal tones.

SYLLABIC STRUCTURE.   The number of syllables in the text line of a melody section. In certain instrumental music, the implied syllabic number according to the skeleton form of the melody section.

TEMPO GIUSTO.   Strict (i.e., non-*rubato*), dance-like rhythm.

TETRACHORD.   A four-tone segment of a scale or mode.

X-CELL.   A chromatic tetrachord of contiguous semitones, used linearly to provide rudimentary motifs, and vertically as chords.

Y-CELL.   A whole-tone tetrachord, used linearly to provide rudimentary motifs, and vertically as chords.

YUGOSLAV CADENCE.   An imperfect (half-) cadence in which the melody ends on the second degree of the scale or mode.

Z-CELL.   A tetrachord consisting of juxtaposed tritones, used linearly to provide rudimentary motifs, and vertically as chords.

BIBLIOGRAPHY

Antokoletz, Elliott. "Principles of Pitch Organization in Bartók's Fourth String Quartet."Ph.D. diss., The City University of New York, 1975.

———. "The Musical Language of Bartók's *14 Bagatelles* for Piano." *Tempo* 137 (June 1981): 8–16.

———. *The Music of Béla Bartók: A Study of Tonality and Progression in Twentieth-Century Music.* Berkeley and Los Angeles: University of California Press, 1984.

———. Béla Bartók: *A Guide to Research.* New York: Garland Publishing, 1988.

———. "Bartók's *Bluebeard:* The Sources of Its 'Modernism.'" *College Music Symposium* 30, no. 1 (Spring 1990): 75–95.

———. *Twentieth-Century Music.* Englewood Cliffs, N.J.: Prentice Hall, 1992.

———. "'At last something truly new': Bagatelles," "Concerto for Orchestra," and "Middle-period String Quartets." In *The Bartók Companion,* 110–123, 257–277, 526–537, ed. Malcolm Gillies. London: Faber and Faber; Portland, Or.: Amadeus Press, 1993.

Austin, William."Bartók's Concerto for Orchestra." *The Music Review,* 18, no. 1 (February 1957): 21–47.

Bartók, Béla. "Székely balladak" (Székely Ballads). *Ethnographia* (Budapest) 19, nos. 1 and 2 (January and March, 1908): 43–52, 105–115.

———. "Die Volksmusik der Araber von Biskra und Umgebung." *Zeitschrift für Musikwissenschaft* 9, no. 2 (June 1920): 399–522.

———. *Bartók Béla levelei* (Béla Bartók letters). Ed. János Demény. Budapest: Művelt Nép Könyvkiadó, 1951.

———. *Bartók Béla. Válogatott írása* (Béla Bartók. Selected writings). Ed. András Szőllősy. Budapest: Művelt Nép, 1956.

———. "Debussyről" (About Debussy). In *Bartók Béla válagatott irásai* (Béla Bartók selected writings), 342–343. Coll. and arr. András Szőllősy. Budapest: "Művelt Nép" Kiadó, 1956.

————. *Slowakische Volkslieder.* Ed. Alica Elscheková, Oskár Elschek, and Jozef Kresánek. Bratislava: Academia Scientiarum Slovaca, vol. 1, 1959; vol. 2, 1971; vol. 3 unpublished.

————. *Rumanian Folk Music.* Ed. Benjamin Suchoff. Trans. E. C. Teodorescu et al. Foreword by Victor Bator. The Hague: Matrinus Nijhoff, 1969–1975. 5 vols. The five volumes appear as vols. 2–6 of the New York Bartók Archive Studies in Musicology series, ed. Benjamin Suchoff: vol. 2: I. Instrumental Music (1967); vol. 3: II. Vocal Melodies (1967); vol. 4: III. Texts (1967); vol. 5: IV. Carols and Christmas Songs (*Colinde*) (1975); vol. 6: V. Maramureș County (1975).

————. "Musique paysanne serbe (No. 1–21) et bulgare (No. 22–28) du Banat: Budapest, 1935." In *Documenta Bartókiana* 4, 221–244, ed. Denijs Dille. Budapest: Akadémiai Kiadó, 1970.

————. *Béla Bartók Letters.* Trans. Péter Balabán et al. from compilation edited by János Demény. New York: St. Martin's Press, 1971.

————. *Turkish Folk Music from Asia Minor.* Ed. Benjamin Suchoff. Princeton and London: Princeton University Press, 1976. Appears as vol. 7 of the New York Bartók Archive Studies in Musicology series, ed. Benjamin Suchoff.

————. *Béla Bartók Essays.* Ed. Benjamin Suchoff. London: Faber and Faber; New York: St. Martin's Press, 1976. Appears as vol. 8 of the New York Bartók Archives Studies in Musicology series, ed. Benjamin Suchoff. Reprint, Lincoln, Nebr., and London: University of Nebraska Press, 1992.

————. *Yugoslav Folk Music.* Ed. Benjamin Suchoff. Albany: State University of New York Press, 1978. 4 vols. Appears as vols. 9–12 of the New York Bartók Archive Studies in Musicology series, ed. Benjamin Suchoff. Vol. 9: I. Serbo-Croatian Folk Songs (with Albert B. Lord); vol. 10: II. Tabulation of Material; vol. 11: III. Source Melodies, Part One; vol. 12: IV. Source Melodies, Part Two.

————. *The Hungarian Folk Song.* Ed. Benjamin Suchoff. Trans. M. D. Calvocoressi. Annotations by Zotán Kodály. Appears as vol. 13 of the New York Bartók Archive Studies in Musicology series, ed. Benjamin Suchoff.

————. *Piano Music of Béla Bartók.* The Archive Edition. Ed. Benjamin Suchoff. New York: Dover Publications, 1981. Series I appears as vol. 14, Series II as vol. 15 of the New York Bartók Archive Studies in Musicology series, ed. Benjamin Suchoff.

————. *XVII and XVIII Century Italian Cembalo and Organ Music.* Ed. László Somfai. New York: Carl Fischer, 1990.

Bartók, Béla, and Zoltán Kodály. *Transylvanian Hungarians: Folk Songs.* Budapest: The Popular Literary Society, 1923.

Bartók, Béla, Jr. "Remembering My Father, Béla Bartók." *The New Hungarian Quarterly* (Budapest) 7, no. 22 (Summer 1966): 201–203.

————. "Béla Bartók's Diseases." *Studia Musicologica* 23 (1981): 427–441.

————. *Apám eletének krónikája* (Chronicles of my father's life). Budapest: Zeneműkiadó, 1981.

Bartók, Ditta. "26. September 1945. Zum 20. Todestag von Béla Bartók." *Österreichische Musikzeitschrift* 20, no. 9 (September 1965): 445–449.

Bator, Victor. *The Béla Bartók Archives: History and Catalogue.* New York: Bartók Archives Publication, 1963. Appears as vol. 1 in the New York Bartók Archive Studies in Musicology series, ed. Benjamin Suchoff.

Berger, Arthur. "Problems of Pitch Organization in Stravinsky." *Perspectives of New Music* 2 (Fall–Winter 1963), 11–42.

Bónis, Ferenc. "Quotations in Bartók's Music: A Contribution to Bartók's Psychology of Composition." *Studia Musicologica* 5 (1963): 355–382.

————. *Bartók Béla élete képekben és dokumentumokban* (Béla Bartók's Life in Pictures and Documents). Budapest: Zeneműkiadó, 1980.

Borroff, Edith. *Three American Composers.* Lanham, Md.: University Press of America, 1986.

Broderick, Richard, ed. *The New York Times Great Latin Songs.* Introduction by José Feliciano. New York: Quadrangle/The New York Times Book Co., 1947.

Brumbeloe, Joe. "Symmetry in Lutosławski's *Trauermusik*" (*Indiana Theory Review* 6, no. 3 (Spring 1983): 3–14.

Carner, Mosco. "Béla Bartók." In *The Modern Age 1890–1960,* ed. Martin Cooper. Vol. 10 of The New Oxford History of Music. London: Oxford University Press, 1974.

Chase, Gilbert. "Albert Ginastera: Argentine Composer." *The Musical Quarterly* 43, no. 4 (1957): 439–458.

Dille, Denijs. *Thematische Verzeichnis der Jugendwerke Béla Bartóks 1890–1904* (Thematic catalogue of Béla Bartók's youthful works 1890–1904). Budapest: Akadémiai Kiadó, 1974.

————. *Béla Bartók. Regard sur le passé.* Ed. Yves Lenoir. Études Bartókiennes, vol. 1. Louvain-la-Neuve: Institut Supérieure d' Archéologie et d'Histoire de l'Art Collège Érasmé, 1990.

Dorati, Antál. "Bartókiana (Some Recollections)." *Tempo* (London) 136 (March 1981): 6–13.

Downey, John W. *La musique populaire dans l'œuvre de Béla Bartók.* Preface by Jacques Chailley. Paris: L'Institut de Musicologie de l'Université de Paris, no. 5 (1966).

Duran, Gustavo. *Recordings of Latin American Songs and Dances* (Washington, D.C.: Pan American Union Music Series no. 3, 1942.

Evans, Peter. "Britten's *War Requiem.*" *Tempo* (London) 61–62 (Spring and Summer 1962): 20{-}39.

Gillies, Malcolm. *Bartók in Britain.* New York: Oxford University Press, 1989.

———, ed. *The Bartók Companion.* London: Faber and Faber; Portland Or.: Amadeus Press, 1993.

Ginastera, Alberto. "Homage to Béla Bartók." *Tempo* (London) 136 (March 1981): 3–4.

Gombosi, Otto. Biography of Bartók (unfinished). Typescript. Collection of Peter Bartók, Homosassa, Fla.

Griffiths, Paul. *György Ligeti.* London: Robson Books, 1983.

———. *Olivier Messiaen and the Music of Time.* Ithaca, N.Y., Cornell University Press, 1985.

Grout, Donald. *A Short History of Opera.* New York: Columbia University Press, 1947.

Hawthorne, Robin."The Fugal Technique of Béla Bartók." *The Music Review* 10 (November 1949): 277–285.

Hsu, Madeleine. "Olivier Messiaen, the Musical Mediator, and his Major Influences: Liszt, Debussy, and Bartók." Ph.D. diss., New York University, 1984.

Kárpáti, János. *Bartók's String Quartets.* Trans. Fred Macnicol. Budapest: Corvina Press, 1975.

———. *Bartók's Chamber Music.* Trans. Fred Macnicol and Márina Steiner. Trans. rev. Paul Merrick. Stuyvesant, NY: Pendragon Press, 1994.

Kerényi, György. *Népies dalok* (Popular Songs). Budapest: Akadémiai Kiadó, 1961.

Kodály, Zoltán. "Mátyusföldi gyűtés" (Mátyusföld Collection). *Ethnographia* (Budapest) 16 (1905): 300–305.

———. *Folk Music of Hungary.* Trans. Ronald Tempest, et al. New York and Washington, D.C.: Praeger Publishers, 1971.

———. *A magyar népzene* (The Hungarian folk music). Ed. Lajos Varygyas. Budapest: Zeneműkiadó, 1973.

———. "Bartók the Folklorist." In *The Selected Writings of Zoltán Kodály,*

102–108, ed. Ferenc Bónis, trans. Lili Halápy and Fred Macmicol. London: Boosey & Hawkes, 1974.

Kovács, János. Notes to *Béla Bartók Complete Edition*, Budapest: Hungaroton SLPX 1142 (n.d.).

Kroó, György. "Unrealized Plans and Ideas for Projects by Bartók." *Studia Musicologica* 12 (1970): 11–27.

———. *A Guide to Bartók*. Trans. Ruth Pataki et al. Budapest: Corvina Press, 1974.

———. "Bartók and Hungarian Music (1945–1981)." In *Bartók and Kodály Revisited*, ed. György Ránki. Budapest: Akadémiai Kiadó, 1987.

Kunst, Jaap. *Ethnomusicology*. The Hague: Martinus Nijhoff, 1959.

Laade, Wolfgang. "The Diaphonic Music of the Island of Krk, Yugoslavia." Recorded in 1961 by Wolfgang and Dagmar Laade. *Music from the Island of Krk, Yugoslavia*. New York: Ethnic Folkways Records FE 4060 (1975): 1–4.

Lampert, Vera and László Somfai. "Béla Bartók." In *The New Grove Modern Masters: Bartók, Stravinsky, Hindemith*, 1–101, ed. Stanley Sadie. New York and London: W. W. Norton, 1984.

Lendvai, Ernő. *Béla Bartók. An Analysis of his Music*. London: Kahn and Averill, 1971.

Lenoir, Yves. *Folklore et transcendance dans l'œuvre de Béla Bartók* [1940–1945]. Preface by Denijs Dille. Louvain-la-Neuve: Institut Supérieure de Archéologie et d'Histoire de l'Art, 1986.

Lesznai, Lajos. *Bartók*. London: J. M. Dent, 1973.

London, Roberta. Liner notes to *Bartók: Concerto for Orchestra*. New York: Columbia Masterworks MS 6141 (n.d.).

Lundergan, E. J. "Benjamin Britten's *War Requiem*: Stylistic and Technical Sources." D.M.A. treatise. University of Texas at Austin, 1991.

Menuhin, Yehudi. *Unfinished Journey*. London: Macdonald and Jane's Publishers, 1977.

Messiaen, Olivier. *Musique et couleur*. (New interviews with Claude Samuel.) Paris: Pierre Belfond, 1986.

———. *Technique de mon langage musicale*. Trans. John Satterfield. Paris: Alphonse Leduc: Éditions Musicales, 1956.

Moevs, Robert. "George Crumb: *Music for a Summer Evening (Makrokosmos III)*." *The Musical Quarterly* 62 (1976): 292–302.

Moreux, Serge. *Béla Bartók*. Trans. G. S. Fraser and Erik de Mauny. Preface by Arthur Honegger. London: The Harvill Press, 1953.

Nüll, Edwin von der. *Béla Bartók. Ein Beitrag zur Morphologie der neuen Musik*. Halle: Mitteldeutsche Verlags A.G., 1930.

Nordwall, Ove. "Ligeti, György (Sándor)." In *The New Grove Dictionary of Musicians* 10, ed. Stanley Sadie. London: Macmillan, 1980.

Nichols, Roger. *Messiaen*. London: Oxford University Press, 1975.

Parker, Beverly Lewis. *Parallels Between Bartók's Concerto for Orchestra* and Kübler-Ross's Theory about the Dying. *The Musical Quarterly* 73 (Fall 1989): 532–556.

Perle, George. "Symmetrical Formations in the String Quartets of Béla Bartók." *The Music Review* 16 (1955): 300–312.

Ránki, György, ed. *Bartók and Kodály Revisited*. Budapest: Akadémiai Kiadó, 1987.

Reti, Rudolph. *The Thematic Process in Music*. New York: Macmillan, 1951.

Reverdy, Michèle. *L'œuvre pour piano d'Olivier Messiaen*. Paris: Alphonse Leduc, 1978.

Richart, Robert W. *György Ligeti: A Bio-Biography*. New York: Greenwood Press, 1990.

Rößler, Almut. *Contributions to the Spiritual World of Olivier Messiaen: With Original Texts by the Composer*. Duisberg: Gilles & Francke, 1986.

Samuel, Claude. *Entretiens avec Olivier Messiaen*. Paris: Éditions Pierre Belfond, 1967.

Schauffler, Robert H. *Beethoven: The Man who Freed Music*. New York: Tudor Publishing, 1946.

Serly, Tibor. "Story of a Concerto." *The New York Times*, December 11, 1949.

———. "Béla Bartók's Last Works." *The Long Player* (New York: Long Player Publications) 2, no. 10 (October 1953): 26–27.

———. "The Reconstruction of a Musical Masterpiece." *College Music Symposium* 15 (Spring 1975): 7–25.

Stevens, Halsey. *The Life and Music of Béla Bartók*. 3d ed. Rev. ed. Malcolm Gillies. New York: Oxford University Press, 1993.

Stucky, Steven. *Lutosławsky and his Music*. Cambridge: Cambridge University Press, 1981.

Suchoff, Benjamin. "Errata in the *Mikrokosmos* Publication." *Piano Quarterly Newsletter* 16 (Summer 1956): 11, 24.

———. *Béla Bartók and a Guide to the Mikrokosmos*. Ann Arbor, Mich.: University Microfilms, 1957.

———. "Some Observations on Bartók's Third Piano Concerto." *Tempo* (London) 65 (Summer 1963): 8–10.

———. "Structure and Content in Bartók's Sixth String Quartet." *Tempo* (London) 83 (Winter 1967/1968): 2–11.

―――. "Bartók's *Rumanian Folk Music* Publication." *Ethnomusicology* 15, no. 2 (May 1971): 220–230.

―――. *Guide to Bartók's Mikrokosmos*. London: Boosey & Hawkes, 1971. Reprint with foreword by György Sándor, New York: Da Capo Press, 1983.

―――. "Bartók and Serbo-Croatian Folk Music." *The Musical Quarterly* 58, no. 4 (October 1972): 557–571.

―――. "Notes on the Music." In *Béla Bartók: A Celebration*. Introduction by Harold C. Schonberg. Camp Hill, Penn.: Book-of-the-Month Club, 1981; The Classics Record Library 81-6407, 41-6444.

―――. "Folk Music Sources in Bartók Works." In *"Weine meine laute . . ." Gedenkschrift Kurt Reinhard*, ed. Christian Ahrens, et al. Laaber: Laaber-Verlag, 1984: 197–218.

―――. "Ethnomusicological Roots of Béla Bartók's Musical Language." *The World of Music* 29, no. 1 (1987): 43–65.

―――. "The Impact of Italian Baroque Music on Bartók's Music." In *Bartók and Kodály Revisited*, ed. György Ránki. Budapest: Akadémiai Kiadó, 1987.

―――. "The Bartók-Kodály Connection." *The New Hungarian Quarterly* (Budapest) 34, no. 118 (Summer 1990): 154–157.

―――. "Fusion of National Styles: Piano Literature 1908–1911." In *The Bartók Companion*," ed. Malcolm Gillies (London: Faber and Faber, 1993); Portland, Or.: Amadeus Press, 124–145.

―――. "Synthesis of East and West: *Mikrokosmos*." In *The Bartók Companion*, ed. Malcolm Gillies (London, Faber and Faber, 1993); Portland, Or.: Amadeus Press, 189–211.

Szegő, Julia. *Bartók Béla népdalkutató* (Béla Bartók the folk song researcher). Bucharest: Állami Iroldalmi és Művészeti Kiadó, 1956.

Szitha, Tönde. "A Conversation with György Ligeti." *Hungarian Musical Quarterly* (Budapest) 3, no. 1: 13–17.

Tallián, Tibor. *Béla Bartók: The Man and His Work*. Trans. Gyula Gulyás. Rev. ed. Paul Merrick. Budapest: Corvina, 1981.

Treitler, Leo. "Harmonic Procedures in the Fourth Quartet of Béla Bartók." *Journal of Music Theory* 3, no. 2 (November 1959): 292–98.

Ujfalussy, Jószef. *Béla Bartók*. Trans. Ruth Pataki. Rev. Elisabeth West. Budapest: Corvina Press; Boston: Crescendo, 1971.

Veress, Sándor. "*Bluebeard's Castle*. In *Béla Bartók: A Memorial Review*. New York: Boosey & Hawkes, 1950: 36–52.

Vinton, John. "Toward a Chronology of the *Mikrokosmos*." *Studia Musicologica* 8, nos. 1–4 (1966): 41–69.

Webster, J. H. Douglas. "Golden-Mean Form in Music." *Music and Letters* 31 (1950): 238–248.

White, Eric W. Benjamin Britten: His Life and Operas. *Berkeley and Los Angeles: University of California Press, 1983.*

Williamson, John. Strauss: *Also sprach Zarathustra*. Cambridge: Cambridge University Press, 1983.

INDEX

A

Abdal tribe, 102
"acoustic scale," 239n.6
Ady, Endre, 62
Aeolian mode or collection, 41. *See also* individual works
Africa, 72, 124
Aggházy, Károly, 13
aksak. *See* Bulgarian rhythm
Algeria, 72
alphorn, 238n.2
Altdörfer, Christian, 13
American Musicological Society, 114
American Society of Composers, Authors, and Publishers (ASCAP), 115
Amsterdam, 84
Anatolia, 102
Ankara, 102
Antokoletz, Elliott, 226n.5, 229n.27, 231nn. 8, 12, 233n.47, 237n.5, 238nn.3, 15, 239n.15
Arab folk music, 71–73, 124, 220, 231n.10, 235n.16
  chromatic melodies, 80
  Qseida type, 133
  style, 127
d'Arányi, Jelly, 75, 77
Ardeleana, 68, 79–80, 105
Argentine folk music, 204, 206, 241n.11
art music, 56, 141, 155, 216, 220
  Baroque, 98
  Middle Ages, 124
  see also Western art music
art song, popular (urban). *See magyar nóta*
atonality, 105, 114, 212, 221
Austin, William, 238nn.12, 14, 239n.7
Austria, 5, 211

B

Austro-Hungarian army, 238n.2
axis of symmetry, 26, 92, 221

Bach, Johann Sebastian, 17, 21, 36, 67, 83–84, 92–93, 221
  WORKS:
    Brandenburg Concertos, 123
    chorales, 146, 236n.14
    Die Kunst der Fuge, 222
    Inventions, 88
    keyboard, 221
    St. Matthew Passion, 67
    The Well-Tempered Clavier, 227n.3
bagpipe. *See* motif: bagpipe
  imitation, 175, 178–179
Balázs, Béla, 62–63
Bánát region, 70, 95
Baroque music
  German, 166
  Italian keyboard, 82, 84, 88
Bartalus, István, 106
Bartók and Reschofsky
  Zongora Iskola (Piano School), 91, 231n.13
  see also Reschofsky, Sándor
Bartók Archives
  Budapest, 2
  New York (NYBA), 2, 5
Bartók, Béla, 1
  centenary, 203
  death, 120
  emigration to the United States, 112
  fatal illness, 114–115, 118, 120, 123–24
  New York estate, 2–5
  piano technique, 227n.3
  WORKS: 2
    Allegro Barbaro, 204, 240n.21

257